Financial Modelling
for Project Fin

Third Edition

Financial Modelling
for Project Finance

Third Edition

Dr Penelope Anne Lynch

Published by Lynch-Ayerst Publishing

PO Box 241,
Hailsham,
BN27 9ER
United Kingdom

Copyright © 2016 Dr Penelope Anne Lynch

ISBN 978-0-9956730-0-7

NOTE: A number of **Excel files** are available to support this text.
To access the files, please go to
www.projfinmod.co.uk

Contents

Contents

About the author

Penny Lynch has worked since 1992 as an independent consultant specialising in project finance modelling. Her career started in the early 1980s, in the financial modelling team at Morgan Grenfell. At this time modelling was done using a mainframe computer housed in a basement in Tabernacle Street, London EC2a, from where carrier bags of computer printout were carried up the road to the altogether plusher bank offices in Great Winchester Street.

Probably the most important result of the introduction of PCs on desks, and the adoption of Lotus 123, was that it finally allowed the modellers to leave the outer darkness and sit in the nice offices with the bankers. Penny spent several years in the nice offices, as a member of the Energy, Export Credit and Project Finance teams, before moving to Project Finance at Chase Investment Bank, where the offices were slightly less plush, but the pay was substantially better.

After twelve years in the City, she decided to gain full control of her surroundings, and set up her office at home, since when she has been providing project finance modelling and training to a wide range of clients including leading banks and consultancies, as well as project sponsors and developers. Her work has included modelling and model review for renewable and traditional energy and power, road, rail, telecom and other infrastructure projects, with BOT, PPP and PFI, as well as traditional project finance funding structures.

In 1997 the first edition of 'Financial Modelling for Project Finance' was published by Euromoney, and the updated second edition was published in 2011. With Euromoney's withdrawal from book publishing in 2016, Penny created Lynch-Ayerst Publishing to continue to make this work available.

The author's website is www.projfinmod.co.uk

1 Introduction

For project finance deals, where everyone's financial security rests on the future performance of a new undertaking, a thorough analysis of the project's cash flows under a range of assumptions is a prerequisite for arranging debt and equity funding.

This analysis is usually performed using a spreadsheet model, and the person preparing the model (the modeller) can expect long hours, the risk of highly public failure, little scope to be seen to make deals happen and – up to and beyond financial close – every opportunity to create disaster! This workbook has therefore been prepared to make the modeller's life easier, and to improve his or her skills, and is intended for those coming to modelling with no previous experience as well as for those already familiar with the modelling process (although, in either case, competence in a standard spreadsheet package, and specifically in 'Excel', is assumed).

While every project will have unique features, certain principles apply generally to the construction of project finance models, and these principles are the main focus throughout this text. The aim is to make the modelling process quicker and easier whilst minimising the risk of errors, and to create a model which is as flexible, robust and understandable as possible.

The techniques discussed follow some basic 'Golden Rules' (see Section 2.3), along with some subsidiary 'golden aspirations'. An attempt has been made at each stage to give an explanation for the approach recommended, rather than just an assertion of its desirability. This is in recognition of the fact that any suggested changes to a modeller's current methods (especially if it appears counter-intuitive) is unlikely to be adopted unless supported by good arguments in its favour. Because the ideals of layout, structure and technique described here all interact to improve the modelling process, it is hoped to encourage adoption of this methodology as a whole package, rather than simply selective use of particular tips and 'wrinkles'. A good understanding of the reasoning behind a particular recommendation can also be helpful when making decisions about the (very rare) occasions when the 'Golden Rules' need to be broken.

Following the main explanatory sections, the final chapters provide a series of exercises and worked examples following development of the model for an illustrative, fictional project, to illustrate and reinforce the earlier chapters.

When first published, this workbook was probably the only definitive reference source in the field. The field is now well served with reference sources, and with various draft standards of 'best practice'. Unfortunately, although offering consistent views on many issues, these frequently conflict with each other on key points. My advice when selecting among the various philosophies on offer (including this one) is to be sure you thoroughly understand the reason for each recommended or prohibited item, and then adopt the methods which you feel best support a flexible and error-resistant modelling process.

1.1 The need for the model

Project finance is essentially the raising of finance for a new project, secured against future revenues rather than an existing corporate balance sheet or other existing assets. The completion of the project and its successful and profitable operation are therefore key concerns for all lenders and investors.

This means that all the elements that influence the costs, revenues and returns from the project are of interest when determining the finance structure. Analysis of the projected cash flows for the deal, from financial close to the end of the concession or useful life, tested under a range of assumptions, is therefore essential.

The results of such analysis can be used to determine whether a project is sound enough to pursue, by:

- giving an initial figure for project internal rate of return (IRR);
- establishing a finance structure that is supportable for the project; and
- quantifying the robustness of the deal under a range of downside assumptions.

In order to do this within a reasonable timescale it is necessary to construct a computer model that processes a comprehensive list of input assumptions and applies the interactions expected of them in real-life to generate useful output values. Once properly set up, such a model can quickly provide results reflecting a range of data variations and hence allowing the effect of a selection of downside variations from the base case assumptions to be assessed.

1.2 Purpose and uses of the model

As a project progresses from the early stages of basic feasibility assessment to achievement of financial close and drawing of funds, the contribution made by the model changes and develops.

1.2.1 Initial assessment of feasibility

The model provides a simple initial analysis, usually based on relatively raw, preliminary data and simplified financing assumptions, to establish whether a given project is worth pursuing further. The required output may be:

- basic project IRR;
- indicative amounts of debt and equity required to fund the project;
- indicative revenue levels required to achieve appropriate returns; and
- the general level of returns achievable with anticipated revenue levels.

1.2.2 Determining financing structure and facility amounts

Once a decision has been made to move forward from the very basic feasibility analysis, work will begin to establish the optimum financing structure for the project. This will consider the various types and amounts of funding potentially available, and the structures and levels of funding supportable by the anticipated cash flows.

When the analysis has established the preferred financing structure, detailed work will be undertaken to establish facility sizes and to explore the robustness of the finance structure under a number of sensitivity assumptions. The facility sizes will usually be based on a case that incorporates some downside assumptions when compared with the anticipated base case; this is to ensure that funding is available to complete the project, even if things do not go precisely to plan. In addition to the main facility amounts, the model may be required to provide an indication of appropriate sizes for standby debt or equity facilities, and achievable repayment/return arrangements for such facilities.

1.2.3 Reflection of developing documentation

As the details of project structure are incorporated into the developing project documentation, they must also be included (in so far as they are relevant) in the model structure. This is to ensure that the figures are a proper representation of the currently agreed project structure.

1.2.4 Establishing critical issues

The production of sensitivity analyses using the model allows the identification of any variables to which the key results are particularly sensitive. Measures for mitigating such risks can then be incorporated in the structure of the deal. The model can in turn test the effectiveness of such risk-mitigation arrangements.

1.2.5 Support of ongoing negotiations

As documentation is negotiated, the model must provide guidance as to a range of values and structures that might be offered or accepted without compromising the proposed funding and returns for the deal.

1.2.6 Provision of figures for bid submission

If used in support of a competitive bidding process, for example on BOT or PFI projects, the model must provide the key figures for inclusion in the bid, together with supporting calculations and any specific variants requested as part of the bid or additionally offered by the bidders. Historically the model itself was regarded as proprietary, and generally not made available in soft form. Now, however, it is standard practice for the model itself to form part of the bid submission, and to be reviewed and possibly manipulated as part of the bid assessment process.

1.2.7 Provision of information memorandum figures

With the target finance structure and other project structures in place, the model must produce figures correctly reflecting these structures, and using the latest assumptions for other inputs and calculations, to support the process of raising funds. The documents produced in support of fund raising will usually incorporate results from the base case and a number of sensitivity cases. The nature of the sensitivity cases will depend upon the precise structure of the deal, and will generally include a banking 'worst case', incorporating a number of downside assumptions, and possibly an 'equity case' showing the upside potential of the deal.

1.2.8 Preparation of sensitivity analyses for potential lenders/investors

Once potential lenders/investors have been approached, many wish to analyse the project using a number of sensitivities of their own. This may be carried out by the project sponsors and their advisers, using the original model, or may be done by the potential funders, either using the original model, or working with their own models.

1.2.9 Use as part of the loan agreement.

Usually, a loan agreement will include a requirement for periodic checks on loan cover factors, with specific agreed amendments to cost, revenue or macroeconomic assumptions. Based on the results of such checks, constraints may be placed on loan drawings, or lock-ins or cash-sweeps may be triggered. For this purpose, an audited version of the final model commonly forms part of the loan agreement and is run at specified dates to provide the required figures.

1.2.10 Use as part of project documentation

When a project involves a complex product price agreement or similar calculated item, which may require adjustment in the light of actual, rather than projected, information, then a version of the model will usually form part of the project documentation, and is run periodically to provide the required figures as needed over time.

1.3 Development over the project life

For any given project, the model will usually be required to fulfil several of the roles listed in the previous section, sequentially and/or concurrently, often developing right through from the feasibility model to the final model used for fund raising. Given that detail and data are often acquired gradually over time, it is important that the first model, written at whatever stage, should be structured to allow easy onward development to the final version. In this way all effort contributes towards the final model, rather than being lost or repeated.

In order to allow the model readily to provide the analyses required at each stage of the project, and to develop smoothly over the project life, it is clearly important that the modeller is well informed about the project throughout its development. The bare information required to specify a particular calculation, without a wider understanding of the deal and the issues involved is not sufficient to support an appropriate and adaptable modelling process. An appreciation of the sources and validity of particular data items, the assumptions that are 'set in stone', those for which an optimum is to be established, and those likely to be negotiating issues, will contribute to the structuring of the model in a format best suited to develop with the project and to provide the required results in a flexible manner.

1.3.1 Feasibility model

This is the first stage of analysis and entails an assessment of whether or not a given project is worth pursuing. For this, the model needs to be prepared quickly and must be able to work with limited data and (probably) very generalised assumptions as to financing, timing of capital expenditure and operations.

Depending upon the nature of the project, the model may be required to give an indication of equity returns given reasonable cost and revenue assumptions, or of the revenue levels needed to meet target levels for cover factor and equity returns.

The feasibility model should be structured to allow easy development for further use if the project is progressed. The structure and layout should follow that detailed later in this book, even though the data and assumptions available at this stage may not appear to justify it. For example, data may be available only on an annual or even multi-annual basis, but the model should none the less be prepared on a semi-annual basis to avoid the need for restructuring as more information becomes available. The basic data can then be converted into a semi-annual format on the simplest basis possible.

1.3.2 Model during project development

During the development of the project after the feasibility analysis the model will be subject to considerable change. It will become much more complex than the feasibility model, incorporating detailed data and assumptions, and possibly reflecting more than one structure for particular calculations (for example, finance, offtake contracts) as options are assessed and reviewed. At this stage the model must be able, at short notice, to incorporate quite significant changes or additions.

1.3.3 Final model for bid submission, raising finance, etc.

Once a final structure has been agreed for the deal, and the majority of the project documentation is in place, the model reaches a final form, established around the base case. The code of the model should require little change from this point on: cases will primarily be run to reflect final changes in data and to provide a range of sensitivity analyses.

At this point the model may well be somewhat simpler than it was during project development since, with the final structure established, alternative structures can be removed from the code. This simplification may of course be offset by very detailed reflection of the final terms of the loan and project agreements.

1.3.4 How much detail at each stage?

When writing or developing the model, it is important to bear in mind what stage the project has reached, and the level of detail available in the data; this information should then be used as a guide to the complexity of the model. The model should not generally seek to apply complex calculations to vague, inaccurate data. On the other hand, if the assumptions for processing the data are clearly defined, and available ahead of firm data, then it is appropriate to prepare the model according to the detailed assumptions, in readiness for the detailed data. The initial poor quality data will allow the model to be run and checked and indicative results to be obtained prior to provision of the better information.

More significantly, it is worth trying to avoid engaging in very complex modelling in the early stages of the project in order to reflect, for example, tentative options for the financing structure. Before starting work on a very complex structure, it is always worth checking whether the complicating elements are fundamental to the option being considered, or whether the analysis can effectively be performed using slightly amended assumptions in order to simplify the modelling requirements. Sometimes structures are proposed by people with little idea of the technical issues involved in modelling a particular concept. It is often worth spending a few minutes in discussion to avoid hours of frustrating and ultimately unnecessary work.

In the final stages the level of detail included in the model code should give regard to the detail available in the input assumptions and the uses of the model outputs. More detail is generally appropriate, for example, for a model which generates the exact figures used for real-world values, such as the actual power price or availability payment charged in each year of the project life. Less precision may be appropriate for a model analysing cover factors and returns based on assumed market prices or forecast sales volumes.

1.3.5 Who will use the model?

When writing the model it is important to be clear as to its function, not only in terms of the analyses to be performed and the results produced, but also as regards its mode of use. Is the model going to be run by the modeller, processing data and providing outputs as required by third parties? If so, the structure of the model can be rather different than would be required if, for example, the people organising the deal want to be able to run the model themselves.

While the model should always be laid out to facilitate its use and development by a competent modeller, this is a rather different task to that of ensuring safe and easy access for a third party with a minimum understanding of the 'nuts and bolts' of the model. If it is possible to anticipate the data items that are likely to be varied during such use, it should be possible to prepare a single page that allows entry of relevant data items and provides a summary of the key results produced. The rest of the model can then be protected to prevent ill-conceived changes being made which could produce anomalous results. Such a page can be prepared in the format of a 'Key inputs and results summary', as described in Section 24. The data items entered on this 'interface' sheet can be picked up by the appropriate cells in the data section, reversing the usual technique of presenting values in the summary that are entered in the data. Having the data section pick up the input values from an adapted summary sheet, rather than moving the input cells to the summary sheet, means that items can be moved or removed (intentionally or otherwise) on the summary sheet without doing any damage to the model, because numeric values can simply be re-entered in the proper data cells if required.

1.4 The need for flexibility, robustness and clarity

As explained above, the model must be structured to allow major changes to the code to be made as quickly and easily, and with as little risk of introduced error, as possible. In addition the model must be robust, accepting and processing any reasonable inputs to give revised base case or sensitivity results. A number of factors can contribute to flexibility and robustness, including the use of layout and time-lines as detailed below.

'Clarity' sounds like a purely cosmetic, presentational issue. However, in addition to contributing to the flexibility of the model, clarity of layout and labelling helps the modeller and any other parties using the model to navigate within the spreadsheet, to identify the items they are looking for and (most importantly) to understand and check the model calculations. Clarity therefore makes errors less likely and contributes much more than just superficial benefits.

The majority of this text is directed to achieving an ideal – a model with a layout that maximises clarity and flexibility, minimises the risk of error and facilitates checking procedures. The techniques applied to achieve this ideal should become second nature to the experienced modeller. In life, however, the ideal is seldom achievable, and compromises must be made while working on any model, between the ideal structure and the constraints imposed by, for example, fixed deadlines.

The process of deciding the optimum approach given all the factors, is a complex and continuing one, but should largely relate to detail. Compromising on basic layout and timescale criteria, for example, is very unlikely to be a wise decision, because the short-term benefit in terms of time saved will almost certainly be more than offset by the significantly increased workload, and increased risk of error, at later stages.

Project finance models are **dynamic,** they have to change and develop to short timescales.
Therefore they must be **easy to change,** and **input values must be easy to update.**

---

2 Model design

2.1 Basic principles

2.1.1 Always, sometimes, never

Of the principles of model design and construction outlined in this book, some are rules, things which should always be done a certain way or things which should never be done a certain way. Some define an approach which should be applied according to the specific circumstances of the project and model being developed.

Care should be given when prescribing or proscribing modelling methods. Clearly for an integrated approach, where each aspect depends for its full effect on other elements of the approach, it is potentially destructive to ignore one precept which may then undermine other parts of the methodology and give rise to unnecessary vulnerabilities to error, or difficulties in making changes and developing the model. Most specifications have a cost, as well as a benefit, however, and this should be considered when adopting a fixed strategy. Throughout this text, an attempt has been made to give the reasons behind the 'always' and 'never' recommendations, and to help the modeller understand the appropriate times for the 'sometimes' methods.

2.1.2 One model for all cases

The model must be able to handle changing inputs as the deal develops, and process alternative inputs for sensitivity cases. It is fundamental to the model's purpose, therefore, that it should be able to run one case as well as another. In practical terms, this basic assumption is supported as a 'Golden Rule' by the disadvantages of maintaining multiple versions of the model in parallel (for example, a 'base case' model, 'delay case' model, etc.).

- **Workload** – every addition and amendment has to be made in multiple models, multiplying the workload associated with every change.
- **Error** – multiplying the number of changes to be made multiplies the opportunity for introducing simple typographical errors, and introduces the possibility of omitting changes, or parts of changes from one or more copies of the model.
- **Checking workload** – each version of the model must be checked separately.

As an illustration of the process of understanding enough to know when to break the rules, if a complex sensitivity case, which (a) will almost certainly be required only once, (b) will require several hours work in order to be incorporated into the model as an option and (c) could be hard-wired into the model as a one-off exercise in under an hour, is required in the next two hours, or by tomorrow and it is already nearly midnight, then the time has come to break the rules. Hard-wire the changes, and save the revised model version as a clearly labelled historical item, never to be used again. Should the run be required again, the same changes can be made to the version of the model current at the time the re-run is required.

2.1.3 The benefits of using a consistent basic layout

There are a number of benefits that flow from using a consistent basic layout for all models:

- incorporates best practice established to date;
- makes old models easier to follow and review;
- makes models easier to share and support between modellers; and
- early stage models automatically incorporate structure suitable for development through to final model version.

2.1.4 Data, calculations, results

It is helpful to conceptually divide model sheets into three categories, **data**, **calculations** and **reports**.

The **data**, comprising usually one worksheet, accommodates all input values, switches, etc.

The **calculation** sheets comprise the sections that process the data in line with the assumptions applicable to the project. Calculation sections are organised primarily for ease of use by the modeller and for clarity of the calculations, although each should give a useable printout to support a detailed audit of the figures in due course.

The **results** sheets are the presentation sheets where values from the data and calculation sections are collected and organised into the format required for output summaries and reports.

This notional categorisation provides a number of benefits in terms of model development and use. Localisation of all inputs allows the input values to be readily found, reviewed, checked, expanded, updated and printed. Separation of calculation sheets from reports allows clarity and ease of calculation to be the primary shaper of the calculation pages, without regard for the constraints of any ultimately required output formats. It also means that the results pages can be structured and amended as required without compromising the safe calculation of the figures.

Each calculation section should be printable for use when carrying out detailed checks or audits, but will primarily reflect the needs and logic of calculation. The reverse is true of the reports, which basically pick up the values calculated elsewhere and arrange them in a format driven by presentational needs. This distinction allows each section to be presented in a format best suited to its role.

While the calculation sheets should all use a consistent timeline and currency, the reports can rearrange the figures for presentation on any timing basis and display them in any currency.

2.1.5 The 'Base Case'

The Base Case is a fundamental concept in project finance modelling. It is essentially the case which all parties agree uses the most reasonable value for each data input. In some instances values are contractually set, and the choice of value for the model is easy. In other cases the only certainty is that the value used in the model will not be equal to the actual value!

The base case gives basic information about the project, expected funding requirements, equity returns etc, but it is only in association with a suitable set of sensitivity cases that it can form part of a sound analysis of the project.

2.1.6 Consistent signs

The model will inevitably contain values that represent costs and revenues – cash flows to and from the project. Some of these appear to have an inherent positive or negative value in relation to the project, and it is tempting to assign a positive or negative sign to such values throughout the model, with totals and sub-totals thus being able to sum together all relevant rows and achieve the correct calculated total.

Experience suggests, however, that it is preferable to essentially present all values in absolute terms, and add or subtract them as required in the formulae that use them. Thus the descriptive title of a row, and its context, will indicate whether a value is an addition to or deduction from project cash flows. Sub-totals, totals, net transfers (to)/from accounts, and other items where it is specifically appropriate, may then show a mixture of positive and negative values, the meaning of which should be clear.

This approach gives figures that are in agreement with row titles. A negative value shown for costs, for example, might reasonably be assumed to represent a positive cash item. More importantly, it means that values will reliably have a consistent sign throughout the model, and can confidently be picked up from any part of the model for use in a formula without uncertainty on this point. Otherwise, values may well require a different sign according to the calculation in which they are being included, and this adds a significant area of possible (and in practice frequently observed) confusion and error to the process of constructing the model.

2.1.7 Real and nominal values

Project finance models usually analyse cash flows over relatively long periods of time, where the effects of inflation can have a significant effect on projected cash flows. Specific cost and revenue items may inflate according to different indices, and debt service is usually unaffected by inflation. For these reasons it is not appropriate to ignore inflation in the model, and all cash flows should be calculated in nominal terms (i.e., including any assumed effects of inflation). Where necessary, real terms figures can then be calculated at a stated value date with a given inflation index. Note that simply setting inflation to 0% does not give real-terms figures, it gives figures assuming zero inflation. An assumed inflation rate would still be required if working with real-terms figures, since debt service is nominally fixed and must be discounted using the assumed inflation rate to provide real-terms values.

For consistency, and to allow inflation assumptions to be updated and sensitised, any values subject to actual inflation must be entered into the model in uninflated terms, at a stated value date, and then inflated in the model using the currently specified inflation assumptions. Using inputs which already reflect inflation assumptions applied outside the model is inflexible, and highly likely to lead to anomalous results when different, incompatible, assumptions are combined in the calculations.

2.1.8 Manual calculation

The relatively large size of project finance models, the dynamics of the development process and the need to identify and remove any circularities in the code mean that it is desirable to maintain specific 'Calculation' settings in Excel whilst working on the model.

In Excel 2003 or earlier, use the Tools, Options Menu to access the required choices. In Excel 2007, Click on the 'Office' button at top left, then select the 'Excel Options' button at the bottom of the dialog box.

In all cases, select Manual recalculation with no Recalculation Before Save, and no Iteration.

Manual recalculation avoids starting the calculation process every time a formula or input value is entered, and keeps the recalculation process very clear when using macros.

Recalculate before save is a dangerous option. If saving prior to removing an unintended circularity with a propagated ERR message, recalculating the model and then saving the recalculated version would disastrously propagate the ERR throughout the model in the saved version. Saving before an impending loss of power or battery failure would also be impeded by a preliminary recalculation of the model. This is therefore best kept under optional control, not set as an automatic choice.

Exhibit 2.1

Specifying calculation options

Excel 2007

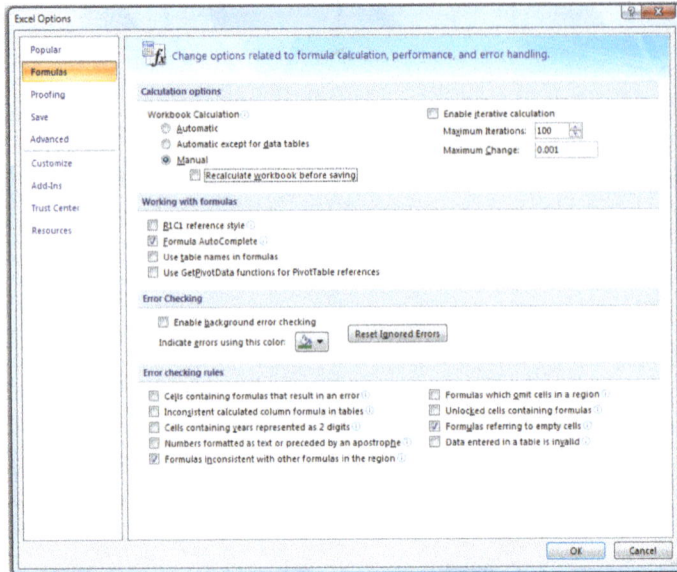

Excel 2003

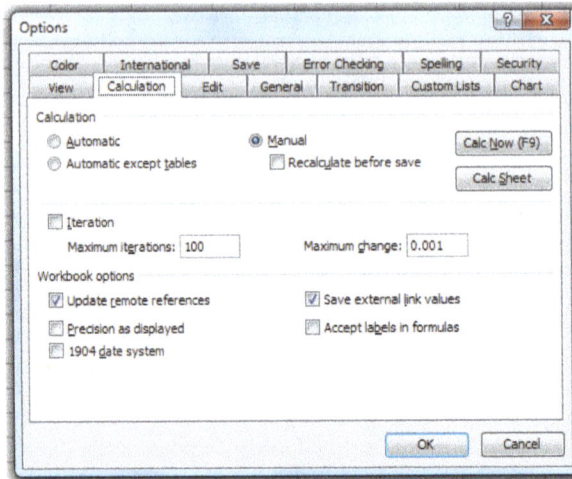

Iteration is only required for circular calculations, switching it off ensures that any accidentally created circularities will be flagged by Excel.

2.1.9 Currency treatment

Many projects involve cash flows denominated in different currencies, and the relative values of those currencies then becomes a key assumption for the project cash flows. The treatment of currencies within the model can follow one of two basic methodologies. Amounts can be calculated in their actual currency, or all amounts can be shown in a single, presentation currency, with amounts adjusted as necessary to properly reflect the changing exchange rates between the presentation currency and the actual currency over time. Each has drawbacks and benefits.

- **Calculations in actual currency:**
  - ○ intuitive, easy to see the actual values assumed;
  - ○ creates duplication, all values must eventually be converted into a consistent currency to calculate net cash amounts;
  - ○ introduces risk of using incompatible values in formulae, for example, adding an amount in dollars to an amount in euros; and
  - ○ inputs and calculations rather rigidly defined as belonging to a particular currency.
- **Calculations in single presentation currency:**
  - ○ needs careful thought to ensure all adjustments made correctly;
  - ○ avoids unnecessary duplication of values;
  - ○ whilst calculations are consistently in one currency, results sheets can present values converted to underlying currencies where required;
  - ○ avoids risk of inappropriate combinations of values in different currencies; and
  - ○ allows flexible allocation of currencies to specific inputs and cash flows.

On balance, and based on experience of writing and using models prepared on both bases, **the use of a single, consistent, presentation currency is recommended**. Details of handling currency-related calculations in the model are given in Section 8.

2.1.10 Circular code

Whilst circular calculations are common and intrinsic to some aspects of project finance modelling, circular calculations need not be handled by creating circular code. Many of the methods and structures described in this text are devised specifically to avoid circularity or to manage circular calculations without circular Excel code. It may seem like a lot of work when Excel is happy to do the job for you, iterating to a solution wherever the code links up into a circular path. There are good reasons for making the extra effort, however. Each is probably a good enough reason on its own, taken together they are overwhelming. The following are some of the drawbacks of circular code:

- loss of control over model calculation path;
- potential for infinite oscillation or repeated cycling through sequential results;
- very limited ability to specify the accuracy to which individual iterative calculations should be solved;
- disappointing outcomes when any error messages arise within a circular calculation; and
- inability to definitively audit a calculation path with no defined start point and end point.

Model design should therefore seek to eliminate circularity wherever possible. This process is supported by a model design in which all but a very few calculations refer to values in higher rows, earlier columns, and/or earlier pages of the model.

For calculations which are inextricably and inherently circular, iteration should be under the modeller's control, and carried out using a simple copy-and-paste-as-values recalc macro (see Section 7.4.2).

2.1.11 Range names

Range names in project finance models are generally a nuisance and an abomination! Although often cited as good practice for Excel spreadsheets, the process of naming cells or ranges of cells is not a positive contribution to the modelling process for the relatively large and complex models typical of project finance.[*]

The classic example of the beneficial use of range names is the spreadsheet for calculation of the salesman's monthly commission. In this instance, it might be easy to follow a formula such as "=Jan_sales*percent_commission", there are few inputs, and the formulae processing them are simple.

In project models, however, aside from the time and effort involved in creating them, profligate use of range names creates the following issues.

- Need to create many range names means they become either very long, rather obscure, or both, making the formulae referencing them also rather long and/or obscure.
- It is harder to trace references in a formula back to source via a range name than via a directly displayed cell addresses.
- Tracing the source of range names becomes increasingly time-consuming and tedious as the list of names to be scrolled through increases in length.
- When copying formulae referencing range names, it is not always clear exactly which cells within the named range are referenced from a given cell.
- When researching a formula, it is not possible to leave the cursor on the cell in question and simply go and look at the components of the formula when they are defined as range names rather than cell addresses.

There have been instances of models rendered effectively unuseable and unauditable by diligent use of range names for input cells. In such cases a great deal of work and time has been invested in rendering the model useless.

The only case where the **use of range names is recommended** is **to define ranges referenced in macros.** Visual basic references are not updated to reflect insertions or deletions in the worksheet. If the macro uses a range name instead of a direct cell address, the range name relocates with the cells to which it refers, and the integrity of the macro is preserved. Of course, macros themselves should be used very sparingly, see Section 6.1.

Range names are also harmless and potentially useful when used sparingly to assist with navigation within the model.

To create a range name, select the cells to be included in the range and click on the 'Name box' (usually displaying the current cell address near the top left corner of the Excel window) and type the required range name. To change the location of an existing range name, or if preferred for some other reason, names can also be created or deleted using Insert, Name, Define or Delete (in Excel 2003), or Formulas, Define Name or Name Manager (in Excel 2007).

---

[*] McKeever, R., McDaid, K. and Bishop, B., 'An exploratory analysis of the impact of named ranges on the debugging performance of novice users', Proc. European Spreadsheet Risk Interest Group, 2009, pp. 69–81.

2.1.12 Off-sheet references

An example of a 'sometimes' method which is sometimes promoted as a 'never' would be the rigid prohibition of the use of 'off-sheet' references in formulae. Since it is clearly necessary to access figures from other sheets in many formulae in the model, this effectively means that values in any rows required by a formula, which originate on another sheet, must be imported into a duplicate row on the same worksheet as the new formula, and accessed from there by the formula. This is sometimes a useful approach, but if applied rigidly has many downsides. The size of the model can be substantially increased with no equivalent increase in information, which makes checking the model more time-consuming. Although all the source cells for a formula may be visible when checking the formula, superficially simplifying the checking process, the actual source of the figures shown in those cells still needs to be followed back to their origin and this now requires an additional step, and that additional step introduces an additional opportunity for error in the model. Further, the insertion of many duplicate rows into the flow of the model calculations, far from increasing clarity, can actually obscure the flow of the calculations and make the 'story' of the model harder to follow.

> There is no intrinsic problem with off-sheet references!

2.2 Maintaining flexibility

Flexibility is critical to the model, both to allow model development over the project life and to support production of sensitivity cases. The principle of maintaining flexibility underlies all aspects of model structure and content.

2.2.1 Avoiding hard-wiring into formulae and model structure

An important factor in maintaining robustness in use is the collection of all data items in a single section of the model where they can easily be found and viewed. This should include all input values, switches and any data relating to the timing of events in the project. These items should therefore not be entered directly into formulae or the model structure, where they are hard to identify, and inflexible.

The exclusion of figures from formulae outside the data section (other than constants such as days per year and hours per day) ensures that the model can be confidently controlled and reviewed from the data section. Even values not expected to change during the model's life are made visible and explicit by entry via the data section. In practice, also, the values expected to remain unchanged have a habit of changing nonetheless!

Timing items, such as financial close, construction period, start of operations, loan repayment periods, etc., are assumptions that may well change during the development of the model and for which sensitivities may be required. Rather than determining such timings by 'hardwiring' them into the timeline, formulae referencing these dates should be consistent across all columns of the model timeline. Timing of events within the timeline should be controlled via formulae using data inputs. Such inputs can be in any format that suits the timeline of the model and the requirements of the project, but should ensure that dependent timings are entered as relative values, not as absolute dates. In practice, this generally means that financial close should be entered as a date, and other timings should be entered as a number of days, weeks, months or years from financial close, or from some other date in turn dependent upon financial close. The exception would be events external to the project with fixed timings unrelated to the project timetable.

Timing can then be controlled via simple changes in the data section. Key to maintaining total flexibility in this regard is the inclusion of the whole analysis period under a consistent timeline, and rigorous adherence to the principle of having consistent formulae across the timeline in every row of the calculation sheets. This applies from the timeline start date, at or before scheduled financial close, to the end of the model timeline, at a date beyond the expected analysis period. There are no benefits and many disadvantages to separate treatment of the construction and operating time periods in the physical layout of the model.

2.2.2 Using 'pinch-points'

Where particular sub-totals need to be used in more than one calculation, they should be calculated explicitly in one row, and used from there in all the dependent calculations. This means that any changes to the sub total can be fed to all relevant calculations simply by updating one row.

A good example is loan interest in a model with multiple loans. Several calculations, for example the cash cascade, tax and profit and loss (P&L) need the total loan interest figure. Calculating this in one place (ideally at the bottom of the Funding sheet) means that, if additional loans are added to the model, or surplus loan calculations are removed from the model, the total interest figure used throughout the model can be updated simply by amending one row.

Exhibit 2.2

Pinch-point example

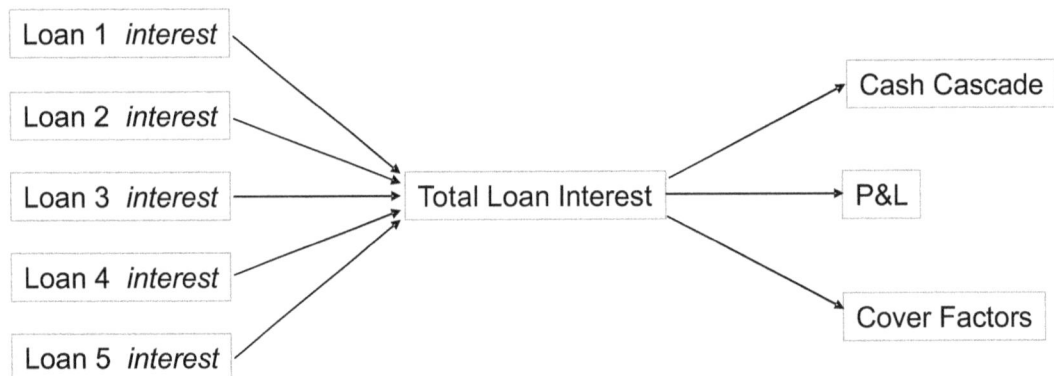

2.3 The Golden Rules!

- **One model** for each project
- **Data in one place**
- Any **value calculated only once** in the model
- **Consistent formula across** any given **row**
- **Consistent timeline on all calculation** sheets
- **No circular code**

2.4 Model layout and structure

The underlying layout of the model provides the essential framework on which the detail can be hung, and can (and should) essentially be the same for the first feasibility model and the model eventually used for Financial Close.

2.4.1 Basic structure

The suggested pages to be included in the model (each of which is described in detail in later sections) are listed in Box 2.1.

Data
  Input sheet(s)

Calculations
  Worklines, masks, factors and counters
  Construction/capital costs
  Funding
  Operations
  Tax
  Profit and loss
  Cash cascade
  Cash deposits
  Investor returns
  Cover factors

Reports
  Net cash flow summary
  One-page key inputs and results summary
  Balance sheet
  Annual summaries, etc.

Other
  Macro support sheet
  Results library

These sheets are generally applicable, but additional sections may be required for specific projects – for example, for the calculation of revenues to meet target cover factor and return requirements.

2.4.2 The flow of logic through the model

Whether the calculations are laid out over a single page or over several pages, it is helpful to consider the order in which sections are included in the model. In general, it is worth laying out the model so that calculations flow consistently across the spreadsheet pages from left to right, down the spreadsheet pages from top to bottom, and from sheet to sheet from left to right. As well as making the model easier to follow and to map mentally, this facilitates the auditing of specific calculations and the tracking down of any introduced 'ERRs'.

    Thus information flows from the data to all subsequent sections, from the worklines to several later sections, from capital costs into funding, from capital costs, funding and operations into tax and profit and loss, and so on.

There will always be exceptions to this – calculated values that necessarily feed into 'earlier' sections of the model – but the aim should be for these to be kept to a minimum. Wherever such 'backward' flows occur they should form a focus of attention with regard to avoidance of circular code.

2.5 Basic page layout

At a more detailed level, model layout includes the organisation of rows and columns within the sheets, and certain guidelines can ensure that these elements are best arranged to support the development, use and presentation of the model.

Exhibit 2.3

Basic page layout

	B	C	D	E	F	G	H	I	J
1	Full Scheme Base Case		*labelled single*		*pre-*	*half years >>>>>>>*			
2	Worklines Sheet		*values or*		*time*	Jul 2011	Jan 2012	Jul 2012	....
3	*All values without labelled units are in millions Sa*		**Totals**		*line*	to Dec '11	to Jun '12	to Dec '12	....
4									
5									
6									
7									
8									
9									
10									

2.5.1 Columns

● Column A is a very narrow column, used to allow headings to help with navigation. If main headings are entered in column A rather than B, then it becomes possible to navigate through a sheet by hopping from one main heading to the next.

● Column B is wide enough to accommodate useful descriptive titles for the rows without taking up too much of the screen when working with the model.

● Column C is narrow and serves to separate the titles from the totals, and from the later columns, when printing. In addition it can be used to contain hidden notes and documentation (for example, giving source and date for data items).

● Column D can contain single input values in the data section, but is particularly used to provide nominal totals for cashflows in the calculation and report sheets (see Section 2.5.3).

● Column E is again narrow and provides an empty 'buffer' between totals and formulae, which is useful when copying formulae back across a row, and when writing formulae that need to reference values in the preceding period.

● Column F, 'Pre-Year 1', will largely be unused, but provides scope for a number of useful values, such as the initial '1.00' required for inflation factor calculations, as well as providing a further empty cell facilitating consistency when writing formulae looking back over the two preceding periods (some annual calculations).

● Column G onwards comprise the timeline, all columns consistently representing sequential six month time periods, over the total timescale covered by the model.

Inclusion of additional columns to the left of the timeline can offer some benefits, but there are costs to offset against them. The additional space for extra inputs or complex structuring of headings also means a lot more blank space between the row headings and the timeline, on the screen and the printed page. This means that either very few timeline columns are visible when working, or, in order to view more, zoom is set so that the displayed and printed text is very tiny. In addition, where the extra columns are used to display values, these commonly end up as unlabelled figures floating in space. When it is necessary to display a single value, it should be given a row, and a heading, of its own.

Note that all rows in the model should run from the chosen start point for the timeline. There should not be a separate timeline layout for construction and operating periods. The project's cash flows must be analysed through the construction and operating periods, many calculations will carry across both phases, construction can overlap with operation, and sensitivities will require the timing of completion and the start of operations to be easily varied. See Section 3.2 for details on varying the timing accuracy of calculations within an overall timescale (for example, including monthly calculations in a semi-annual layout).

2.5.2 Rows

All input and calculation sheets should consistently use a set of rows at the top of the sheet to give, in columns A or B:

- project title;
- run description;
- page title; and
- units.

These rows can also include, in later columns:

- heading for 'totals' column; and
- timeline headings.

These rows can then head the cells being observed on screen (using 'freeze panes') or printed (using 'rows to repeat at top of sheet'), making time periods easy to identify, and ensuring that printed figures are associated with an appropriate run description.

2.5.3 Including nominal totals

Although there are obviously drawbacks to the totalling of projected nominal values over long periods of time, the inclusion of a column of such totals for most rows of the model has a number of benefits:

- for values fixed in nominal terms (such as loan calculations) the totals have intrinsic meaning;
- for many calculations, totals provide quick checks on the validity of figures;
- totals help comparison between runs, where the figures affected by a given sensitivity can quickly be identified by a comparison of corresponding totals;
- the origin of ERRs accidentally introduced during model development can be quickly identified by checking through the total column; and
- information about the whole timeline is brought into view alongside row headings and the start of the timeline when printing or working with the model.

The totals column can also be used to display specific single values, as long as these are clearly labelled. When displaying totals, however, they must always be the total of the values in the row to which they belong, not a subtotal calculated from other figures in the 'totals' column. This rule ensures that the totals can serve as a meaningful cross check on the calculations, and that they tell us something useful about the rows which they summarise.

2.6 Timeline

The model provides an analysis of values in the context of their relationship over time. To place values in time, the model has a timeline – a header that indicates the point in the analysis represented by each column. This indicator can be in any format, provided it indicates clearly the timing of each period. The timeline should be consistent on all calculation sheets.

2.6.1 Frequency of model periods

Given that initial data will often be annual (at best) and final data may well include monthly expenditure profiles, what timescale should be selected for the model?

Experience suggests that using each column to represent a six-month period will provide the best balance between practicality and accuracy, bearing in mind that monthly accuracy can readily be incorporated into a semi-annual model, when first building the model or as a later development (see Section 3.2). Six-monthly periods usually work well with finance calculations, allow seasonal or other cash flow variations within the year to be reflected, and allow most project lives to be modelled in a manageably sized model.

2.6.2 Consistency of timescale within the model

With the exception of the reports sections, the model should have a consistent timescale – i.e., every column should represent the same length of time (for example, six months) and a given column should always represent the same point in time (for example, '2nd half Year 3'). This offers a number of benefits:

- reduces risk of error in formulae referencing other model sheets;
- the timeline at the top of the page applies to all columns on that page, and can be fixed for printing or viewing without risk of error or confusion; and
- NPV and IRR calculations can easily be calculated across the timeline.

As explained below, it is still possible to perform calculations based on a time period other than that selected for the columns, and figures can be converted to any time basis for presentation in the report sections.

2.6.3 Period included in the timeline

The timeline should start on or before the earliest possible anticipated date for financial close and run through to a date several years after the latest expected end of the analysis period. This allows changes to financial close or to concession length, project life, or start of operations to be reflected easily by simple changes to input data. See Section 3 for detail regarding control of timings relative to the timeline.

2.6.4 Extending the period covered by the model timeline

When in the chronicle of wasted time, spreadsheets were written on a single page, it was a simple matter to extend the timeline included in a model. With multiple sheets this has become a much more complicated and error-prone process, and one best avoided if at all possible. If it becomes absolutely necessary to extend the period covered by the model, then the following procedure is suggested. This is intended to produce corrected ranges in formulae for totals, etc., and to ensure that the correct formulae apply across the new columns. In the explanation, the term 'move' is equivalent to 'cut and paste', while 'copy' means simply 'copy and paste'. The former will transfer formulae unchanged from one location to another, and will adjust all formulae referring to the 'moved' cells to ensure that they continue to reference the moved formulae in their new location, while the latter simply copies a formula to a new cell, making no adjustment to other cells.

To extend the model timeline, use the following procedure.

1   Recalculate the model, save and then save again under a new name.
2   Using the renamed model, on all pages of the model incorporating a timeline, including the Data sheet, select the original final column of the timeline, and insert the required number of new columns to its left This should adjust all 'SUM' and similar array-based formulae covering the original timeline to include the additional new columns.
3   Inserting the new columns will have changed any formulae which reference forward to a later column wherever such formulae were using the original end period. These formulae will now be looking ahead many columns instead of simply one or two. In addition to populating the new columns, therefore, it is also necessary to re-instate the original formulae in later periods. It is therefore advisable to copy from an early column of the timeline, taking care, however, not to overwrite any special headings or calculations included as single item entries or as table headings, etc. The procedure is therefore, on each page with a timeline, to copy the cells in an early column, for all rows down to the last row used, and paste across all later columns up to and including the new final column, breaking the process down, if necessary, to omit any rows with unique entries in specific columns. The pasted formulae should overwrite the formulae moved into the new final column in stage 1 above.
4   Recalculate the model and check (by comparison with original version of the model) that results remain unchanged.
5   Change the inputs controlling the length of the analysis period and, again by comparison with the original version, as well as by direct observation of the new columns for all sheets, check that the extended calculations are working. Take particular care to check that calculations such as IRR and NPV have updated correctly, and that single calculations on summary sheets have maintained their integrity.

3 Handling timings

3.1 Flexible timings

In order to preserve the concept of consistency and flexibility, the timing of events in the model needs to be controlled flexibly via input values, not hard-wired into the model structure. This process is supported by the 'rules' that all data is entered as explicit values on the 'Data' sheet, and that all formulae are consistent across the whole timeline for each row.

3.1.1 Data inputs to control all timings

The timing of most project events happens relative to the timing of some other event. The start of operations depends on completion of the operating unit; completion date depends on the start date for construction and the length of the construction period, and so on. Generally, the key independent timing event is Financial Close, and all other timings flow from there. The model inputs therefore need to specify an absolute date for financial close and relative dates for subsequent events. The exception would be events external to the project whose timing will remain unchanged irrespective of the assumptions made about project timings, and these should clearly also be entered as absolute dates.

Excel handles dates simply as numbers, the number of days from 1st January 1900. Formatting a cell as a date will cause these numbers to be displayed as a recognisable date (for example, 40,266 gives 29th March 2010), but the underlying value continues to be a large integer. This means that we can use date values with mathematical operators. One date minus another gives the number of days between the two dates; a date value less than another date will be an earlier date; adding an integer to a date value gives a date later by the added number of days, and so on.

3.1.2 Defining the timeline

In order to allow calculations to access timing information on the model timeline, two key rows are included in the 'Work' sheet, the Start Date and End Date for each column. These are used, formatted as required, to generate the Timeline heading on all sheets, and provide the reference source for all timing calculations in the model.

3.1.3 Positioning events relative to the model timeline

In order to convert the information input in the Data sheet to actual positions and proportions on the timeline, it is often helpful to represent the timing information in a 'mask' which can then be used as needed in other calculations. Separating out the timing part of the calculation in this way serves a number of purposes.

- Timings applied in several places are only calculated once.
- The timing calculations can be reviewed, checked and updated separately from other elements of the calculation.
- Formulae are not made excessively complicated by trying to combine timing calculations with the other elements of a calculation.

Timings take several forms. There can be single point events, such as the occurrence of Financial Close. These are generally best and most simply represented by a formula giving zero in all periods except the one in which the event occurs. Any values which are required in this period only can then be positioned simply by multiplying the formula for the required amount by the value of the mask in each period. Such calculated timing multipliers are referred to throughout this book as 'masks'. You may also see them called 'flags' in some models.

Other timings apply over a particular set of periods, for example, the periods during which a loan can be drawn. For these a simple '1' or '0' result in any period is again the simplest solution, once more providing a 'mask' by which the calculated amounts can be multiplied to ensure that values are zero outside the specified period. If any values are required in all periods *except* those specified by the mask, formulae can be multiplied by (1 – mask value in period).

More detail can be included as necessary, for example an operating mask might give the proportion of each period falling within a concession period, running from start of operations for a specified number of years.

In order to position a fixed sequence of values changing across time periods (for example, construction expenditure, production profile), a combination of a calculated 'counter' and the SUMIF(...) or INDEX(...) functions can be used. The profile is input in the data sheet on a clearly labelled specific timeline for example, 'half years from Financial Close'. A counter is calculated to give a count which starts in the period of the model timeline corresponding to the start of the input timeline, for example, counting from 1 in the half year of Financial Close. To use SUMIF(...), a simple counter starting in the first period of the model timeline is also required.

Exhibit 3.1

Positioning an input profile

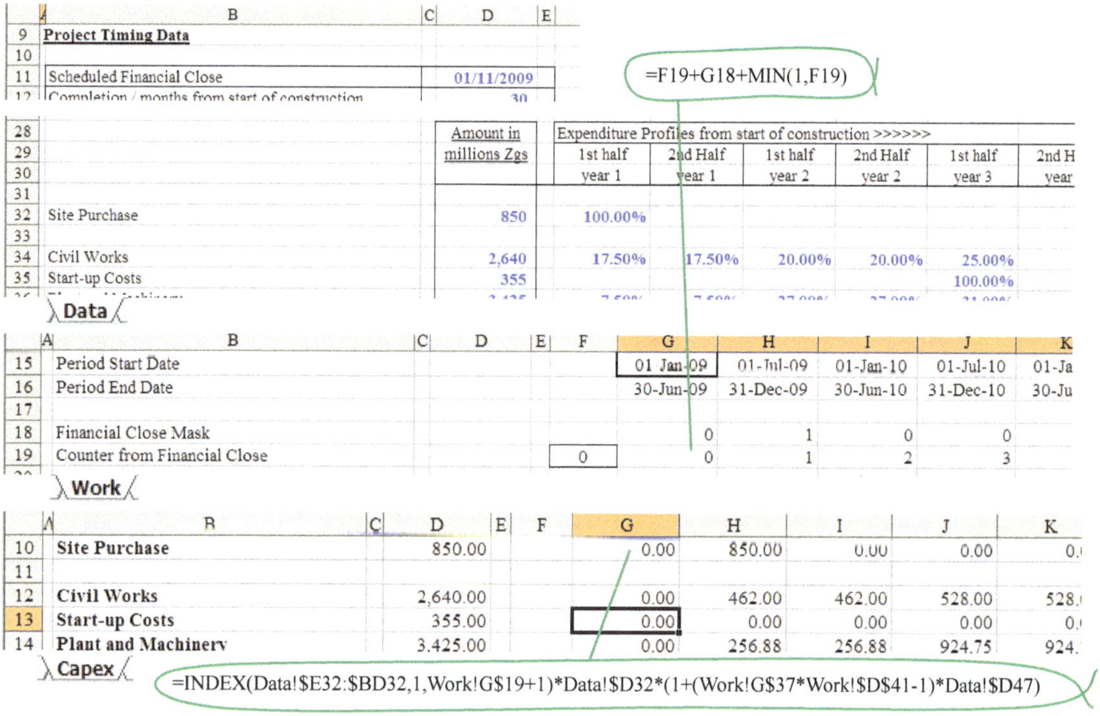

	B	D
9	**Project Timing Data**	
10		
11	Scheduled Financial Close	01/11/2009

	B	Amount in millions Zgs	Expenditure Profiles from start of construction >>>>>> 1st half year 1	2nd Half year 1	1st half year 2	2nd Half year 2	1st half year 3	2nd H year
31								
32	Site Purchase	850	100.00%					
33								
34	Civil Works	2,640	17.50%	17.50%	20.00%	20.00%	25.00%	
35	Start-up Costs	355					100.00%	

Data

=F19+G18+MIN(1,F19)

	B	F	G	H	I	J	K
15	Period Start Date		01 Jan 09	01-Jul-09	01-Jan-10	01-Jul-10	01-Ja
16	Period End Date		30-Jun-09	31-Dec-09	30-Jun-10	31-Dec-10	30-Ju
17							
18	Financial Close Mask		0	1	0	0	
19	Counter from Financial Close	0	0	1	2	3	

Work

	B	D	G	H	I	J	K
10	**Site Purchase**	850.00	0.00	850.00	0.00	0.00	0.
11							
12	**Civil Works**	2,640.00	0.00	462.00	462.00	528.00	528.
13	**Start-up Costs**	355.00	0.00	0.00	0.00	0.00	0.
14	**Plant and Machinery**	3,425.00	0.00	256.88	256.88	924.75	924.

Capex

=INDEX(Data!$E32:$BD32,1,Work!G$19+1)*Data!$D32*(1+(Work!G$37*Work!$D$41-1)*Data!$D47)

3.2 Increasing the number of time-periods per Column

Using a semi-annual model timeline (as recommended) generally provides sufficient detail during the operating period, and for all periods at the feasibility model stage. The drawdown schedule for equity and debt, and hence the construction period costs, are, however, generally required at some stage on a monthly or quarterly basis.

A straightforward way to incorporate this extra detail is to break down the half year over a number of rows. For example, six rows can represent the months within the half-year. The values in the monthly rows can then easily be totalled into semi-annual values for easy compatibility with the semi-annual calculations in the rest of the model. This also allows easy upgrade of working semi-annual feasibility models to include monthly detail as required since the new monthly rows can simply be totalled into the rows previously used to calculate the semi-annual values. This allows the new values to flow seamlessly into the existing semi-annual calculations.

When including monthly calculations, it is worth giving careful consideration to which figures actually need to be calculated on the more detailed basis. For example, if loan drawings are to be calculated to reflect monthly construction costs then the rest of the loan calculation can probably continue to be calculated on a semi-annual basis, provided that the interest calculation uses an average balance which reflects the monthly drawdown schedule.

Because the more detailed timing breakdown is generally only required for a limited number of items it should not prove a particularly cumbersome way of incorporating monthly values whilst maintaining full flexibility in the model timing assumptions. This method also eliminates all the issues regarding flexibility, repetition and integration which commonly arise from attempts to separate the construction and operating period analyses onto separate timelines, one monthly, one semi-annual.

See Exhibit 14.1 for an illustration of including monthly costs.

3.3 Reducing timescale within calculations

It is sometimes necessary to calculate values based on a longer time period than that selected per column in the model. A common example of this would be the annual calculation of tax within a semi-annual model. An easy way to handle this is by using a simple annual mask to switch the calculations on or off as required, as illustrated in Exhibit 3.2.

3.4 Changing timescale for presentation pages

For the report pages there may be a requirement to show values grouped to a lower frequency than that upon which the calculations are based – for example, an annual presentation of figures from a semi-annual model. Conversely, there may be a need to present values with a timeline more frequent than that used for the calculations – for example, monthly columns showing figures included in a semi-annual model.

Both these adjustments can be made easily using a combination of special counters and the INDEX(...) or SUMIF(...) functions.

The SUMIF(...) function calculates the total of all values in a range which are at the same positions as values in another range, of the same size and shape, which meet a specific criterion. Values on the model timeline can thus be totalled when they match the position on the timeline of a given year number. The annual summary can start from a fixed year or from the year of a specific event, such as Financial Close. The year number in each annual column then provides the criterion to be matched in the SUMIF(...) function (see Exhibit 3.3).

Exhibit 3.2

Grouping of values for annual calculations

	B	C	D	E	F	G	H	I	J	J	M
1	**Full Scheme Base Case**		*labelled single*		*pre-*	*half years >>>>>>*		*>>>*			....
2	**Worklines Sheet**		*values or*		*time*	**Jul 2011**	**Jan 2012**	**Jul 2012**	**Jan 2013**	**Jan 2014**	....
3	*All values without labelled units are in millions $a*		**Totals**		*line*	to Dec '11	to Jun '12	to Dec '12	to Jun '13	to Jun '14	....
	⁝⁝										
11	Simple annual mask *(start year)*				0	1	0	1	0	1	....

=1-G11

	B	C	D	E	F	G	H	I	J	J	M
1	**Full Scheme Base Case**		*labelled single*		*pre-*	*half years >>>>>>*		*>>>*			....
2	**Tax Calculations Sheet**		*values or*		*time*	**Jul 2011**	**Jan 2012**	**Jul 2012**	**Jan 2013**	**Jan 2014**	....
3	*All values without labelled units are in millions $a*		**Totals**		*line*	to Dec '11	to Jun '12	to Dec '12	to Jun '13	to Jun '14	....
	⁝⁝										
26	Taxable profits		34,866			0.00	0.00	32.40	64.30	58.20	....
28	Annual Taxable profits		34,866			0.00	0.00	32.40	0.00	122.50	....

=(H26+I26)*Work!I11

The 'INDEX' function can be used when annually spaced values, rather than the total for the year are required, for example, balances on loans or deposits. In this case a counter is needed on the annual sheet starting with a value equal to the position in the semi-annual figures of the first required value, counting in half years from the start of the model timeline. Subsequent values are calculated simply

Exhibit 3.3

Annual summary

	B	C	D	E	F	G	H	I	J	J	M
1	**Full Scheme Base Case**		*labelled single*		*pre-*	*half years >>>>>>*		*>>>*			....
2	**Worklines Sheet**		*values or*		*time*	**Jul 2011**	**Jan 2012**	**Jul 2012**	**Jan 2013**	**Jul 2013**	....
3	*All values without labelled units are in millions $a*		**Totals**		*line*	to Dec '11	to Jun '12	to Dec '12	to Jun '13	to Dec '13	....
	⁝⁝										
11	Year Counter					2011	2012	2012	2013	2013	....

	B	C	D	E	F	G	H	I	J	J	M
1	**Full Scheme Base Case**		*labelled single*		*pre-*	*half years >>>>>>*		*>>>*			....
2	**Funding Sheet**		*values or*		*time*	**Jul 2011**	**Jan 2012**	**Jul 2012**	**Jan 2013**	**Jul 2013**	....
3	*All values without labelled units are in millions $a*		**Totals**		*line*	to Dec '11	to Jun '12	to Dec '12	to Jun '13	to Dec '13	....
	⁝⁝										
26	Interest Payments		68,798			0	0	1,822	3,988	3,686	....
27	Loan Balance Outstanding					0	60,734	132,933	122,871	110,652	

	B	C	D	E	F	G	H	I	J	J	M
1	**Full Scheme Base Case**		*labelled single*								
2	**Annual Summary**		*values or*								
3	*All values without labelled units are in millions $a*		**Totals**			2012	2013	2014	2015	2016	....
4	*Simple annual counter*					3	5	7	9	11	....
	⁝⁝	=(G3-Work!$G$11)*2+1				=SUMIF(Work!$G11:$BC$11,G3,Fin!$G26:BC26)					
18	Interest Payments		68,798			1,822	7,674	2,871	2,306	1,978	....
19	Loan Balance Outstanding					132,933	110,652	80,762	72,963	58,934	....

=INDEX(Fin!$G27:$BC27,1,G$4)

by adding 2 in each period. An index function can then select the values at the specified positions in the semi-annual timeline, as illustrated in Exhibit 3.3.

For further guidance on creating annual summaries see Section 32.3.

Exhibit 3.4 shows the situation where a monthly summary is required for values included in stacked rows in a semi-annual model. Here, a simple monthly counter across the report sheet timeline can be compared with a stacked monthly counter in the semi-annual sheets, and the required values selected for each column using the SUMIF(…) function.

Exhibit 3.4

Quarterly summary

	B	C	D	E	F	G	H	I	J	J	M
1	Full Scheme Base Case		labelled single		pre-	half years >>>>>>>		>>>			
2	Worklines Sheet		values or		time	Jul 2011	Jan 2012	Jul 2012	Jan 2013	Jul 2013	....
3	*All values without labelled units are in millions $a*		Totals		line	to Dec '11	to Jun '12	to Dec '12	to Jun '13	to Dec '13	....
	⑀										
12	Simple monthly counter in 1st month of half year					1	7	13	19	25	....
13	Simple monthly counter in 2nd month of half year					2	8	14	20	26	....
14	Simple monthly counter in 3rd month of half year					3	9	15	21	27	....
15	Simple monthly counter in 4th month of half year					4	10	16	22	28	....
16	Simple monthly counter in 5th month of half year					5	11	17	23	29	....
17	Simple monthly counter in 6th month of half year					6	12	18	24	30	....

	B	C	D	E	F	G	H	I	J	J	M
1	Full Scheme Base Case		labelled single		pre-	half years >>>>>>>		>>>			
2	Funding Sheet		values or		time	Jul 2011	Jan 2012	Jul 2012	Jan 2013	Jul 2013	....
3	*All values without labelled units are in millions $a*		Totals		line	to Dec '11	to Jun '12	to Dec '12	to Jun '13	to Dec '13	....
	⑀										
32	Loan drawdown in 1st month of half year					0	0	6,745	543	0	....
33	Loan drawdown in 2nd month of half year					0	0	18,643	12,786	0	....
34	Loan drawdown in 3rd month of half year					0	0	27,662	4,392	0	....
35	Loan drawdown in 4th month of half year					0	20,246	18,934	0	0	....
36	Loan drawdown in 5th month of half year					0	14,244	42,864	0	0	....
37	Loan drawdown in 6th month of half year					0	26,245	18,995	0	0	....

=SUMIF(Work!$G$12:$BC$17,G4,Fin!$G$32:$BC$37)

	B	C	D	E	F	G	H	I	J	J	M
1	Full Scheme Base Case		labelled single		pre-	>>>		>>>			
2	Annual Summary		values or		time						
3	*All values without labelled units are in millions $a*		Totals		line	April '12	May '12	June '12	July '12	August '12	....
4	*Monthly counter*					*10*	*11*	*12*	*13*	*14*	....
	⑀										
18	Loan Drawings		68,798			20,246	14,244	26,245	6,745	18,643	....

4 Inflation

To properly reflect the relationship between values fixed in nominal terms and those subject to inflation, and between those subject to inflation at different rates, the model must include assumptions about inflation rates during the analysis period, and must apply them on a consistent basis.

Where construction costs are subject to indexation, high inflation during construction increases the investment costs of the project and hence can have a detrimental effect on returns and cover factors. During the operating period, high inflation increases revenues relative to nominally fixed debt service, and so is beneficial to returns and cover factors. It is therefore generally useful to include the option for at least two inflation rates over the project life, to allow these differing effects to be sensitised, i.e., testing higher rates during construction and lower rates during operations.

4.1 Value dates

In order to apply inflation to an input value it is necessary to know the date from which the value is to be inflated, that is the date at which the input monetary value correctly represents the cost or value of the item in question. For a feasibility model it may be that all values are taken from a single study or data source and are at a single given value date. More commonly particular sets of costs will be provided at various value dates, and the model must be able to apply inflation from the appropriate date. The simplest way to deal with this in the model is to have all general inflation factors calculated from the timeline start date, and apply specific single adjustments to each category of cost to inflate or deflate it to the timeline start date.

The complexity of this calculation depends on the relationship between the value dates, the timeline start date, and the inflation rate inputs.

If it is reasonable to assume that the initial inflation rate input into the model will apply during the period between any specified value date and the start of the model timeline, then the value date adjustment can be calculated very simply as

$$=(1 + \text{initial inflation rate \% p.a.})^\wedge((\text{model timeline start date} - \text{value date})/365)$$

This calculates the daily inflation factor as $(1+\text{annual rate})^\wedge(1/365)$, then applies it for the number of days between the value date and the model start date. If the value date is greater than the start date, the calculated days for which the rate is applied will be a negative value, the result will be the reciprocal of the inflation adjustment over the period (since $n^{-x} = 1/n^x$) and the calculated adjustment will be less than 1.00, deflating the input value back to the start of the model timeline. Otherwise it will be > 1.00 and will inflate the value to the start of the timeline.

This simple formula depends upon the following assumptions:

- The initial inflation rate can be assumed to apply between the start of the timeline and the value date.
- The adjustment period is sufficiently short that assuming 365 days per year will not cause material disparities as a result of leap years.

When these assumptions are not valid, other adjustments must be included.

For value dates prior to the start of the model timeline, additional inflation inputs may be required. It may be appropriate to apply all available historic inflation to the input value, specifying the value date accordingly, and have a 'pre-timeline' inflation rate assumption(s) for projected inflation rates between the value dates and the start of the model timeline. The value date adjustment would then be calculated differently if the value date is before (less than) the timeline start date, calculating inflation between the two dates using the pre-timeline rate.

For value dates substantially after the start of the timeline, to eliminate problems with changing inflation rates and year lengths, it may be necessary to include a new row to calculate the required adjustment with a formula in each time period as follows:

= IF (AND (this period start date <= value date, this period end date >= value date),
last period's end point inflation factor∗ (1+ this period's inflation rate %p.a.)^
((value date − last period's end date)/365), 0)

This formula will give zero in all periods except the period in which the value date falls. In the period of the value date it will give the inflation adjustment from the start of the model timeline up to the value date.

The value date formula can then be:

= IF (value date < timeline start date, (1 + % p.a. inflation rate prior to start of model timeline)^
((timeline start date − value date)/365), SUM(row used to calculate value date adjustment if value
date after timeline start date))

The relevant cost and revenue items are then multiplied by the inflation factor (see below), inflating from the start of the model timeline, and by the value date adjustment which either applies additional inflation, from the start of the timeline back to an earlier value date, or applies a factor which removes the inflation applied between the start of the timeline and a later value date.

4.2 Inflation factors

Inflation factors provide in each period the factor by which values should be multiplied in order to apply a particular inflation adjustment.

To maintain flexibility in the model, the factor calculations should allow for inflation rates which vary over time. A simple way to incorporate this is to have a row containing the percentage per annum inflation rate which applies in each half year of the model timeline. The factors can then use these rates, and any change in the way rates are input (for example, moving from a single input to an option for different rates during different time periods) can be included simply by changing the formula in the row containing the rates.

Inflation in real life is generally a rather volatile and elusive measure. In the model we need to find a reasonably consistent way of treating the input percentage per annum values when calculating inflation factors. When attempting to reflect 'natural' inflation of costs or revenues, unless specific information is available about when prices are likely to adjust, it seems reasonable to assume that inflation is consistent at the given rate during each model period, rather than occurring in a single jump at the beginning or end of a period. On this basis, during any half year, a value will begin at one level, and increase at a steady rate until the end the period. Generally the mid-period value gives an acceptable approximation to the average value produced by this process, with a fairly simple and transparent calculation methodology.

For conversion to real-terms values of end period figures such as dividends, and for convenience of calculation, it is generally helpful to calculate end point as well as mid-point factors (end-point value of one period is start-point value of next period).

In order to inflate to the midpoint of any period (half year, quarter, month) it is necessary to decompound the annual adjustment (see 4.2.1). For semi annual inflation factors, therefore, we have the calculations illustrated in Exhibit 4.1.

Exhibit 4.1

Simple inflation factors

Input Sheet		

23				to end	
24		Pre timeline		2015	thereafter
25	UK Inflation % p.a.	2.00%		3.00%	3.50%

=IF(G17<=Input!$F$24,Input!$F$25, Input!$G$25)

	B	C	D	E	F	G	H	I	J
2	Full Scheme Base Case		labelled single		pre-	half years >>>>>>>			
3	Worklines Sheet		values or		time	Jul 2011	Jan 2012	Jul 2012	....
4	All values without labelled units are in millions $a		Totals		line	to Dec '11	to Jun '12	to Dec '12	....

=F59*(1+G$57)^0.25

| 17 | Calendar year applicable to half year | | | | | 2011 | 2012 | 2012 | 2013 |

=G58*(1+G$57)^0.25

57	UK Inflation rate % p.a.					3.00%	3.00%	3.00%	....
58	UK Inflation Factor to mid period					1.007	1.022	1.038	....
59	UK Inflation Factor to end period				1	1.015	1.030	1.045	....

1.00

4.2.1 Decompounding

This is a concept relevant to many calculations in the project finance model, so it may be helpful to review it here.

Inflation is generally quoted as a percentage per annum increase. That is, during the course of a year, an inflated value will have increased by the given percentage.

If we assume that the rate of change remains constant through the year, then the percentage change over any specific time period (for example, month, quarter, half year) within the year, will always be the same.

So, for example, for inflation of 10.25% per annum an inflated value will have increased after one year by a factor of 1.1025. How much will it have increased after just six months? We know that:

(proportionate increase in value during 1st 6 months) × (proportionate increase in value during last 6 months) = 1.1025

Because we are assuming a steady rate of increase we also know that:

(proportionate increase in value during 1st 6 months) =
(proportionate increase in value during last 6 months)

So:

(proportionate increase in value during 1st 6 months)^2 = 1.1025

and hence:

(proportionate increase in value during 1st 6 months) = $\sqrt{1.1025}$ = $1.1025^{0.5}$ = 1.05

And the increase in value over six months = $1.05 - 1.00 = 0.05 = 5\%$.

We can generalise and say that, for any period for which an annual inflation rate of $r\%$ per annum applies, the factor reflecting the change in a value during that period, assuming a constant rate of change during the period, is given by:

(1+annual rate)^(number of years for which rate is applied)

For example, for three months' inflation at 15% per annum, i.e., 0.25 of a year at 15% per annum.

Factor applicable to reflect three months' inflation at 15% per annum = $1.15^{0.25}$ = 1.0276 (*answer shown rounded to 4dp*).

If we need the percentage change, rather than the factor, we perform the same calculation and just subtract 1 from the result.

4.3 Average inflation

For most purposes, use of the mid-point inflation factor to approximate the average value is sufficiently accurate. However, small disparities will appear if, for example, a series of six equal monthly costs are inflated to the mid-point of each month, then the total for the half year is converted back to real terms at the original value date, using the semi-annual mid-point inflation factor. To avoid problems of this sort the average inflation factor can be calculated correctly. Clearly this calculation could simply be used in all circumstances. Experience shows two downsides, however. Firstly the calculation is slightly more complicated and hence is often less popular with, and less well understood by, other model users. Secondly, if using the average then, in order to maintain true consistency, one ought, for example, to calculate the average for the months during which operation actually occurs where this is less than the full half year. This means that use of average inflation factors tends to generate a surprising amount of additional calculation for what is generally a very small numerical change.

The formula for the average inflation factor for any given time-period, expressed in years, during which a constant inflation rate of r percent per annum applies is:

$$((1/ ln(1+r)) * exp(\text{time-period} * ln(1+r)) - (1/ ln(1+r))) / \text{time-period}$$

For example, the average inflation adjustment applicable during a three month period, assuming inflation of 10% per annum can be calculated as follows:

$$=((1/ LN(1.1)) * exp(0.25 * LN(1.1)) - (1/ LN(1.1))) /0.25$$

4.4 Contractual inflation

Rather than adjusting with general inflation, some specific costs and revenues may be subject to defined inflation adjustments applied at specified intervals.

Where such adjustments can be assumed to correspond to model periods the calculation of inflation factors is simple. Using a suitable annual mask (for example, 1 in first half of each year, 0 in other periods), the inflation factor in each half year is simply that from the previous period increased by the applicable annual inflation percentage in adjustment periods only, i.e., multiplied by the simple annual mask. If an inflation factor is calculated for a very specific use, then it may also be appropriate to reflect the relevant value date directly in the factor, rather than inflating from the start of the timeline and then deflating again with a separate value date adjustment.

Exhibit 4.2

Adjusting inflation annually

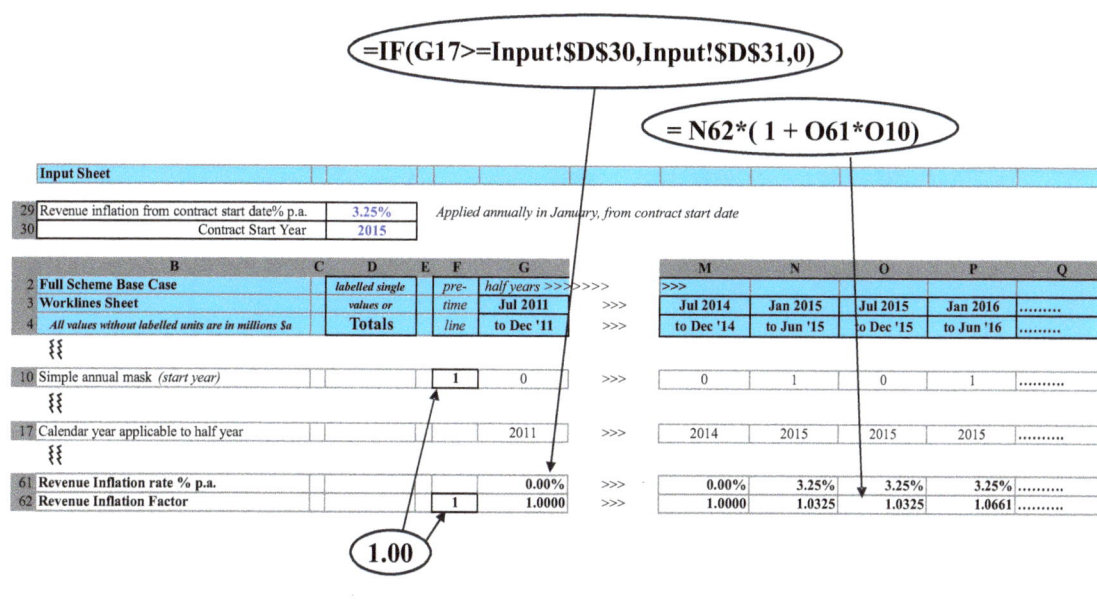

For more complex timing adjustments, for example, inflation applied annually on the anniversary of a flexibly specified date, a slightly more complex adjustment may be required. In this instance it may be necessary to calculate a mask, with 1s only in periods where inflation adjustments should be made, and to calculate a value for the proportion of the half year which falls before the adjustment, in periods when an adjustment is made. The appropriate weighted factor for each period can then be found by first calculating the inflation factor applicable in each half year before any adjustment, and the factor applicable after the adjustment. In periods where no adjustment is due (if any) the beginning and ending factors will be the same. The overall factor is then equal to the beginning factor multiplied by the proportion of the period pre-adjustment, plus the ending factor multiplied by the proportion of the period after the adjustment, as illustrated in Exhibit 4.3.

Exhibit 4.3

Adjusting inflation annually, part-way through a period

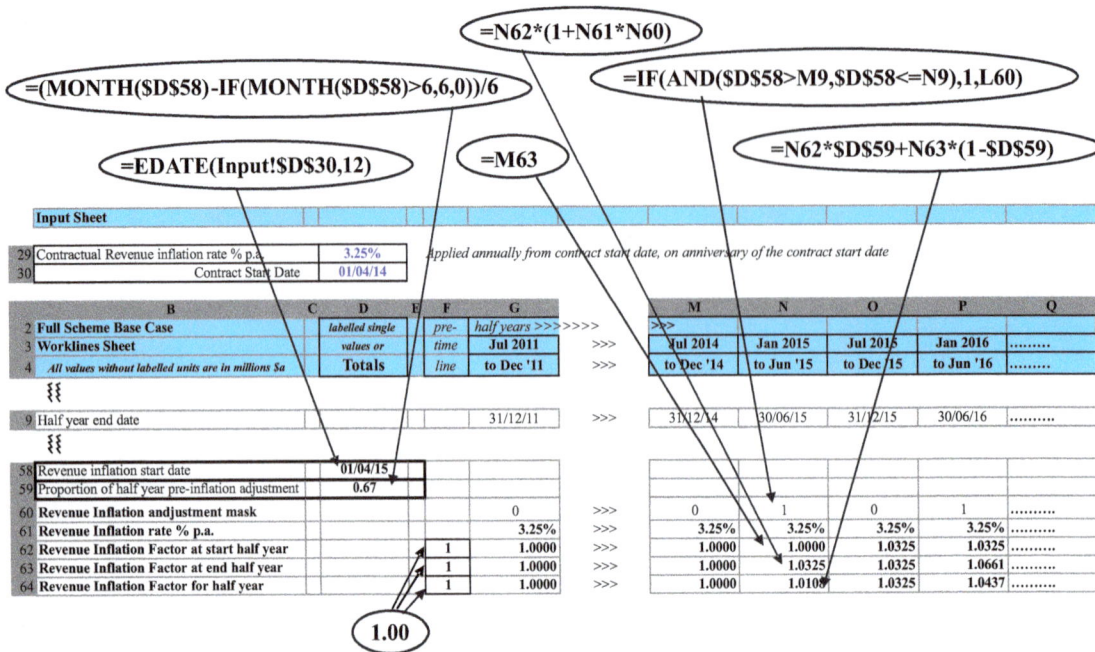

$=\text{N62}*(1+\text{N61}*\text{N60})$

$=(\text{MONTH(\$D\$58)}-\text{IF(MONTH(\$D\$58)}>6,6,0))/6$

$=\text{IF(AND(\$D\$58}>\text{M9,\$D\$58}<=\text{N9),1,L60)}$

$=\text{EDATE(Input!\$D\$30,12)}$

$=\text{M63}$

$=\text{N62}*\text{\$D\$59}+\text{N63}*(1-\text{\$D\$59})$

Input Sheet											
29	Contractual Revenue inflation rate % p.a.		3.25%			Applied annually from contract start date, on anniversary of the contract start date					
30	Contract Start Date		01/04/14								

	B	C	D	E	F	G		M	N	O	P	Q
2	**Full Scheme Base Case**		*labelled single*		pre-	half years >>>>>>		>>>				
3	**Worklines Sheet**		*values or*		time	**Jul 2011**	>>>	**Jul 2014**	**Jan 2015**	**Jul 2015**	**Jan 2016**	....
4	*All values without labelled units are in millions \$a*		**Totals**		line	**to Dec '11**	>>>	**to Dec '14**	**to Jun '15**	**to Dec '15**	**to Jun '16**	....
	⁜											
9	Half year end date					31/12/11	>>>	31/12/14	30/06/15	31/12/15	30/06/16	....
	⁜											
58	Revenue inflation start date		01/04/15									
59	Proportion of half year pre-inflation adjustment		0.67									
60	Revenue Inflation andjustment mask					0	>>>	0	1	0	1	....
61	Revenue Inflation rate % p.a.					3.25%	>>>	3.25%	3.25%	3.25%	3.25%	....
62	Revenue Inflation Factor at start half year				1	1.0000	>>>	1.0000	1.0000	1.0325	1.0325	....
63	Revenue Inflation Factor at end half year				1	1.0000	>>>	1.0000	1.0325	1.0325	1.0661	....
64	Revenue Inflation Factor for half year				1	1.0000	>>>	1.0000	1.0109	1.0325	1.0437	....

1.00

4.5 Real terms values

It is commonly necessary to provide selected results as 'real terms' values. Real terms values are not values assuming zero inflation, they are values expressed in monetary terms which have consistent value, assessed with respect to a given inflation measure, at a specific date.

To convert the nominal figures calculated in the model to real terms values they can be divided by an appropriate inflation factor, essentially the factors calculated using the general inflation rate(s) for the currency in which the figures are calculated. Real terms figures are as at a given date; dividing by inflation factors calculated from the start of the model timeline gives values as at the timeline start date. For real terms values at any other date, the value date must be specified and the results adjusted appropriately by an additional factor.

Real terms figures for IRR calculations do not need to be adjusted to any specific value date. IRR is a relative calculation, so all that is required is that the real terms cash flows all be at the same value date, not at any specific value date.

5 Controlling choices and options in the model

5.1 The use of switches to control data choices

A number of issues require alternatives to be addressed by the model. This may simply be a choice between different sets of data (for instance between data based on low, medium or high traffic forecast cases in a road project), or between different assumptions that require separate coding (for example, alternative financing structures). For simplicity, consistency, and to reduce the risk of run-time errors, choices of this type should be driven from the data using switches.

When specifying a switch there is much to recommend using a simple numeric input to select between the available options. This is clear, unambiguous, and often suitable for direct use as a parameter in the formulae using the switch. Text inputs, or even drop-down lists, lose one or both of these benefits.

Switches: example 1

Let us take as an example a road project, for which figures are being analysed based on three traffic forecasts, identified as low, medium and high forecasts. Each forecast traffic level gives rise to different values for projected traffic and maintenance costs. Revenue and variable operating costs are calculated by the model based on the projected traffic figures, so will automatically adjust for each case.

Obviously the two items could be changed manually each time a different forecast is to be used. The drawbacks with this approach are that it is relatively time consuming, and there is scope for error if any item is not changed correctly, giving rise to an inconsistent set of data. These problems can both be resolved by using a single switch to select the data to be used for the run (see Exhibit 5.1).

Exhibit 5.1

Switches to control data choices

=Work!$B$8&" with "&CHOOSE($D$47,"Low","Medium","High")&" Traffic Forecast"

	B	C	D	E	F	G	H	I	J	K	L	M
	Full Scheme, Base Case with Low Traffic Forecast											
	Input Sheet											
	All values without labelled units are in millions $a											
47	Traffic Forecast (low=1, medium=2, high=3)		1									
48												
49					From start of operations >>>>>							
50	Traffic Units per day				year 1	year 2	year 3	year 4	year 5	year 6	year 7	....
51	Low Traffic Forecast				4,560	4,720	4,885	5,056	5,233	5,416	5,605	....
52	Medium Traffic Forecast				5,840	5,957	6,076	6,197	6,321	6,448	6,577	....
53	High Traffic Forecast				6,244	6,338	6,433	6,529	6,627	6,727	6,827	....
55	Selected Traffic Forecast				4,560	4,720	4,885	5,056	5,233	5,416	5,605	....
56												
57					From start of operations >>>>>							
58	Major Maintenance Costs				year 1	year 2	year 3	year 4	year 5	year 6	year 7	....
59	Low Traffic Forecast Maint Costs				58	300	132	58	358	432	190	....
60	Medium Traffic Forecast Maint Costs				59	310	287	59	369	597	346	....
61	High Traffic Forecast Maint Costs				88	310	350	88	398	660	438	....
63	Selected Major Maintenance Costs				58	300	132	58	358	432	190	....

=INDEX(F51:F53,$D$47,1)

=INDEX(H59:H61,$D$47,1)

The value set for the switch, 0, 1 or 2 is used to select between the three input values for each data item. The model then picks up the selected values for use in the calculations.

This technique also works very well when introducing multiple data choices into a model currently offering only one option, because the existing single row or value used for direct input can contain the formula selecting the required value from the new multiple inputs, allowing the selected values to feed instantly into the model calculations. Similarly, it makes it very simple to 'tidy up' the data section if options become redundant, as the final value can be entered directly into the row or cell picked up in the code and the alternative values erased without any changes being required outside the data section.

5.2 The use of switches to control model calculations

Switches: example 2

At the early stages of project development, two possible financing structures are under consideration. Other areas of the model are being continually refined, and trying to create separate versions of the model to include each financing option would result in a great deal of additional work in making all updates to two models rather than one, checking each change in both models, etc. The best approach therefore is to incorporate the two financing options into a single model, and to select between them using a switch in the data.

The two strategies differ in relation to the timing of equity input and the assumed loan structure achievable. In Case 'A' equity is drawn up-front as needed, two export credit agency (ECA) loans are assumed to be available, and a debt:equity ratio of 80:20 is required. In Case 'B' equity is drawn pro rata to debt, with a single export credit loan being available and a 75:25 debt:equity ratio is required. In both cases, equity and export credits are supplemented by a single commercial loan drawn as needed to meet any remaining funding requirement. Because each differing element of the structure will need to be driven by a switch, flexibility can be maximised by providing a separate switch for each item, with an overriding 'master switch' selecting between the two cases as currently comprised (see Exhibit 5.2).

The value set for the master switch in the data controls the values selected for each of the three elements that differ between Case A and Case B via formulae in the 'Selected value' column. The formulae select between the values in the Case A column or the Case B column according to the value entered for 'Finance Case A or B (1 or 2)'.

For the equity, both up-front and pro rata equity calculations are included in the finance calculations section, with one or the other being simply set to zero, based on the value selected in data for the 'Equity up-front or pro rata (0 or 1)' switch. For each calculation, the debt:equity ratio is calculated at the level selected in the data. See Sections 15.2.1.2 and 15.2.2.3 for debt equity and pro-rata debt equity calculations.

For the loans, the finance calculations will include calculations for two ECA loans, together with any supporting calculations in the worklines section. The first loan will use the parameters entered for either ECGD or Coface, selected in the data according to the value set for the 'ECGD and EXIM or Coface (0 or 1)' switch, which will in turn be determined by the value entered for the master switch. The second export credit loan will use the parameters entered for EXIM or be set to zero, according to the applicable value for 'Loan Used for this run' in the Exim Loan column, also determined according to the value entered for the master switch.

Exhibit 5.2

Switches to control calculations

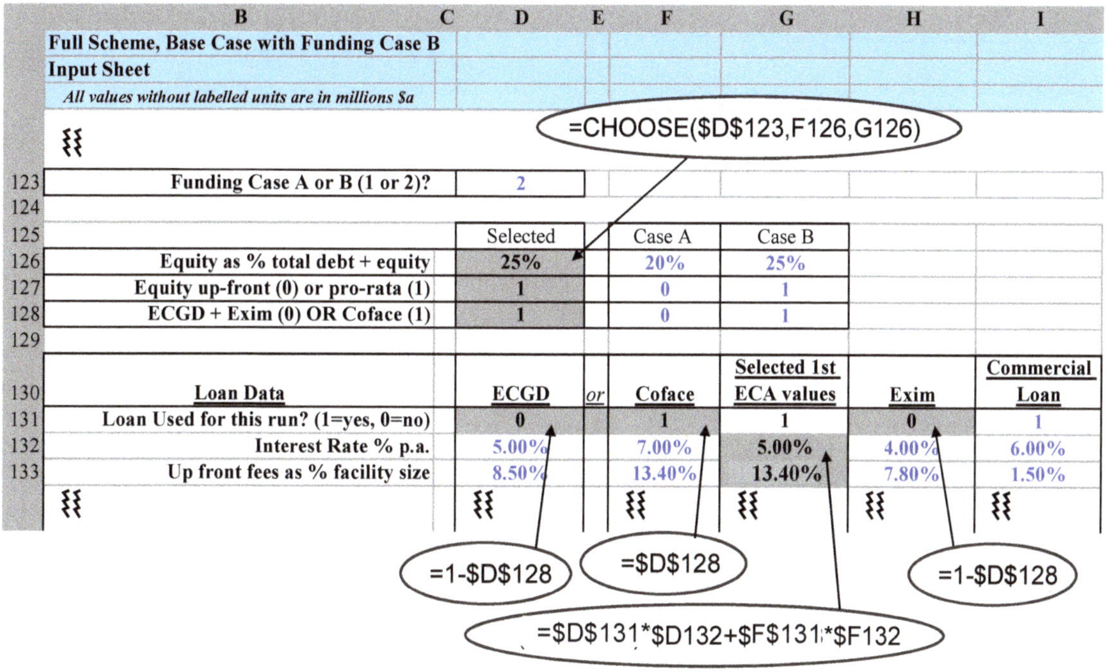

	B	C	D	E	F	G	H	I
	Full Scheme, Base Case with Funding Case B							
	Input Sheet							
	All values without labelled units are in millions $a							
			=CHOOSE($D$123,F126,G126)					
123	**Funding Case A or B (1 or 2)?**		2					
124								
125			Selected		Case A	Case B		
126	**Equity as % total debt + equity**		25%		20%	25%		
127	**Equity up-front (0) or pro-rata (1)**		1		0	1		
128	**ECGD + Exim (0) OR Coface (1)**		1		0	1		
129								
130	**Loan Data**		**ECGD**	*or*	**Coface**	**Selected 1st ECA values**	**Exim**	**Commercial Loan**
131	**Loan Used for this run? (1=yes, 0=no)**		0		1	1	0	1
132	**Interest Rate % p.a.**		5.00%		7.00%	5.00%	4.00%	6.00%
133	**Up front fees as % facility size**		8.50%		13.40%	13.40%	7.80%	1.50%

=1-$D$128   =$D$128   =1-$D$128

=$D$131*$D132+$F$131*$F$132

Throughout the model, the descriptive title for the first ECA loan, and the inclusion of values in reports for ECA loan 2 can also be controlled with reference to the appropriate switches in the data. Similarly, the value of the master or other switches can be used to control a string or text item that is incorporated in the print header in order to identify which finance case has been used in the production of any printed figures.

6 The use of macros in project finance models

The use of Visual Basic for Applications (VBA) programs to control some part of the spreadsheet's operation can offer good solutions for specific problems, but should be approached with care.

6.1 Why macros are a bad idea

6.1.1 Flexibility

The profligate use of macros can greatly reduce the flexibility of the model. Macros which are tightly linked to the physical layout of specific sheets, for example, can make it much more difficult and/or risky and/or time-consuming to make what would otherwise be simple model changes and updates. Although it looks sophisticated, any tendencies to create an 'all-singing, all-dancing' macro-driven user-interface should be firmly suppressed. The process generates extra work, makes the model less flexible, and rarely achieves anything which couldn't be achieved by intelligent use of Excel functions directly on the spreadsheet.

6.1.2 Transparency

Any calculations performed in visual basic, or any values entered directly into the visual basic code, are not transparent when working with the model. This makes the model more difficult to check, calculations harder to follow, and errors more likely when amending and updating the model.

Operations carried out by macros on elements of the spreadsheet can form an invisible part of the calculation path and, unless very clearly documented, can easily create errors where required macro operation is omitted, the source of numbers is obscured, or changes to model layout and structure disable critical but invisible macro operations.

6.2 Why macros are a great idea

Where a manipulation is required as part of the essential and unavoidable process of using the model, macros allow such manipulation to be defined, standardised and formalised as an intrinsic part of the model. The most common example in project finance modelling is a situation where calculated values need to be fixed for some reason, requiring a copy-paste-as-values operation.

6.3 Some simple rules about macros in project finance models

- Keep macro use to a minimum.
- Keep all calculations on the spreadsheet – preserving transparency.
- Isolate areas of the spreadsheet where macros carry out manipulations, ideally on dedicated sheets, for example, macrosupport sheet – preserving flexibility.
- Wherever possible link VBA to spreadsheet areas using range names rather than direct cell addresses – preserves flexibility as cell addresses in VBA are not updated when, for example, rows are added or removed on a worksheet.

6.4 Using macros

6.4.1 Running macros

Macros can be run in four ways.

1　A full list of macros in one or all open workbooks can be found at Tools, Macro, Macros (for Excel 2003) or Developer, Macros (in Excel 2007). Any macro can be run by selecting it on the drop-down list then clicking 'run'.
2　From the visual basic editor (see Figure 6-1), the currently selected macro can be run by clicking 'run' on the menu bar.
3　If a shortcut has been assigned to a macro, it can be run using the shortcut, a combination of the 'ctrl' key and the selected lower or upper case letter.
4　If a macro has been assigned to a button (see Section 6.6) it can be run by clicking on the button.

6.4.2 Stopping macros

If a macro is running incorrectly, accidentally or unendingly, it can be interrupted by pressing 'Esc' (note, it may be necessary to press 'Esc' repeatedly). This will produce a dialog box stating that code execution has been interrupted and offering the following options.

- Continue – allows the macro to resume operation from the point in the code where it was stopped.
- End – stops macro execution.
- Debug – displays the macro code in the visual basic editor, with a yellow block at the point where execution of the code was stopped. Note that after selecting 'Debug', the visual basic editor must be closed or the blue 'reset' square on the menu bar clicked before the macro can be run normally.

6.5 How to add a new macro to a model

6.5.1 Recording macros

A simple and convenient way to create a new macro is to record some parts of the macro, then edit or copy-paste the required code into the new macro shell.

To start recording use the menu options Tools, Macro, Record new Macro (in Excel 2003) or Developer, Record Macro (Excel 2007). **Beware!** Once you start recording, all actions will be recorded until you specifically stop recording. You can stop recording by clicking on the blue square labelled 'stop recording' or using Tools, Macro, Stop recording (in Excel 2003), Developer, 'stop recording' (Excel 2007).

Note, if the 'Developer' item is not shown in Excel 2007, click on the 'Office' button at top left of the screen, click on 'Excel Options' and tick 'show Developer tab on the ribbon'.

When you switch on Macro record, you will see a dialog box prompting you for:

- macro name;
- shortcut key;
- macro location; and
- macro description.

Make the name something clear and descriptive, and fairly short. If the macro is one you will want to run often, and from many locations in the model, it is useful to assign it a shortcut key. This is a key which, when pressed in combination with the 'ctrl' key will run the macro for you. It is clearly best to avoid keys used for other purposes, such as 'c' or 'v'. In general, capital letters are more likely to be free of existing applications (shortcuts are case-sensitive). Generally the default location 'This workbook' will be perfect for macros in project finance models. The description should be brief and helpful!

Once the dialog box disappears you can start recording the Visual Basic code you need for your macro. Carry out all the operations which you will want the macro to perform, ideally in the order in which you want them done. Some macros can be fully specified in this way (see Section 9.5), in which case, once 'stop recording' has been clicked, your work is done, your macro is set up and should be ready to use. It is nonetheless advisable always to save the file before running a macro for the first time. That way, if it runs riot and you have to abort the Excel session, you will have saved the VBA code and you can start trying to improve it and make it work, rather than having to start all over again and record it from scratch.

6.5.2 Editing macros

If your recorded macro is not sufficient as recorded to do what you need, you can access and amend the VBA code via the visual basic editor (Tools, Macro, Macros, select relevant macro, Edit, in Excel 2003, or Developer, Macros, select relevant macro, Edit in 2007). You can edit your VBA code as if

---

Exhibit 6.1

Visual basic editor

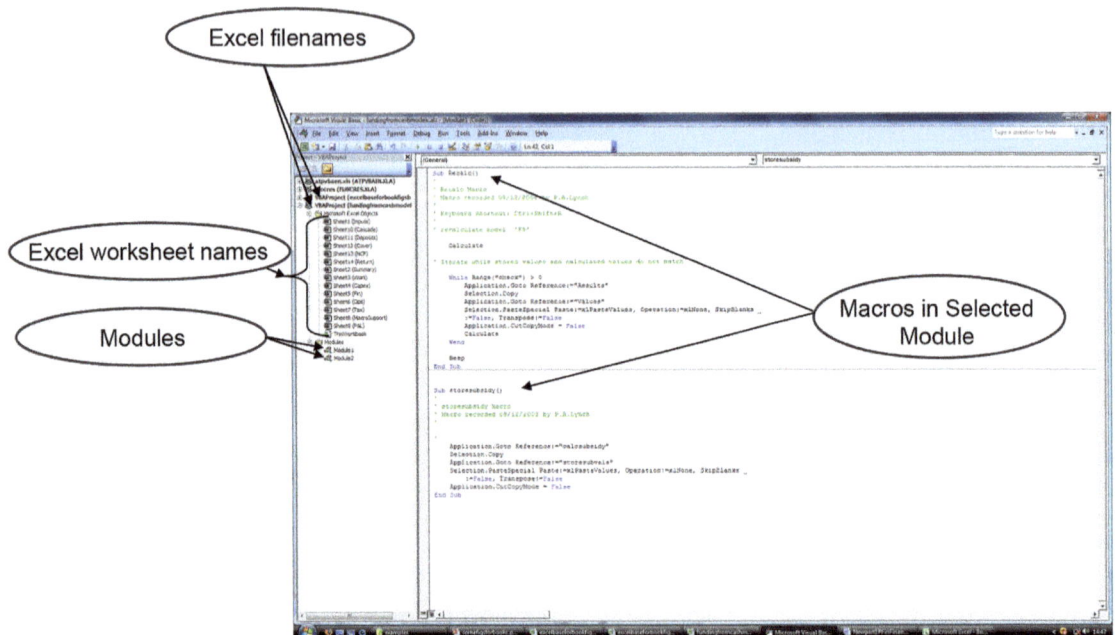

---

the editor were a word processor, and the code you have edited is the code which will run when you next run the macro, there is no intermediate stage of compiling, updating or saving the new code. For examples of the macro editing process see Section 7.4.2.

To access the code for a different macro from within the visual basic editor, find, in the left hand window, the Excel file in which the macro is saved, then look in the 'Modules' for that file. Excel stores macros in 'modules' and creates a new one in any session during which you create a new macro. To see the macros in a given module, double click on the module name. Whole macros can be copied between modules, and code can be copied between macros within one or more modules.

6.5.3 Copying macros between models

Open the file containing the macro (source file) and the model into which the macro is to be copied (destination model), and create or copy any essential supporting sheets and range names into the destination model. If the destination model already includes one or more macros, simply open the visual basic editor and copy the entire code for the required macro (from 'sub' to 'end sub') from a module in the source file, and paste into any existing module in the destination model. Make sure that the new code is inserted above, below or between existing macros, not into the body of an existing macro's code. Save the destination model (perhaps with a new name), and test the macro.

6.6 Using buttons to run macros

Macros can be assigned to labelled 'buttons' on the worksheet, and will run when the buttons are clicked. To be able to create buttons you need the 'button' icon to be visible. This can be done in Excel 2003 by using View Toolbars Customise and selecting it from the 'forms' icons and dragging onto the menu bar (see Exhibit 6.2). Alternatively, tick the 'forms' option on the View, Toolbars menu to display all forms icons, including the button icon. In Excel 2007 the icon is found on Developer, Insert.

Exhibit 6.2

Finding the 'Button' icon in Excel 2003

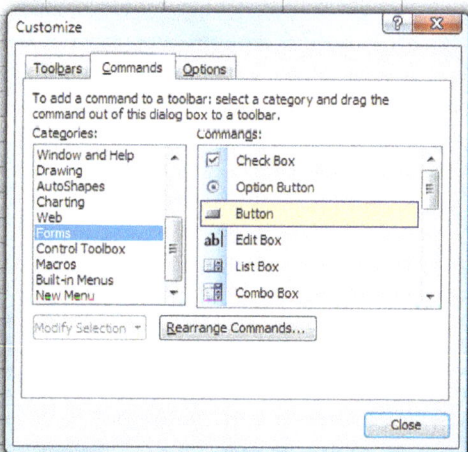

To position a button on the spreadsheet, click on the 'button' icon, then click and drag a rectangle to the required size in the required position on the worksheet. You will immediately be prompted to select a macro from a dialog box. Having selected a macro you can enter the text of your choice to be displayed on the button. To change or format the text displayed on the button, or to assign a different macro to the button, right-click on the button.

Exhibit 6.3

Right-click drop-down box for button

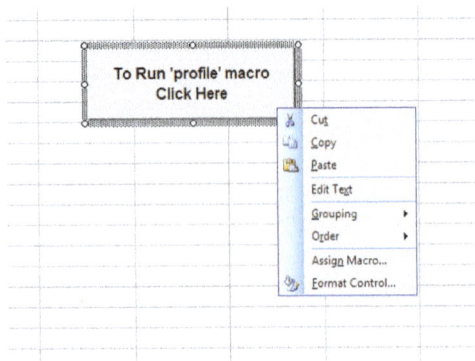

---

7 Treatment of circular and iterative calculations

7.1 Circularity in project finance calculations

There are a number of calculations in project finance analysis which are inherently circular. The most commonly encountered of these are the calculation of equity drawings based on a target debt:equity ratio, and the calculation of loan up-front fees when loans are sized by funding requirement, including fees.

Exhibit 7.1

Some project finance calculations are inherently circular

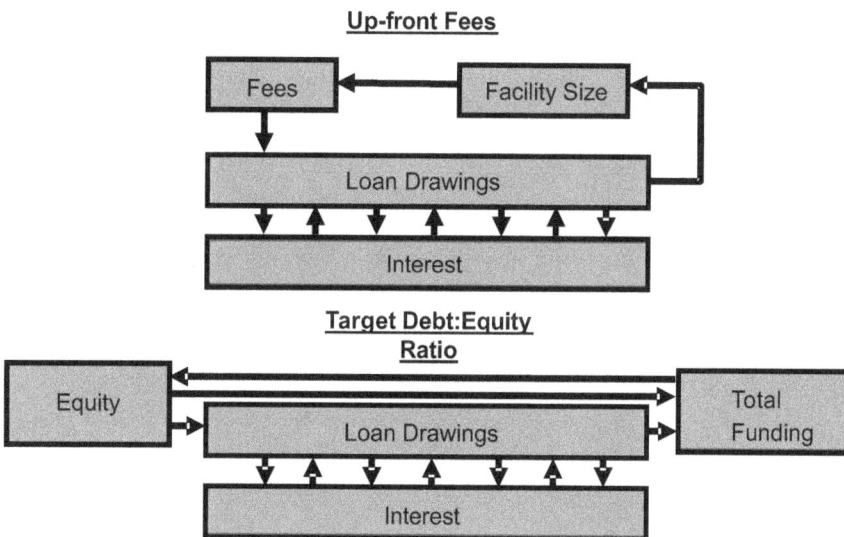

7.2 Drawbacks of circular code

There are a number of disadvantages to simply writing circular code. Although individually these may seem minor issues, taken in total they present sufficient incentive to spend considerable time, if necessary, in modelling circular calculations in a way that avoids simply using circular code, and trusting to the internal mechanism of the spreadsheet or manually repeated iteration to produce consistently correct results. Excel allows a choice between permitting iteration of the calculations in the spreadsheet, up to a maximum number of repetitions and a specified level of accuracy, or prohibiting iteration of code, in which case Excel will issue a warning if a circular path is created in the model (these settings can be accessed via Tools, Options, Calculation in Excel 2003, and via the 'Office button', Excel Options, Formulas in 2007).

The disadvantages of writing circular code are discussed in 7.2.1 to 7.2.5 below, and are considered sufficiently overwhelming to justify all the work required to avoid having any circular code in the model. The option for iteration should therefore always be unticked (see Exhibit 2.1).

7.2.1 Losing control of the model

If circularity is written into the spreadsheet code the modeller loses control of calculations, particularly if more than one circular path is included. It is no longer possible to be certain that the model has resolved to a correct solution, or that exactly the same solution will be produced each time a particular run is performed. If the iterative calculation is cyclical or oscillating then the model will never reach a solution and will simply stop iterating at an arbitrary point. There is no clearly defined point in the model at which such problems can be observed and resolved.

7.2.2 Calculation time

Iteration of circular code is time-consuming. The iteration of circular code may take longer than the iteration of a recalc macro (see below) If the iteration is cyclical or oscillating then the model will cycle to the maximum number of iterations specified in the calculation options, which may be a very prolonged process in a large model, and will still not produce a completed calculation.

7.2.3 ERR propagation

With built-in circularity, any error messages (such as 'ERR', 'NAME' or 'VALUE') on the circular path will propagate throughout the model. Once distributed around the circular calculation path, elimination of the original problem will not clear the messages, as all cells in the circular calculation are now referencing other cells displaying error messages. In this situation it may be necessary to revert to the last-saved version of the model, abandoning changes made meanwhile. At the least it is usually necessary to delete rows until the circularity is broken, and then rebuild the calculations. Thus hours of work can be lost due to a single simple error.

The risk of generating an error message and an accidental circularity whilst building a model is a prime consideration behind the choice to work with 'recalculate before save' disabled. With manual recalculation selected, it may be possible to resolve an error before it propagates through the model. Saving a version of the file to drop back to if things go wrong makes sense, but will be disastrous if the file is automatically recalculated (spreading the error) and then saved.

7.2.4 Control of accuracy

With circular Excel code it is not possible to specify different levels of accuracy for specific iterated solutions. Thus iteration must continue until all values are solved to the level of accuracy required for the most sensitive iterated value.

7.2.5 Ability to check and audit model

It is not possible to confidently check a calculation which has no fixed start or end point, for which every value is correct only if the previous value was correct, and the previous value is correct only if the next value is correct. Even with a single circular path, calculations can become difficult to verify. With multiple circular paths it can become impossible to give a confident validation of the results.

In addition to undermining the normal checking procedure required as part of the model development process (see Section 28), circular code can also disqualify a model for auditing by some organisations, undermining its ability to support the deal through financial close.

7.3 Avoiding circular calculations

7.3.1 Careful coding

Although a small subset of calculations are inherently and unavoidably circular, many circularities in models arise with respect to items which need not be circular at all.

The avoidance of circularity should be a basic driver of model design, from high level structure to detailed formulae. Adherence to the idea of logical flow through the model, from left to right across rows, from top to bottom within sheets, from left to right across sheets, helps avoid unnecessary introduction of circularity. The few calculations which need to flow against this pattern can be treated with extra care as potential sources of risk for circularity.

In addition to general care with model structure, specific methods can be used to manage potential circularity.

Calculations can be broken down into their component parts to avoid 'lumping together' independent items unnecessarily. Interest during construction provides an excellent example of this. Loan interest is payable on specified dates; in the model, the payment dates will be assumed to fall at the end of the given time period, for example, every six months at the end of the model half year periods. Interest is payable on the daily loan balance during the period between interest dates. During construction interest is frequently paid by making an additional drawing on the loan. Thus the interest amount depends on the average balance outstanding over the period, a calculation which uses the loan drawings during the period. If the drawing to pay interest is included in this calculation, clearly the whole thing is very circular. However, in reality the drawings to fund interest payments will not comprise part of the loan balance during the period to which the interest payment relates. Simply separating these additional drawings from all other kinds of drawings on the loan allows appropriate calculation of the average balance on which to charge interest, inclusion of the additional drawings in the loan balance for the following period's interest calculation, and avoids generating any problematic circularity issues.

Unnecessary connections can be eliminated where they would produce circularity. For example, if a project generates some small revenues during the construction period, and the available cash produced is to be used to pay construction costs and reduce the funding requirement, the connection between tax, drawings and interest might give rise to circularity. If, however, it can safely be assumed that no net tax payments will be required during the construction period, then the calculation can use pre-tax revenues, and no spurious circularity is produced.

7.4 Handling circular calculations without circular code

7.4.1 Successive approximation

For some of the circular calculations required in the context of modelling project finance deals, elimination of the inherent circularity is either impossible or impractical. Circular code can however be avoided, and control of the calculation achieved using successive approximation under the direct and transparent control of the modeller, rather than via iterative operation of Excel. This involves breaking a circular calculation at a suitable point, ideally at a point where the calculation path involves a single value, and repeatedly entering, recalculating and re-entering the value for a given element on the circular path. This process should iterate towards a solution until the required level of accuracy is achieved for each value. This has a number of advantages over using Excel's built-in iteration facility:

- modeller has complete control over the calculation;
- independent control over required level of accuracy for each of several circular calculations;
- a clear calculation path, hence a clear audit trail when checking code or output; and
- easy prevention of the irreversible propagation of ERRs throughout the model.

Whilst the calculation remains circular, the code becomes linear, with a clearly identified start and end point.

Exhibit 7.2

Successive approximation

With widely differing start values for ' a ', the iterative calculation rapidly approaches a theoretical solution, giving results consistent to eight decimal places after seven iterations.

Successive Approximation		$a = (d - c)^+$	$c = a + d / a$

iterative calculation is $a_n = (d - c_{n-1})^2$ $c_n = a_n + d / a_n$

	$b = 10$			$b = 10$			$b = 10$	
	$d = 20$			$d = 20$			$d = 20$	
	$a_0 = 5$		$a_0 =$	200		$a_0 =$	3,000,000	

n	a_n	c_n	a_n	c_n	a_n	c_n
0	5	9.	200	200.1	3,000,000	3.00E+06
1	121.	121.16528926	32,436.01	32,436.0106166	9.00E+12	9.00E+12
2	10,234.41575029	0.00195419	1.05E+09	0.00000002	8.10E+25	2.47E-25
3	399.92183619	0.05000977	399.99999924	0.05	400.	0.05
4	398.00211008	0.05025099	398.0025	0.05025094	398.0025	0.05025094
5	397.99248557	0.05025221	397.99248753	0.0502522	397.99248753	0.0502522
6	397.99243708	0.05025221	397.99243709	0.05025221	397.99243709	0.05025221
7	397.99243684	0.05025221	397.99243684	0.05025221	397.99243684	0.05025221
8	397.99243684	0.05025221	397.99243684	0.05025221	397.99243684	0.05025221
.....	.....	.....	.....	.....	.....	.....

7.4.2 Automating iteration – the recalc macro

The process of successive approximation can be automated and controlled using a simple macro to recalculate the model instead of the usual F9 'calc' key. Such a macro can handle any number of separate circular calculations, and will iterate all values simultaneously: this is helpful where the figures from one circular calculation feed into one or more other circular calculations.

The essential element of such a macro is that for each circular calculation it picks up the calculated value for the figures selected for iteration and converts them to numeric values in another cell of the spreadsheet. The calculations in the model use the numeric value, rather than referencing a formula calculating the figure. Thus, there is no circularity built into the code.

The macro recalculates the model and checks the difference between calculated and numeric values. Until this is reduced to a specified level for each value passed through the macro, the numeric values are updated with the revised calculated figures and the process repeated.

An example layout of the spreadsheet items used with the recalc macro is shown in Exhibit 7.3, where 'Calculated results' pick up or calculate values from the calculation section of the model; 'Results as Values...' contain numeric values copied by the macro from the row of calculated figures above; and where the 'Check' row has a formula in each column that takes a value of 1 if the absolute difference between calculated and input values in the column is greater than a specified amount. The outlined value to the left simply totals the 'Check' row. While the total of the 'check' row is greater than zero, the macro will continue to iterate.

Exhibit 7.3

The recalc macro

	B	C	D	E	F	G	H	I	J	K	L	M
1	Full Scheme Base Case											
2	Macrosupport sheet											
3	*All values without labelled units are in millions $a*											
4						Supportable Debt	Total Funding (excl. rolled up sub debt)	NPV at completion of cash for investors	Supportable Equity	Initial Funding of Accounts	Total Senior debt drawings	Projected sub debt drawings	
5	Calculated Results					254,256,350	768,756,289	29,554,382	29,538,123	12,885,432	254,256,350	28,040,915	
6	Results as values, pasted from top row by recalc macro					254,256,350	768,756,289	29,554,382	29,538,123	12,885,432	254,256,350	28,040,915	
7	Check	0				0	0	0	0	0	0	0	0

=SUM($F$7:$AA$7)

=IF(ABS(F$5-F$6)>0.001,1,0)

range name 'check'

range name 'Results'

range name 'Values'

```
Sub Recalc()
'
' Recalc Macro
' Macro recorded 09/12/2008 by P.A.Lynch
'
' Keyboard Shortcut: Ctrl+Shift+R
'
' recalculate model 'F9'

    Calculate

' Iterate while stored values and calculated values do not match

    While Range("check") > 0
        Application.Goto Reference:="Results"
        Selection.Copy
        Application.Goto Reference:="Values"
        Selection.PasteSpecial Paste:=xlPasteValues, Operation:=xlNone, SkipBlanks _
        :=False, Transpose:=False
        Application.CutCopyMode = False
        Calculate
    Wend

    Beep
End Sub
```

VBA code for recalc macro

The steps taken by the macro, controlled by the visual basic code illustrated in Exhibit 7.3 are as follows.

1	Recalculate the model (F9).
2	If the value of 'Check' equals zero, i.e., all items are solved, quit macro.
3	Copy the calculated results on to the row below, pasting as numeric values.
4	Recalculate the model (F9).
5	Repeat macro from '2'.

It can be helpful to include some signal (for example, a series of beeps) prior to quitting the macro, to indicate that the macro has run and has finished operation.

In order to use the Recalc macro efficiently, the spreadsheet recalculation settings should be for manual rather than automatic recalculation, and should recalculate only once – i.e., no automatic iteration. These are, in any case, the appropriate settings for use when developing large, complex models. In addition to breaking circular calculations, once in place the Recalc macro can also be used to automate other iterative calculations, such as the calculation of a fixed input tariff to achieve a specified target IRR (see Section 11).

To create a new Recalc macro in the model, begin by setting up the required range names on the Macrosupport sheet. The 'Results' range should include sufficient columns to accommodate all required values, it doesn't matter if it includes columns which are initially empty. The 'Values' range should either name only the cell immediately below the leftmost cell of the 'Results' range, or should be the same size and shape as the 'Results' range, so that it will work as a specified range for pasting the contents of 'Results'. The 'check' range should include only the cell giving the total of all the individual check formulae. Thus, this figure will only be zero if all items have iterated to an acceptably stable solution.

The formulae in the 'check' row should be copied across the same number of columns as are include in the 'results' range to help make it clear where values will and will not automatically be iterated by the macro. The check formulae compare the magnitude of the difference between the value currently being used by the model, in the 'values' row, and that calculated for the current iteration, in the 'results' row. This value will reduce as the item iterates towards a solution and essentially sets the required level of accuracy for each calculation. An initial default value can be included in the formula when setting up the sheet, but the value can be individually adjusted for specific items which need to be solved to greater or lesser accuracy.

Once the Macrosupport sheet is prepared, and the range names are in place, create the VBA code for the macro (see Section 6.5). This can be done in a number of ways. A simple and convenient way to create a recalc macro from scratch is to record some parts of the macro, then edit the recorded code into a complete macro. The things which can be recorded are moving the cursor (from anywhere in the model) to the macrosupport sheet and selecting the 'results' range containing the calculated results. This is most simply done using 'F5' the goto command, and selecting the results range. Copy the selected range (click on the copy icon or press 'ctrl'+'c'), select the range where the values are to be pasted, F5 'values', and paste as values by clicking on paste-as-values icon or using Edit, Paste Special, Values (Excel 2003), or Home, Paste, Paste Values (Excel 2007). Press 'esc' then press F9 to record the 'calculate' instruction. Stop recording at this point, and open the macro recorded so far in the visual basic editor. The recorded code should look like Exhibit 7.4.

Exhibit 7.4

Recorded VB for recalc macro

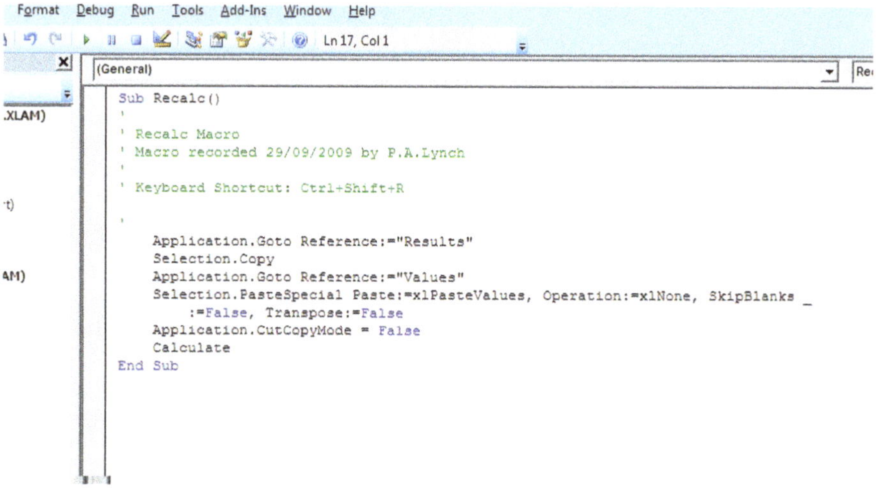

```
Format  Debug  Run  Tools  Add-Ins  Window  Help

                                              Ln 17, Col 1

(General)                                                          Re

        Sub Recalc()
        '
        ' Recalc Macro
        ' Macro recorded 29/09/2009 by P.A.Lynch
        '
        ' Keyboard Shortcut: Ctrl+Shift+R
        '
        '
            Application.Goto Reference:="Results"
            Selection.Copy
            Application.Goto Reference:="Values"
            Selection.PasteSpecial Paste:=xlPasteValues, Operation:=xlNone, SkipBlanks _
                :=False, Transpose:=False
            Application.CutCopyMode = False
            Calculate
        End Sub
```

The code needs to be slightly rearranged and expanded. An additional 'calculation' instruction is needed at the start of the macro to see whether or not changes mean that the model needs to be iterated to a solution. The macro then needs to repeat the copy-paste-calculate cycle until everything is satisfactorily solved. This can be achieved using a 'While loop', which sets a condition with a 'While' command, code between the 'While' and a 'Wend' instruction is then repeated until the condition is no longer fulfilled. After these changes the VB code for the macro should essentially match that shown in Exhibit 7.3.

Alternatively, once you have a model with a working recalc model, you can simply copy it into new models as required (see Section 6.5.3), being careful to ensure consistency between range names on the spreadsheet and in the macro.

8 Currency calculations

For most international projects, costs and/or revenues will be denominated in more than one currency, and the model must be able to cope with this. The most obvious approach is to prepare all figures in their underlying currency, then convert them as required when different currencies have to be combined for calculation purposes. There are, however, advantages to adopting a rather different technique. Instead of including figures in a variety of currencies, the model can be produced in a single, presentation currency, with key figures being converted back into their underlying currency as needed for presentation in the results sections. Obviously, careful thought is required when setting up the model on this basis to ensure that currency issues are properly treated, but overall such models should be simpler and less error-prone than those combining calculations in different currencies.

- Formulae can address any cell in the calculations without risk of mixing amounts in different currencies.
- Figures in the model can easily be audited without repeatedly having to convert values or having to duplicate values in two or more currencies throughout the model.
- Flexible assignment of currency to specific costs, loans, deposits, etc., is much easier.

Input values can be entered in the underlying currency and immediately converted on the input sheet at the initial exchange rate.

In order to produce correct figures using a single presentation currency, the devaluation of underlying currencies versus the presentation currency must be calculated. This can be accomplished using a combination of the assumed general inflation rates for each currency and any assumed real appreciation or depreciation between them. Factors calculated on this basis can then be used directly to adjust calculated values, or to calculate exchange rates. It is useful to calculate such values for end and mid-periods. Real appreciation/depreciation can be specified in a number of ways, for example as a single per annum rate, as a series of per annum rates, or as inputs on the timeline representing percentage adjustments applied in full at the start of the timeline period for which they are input.

Assuming no real appreciation or depreciation (i.e., purchasing power parity), the nominal devaluation of the presentation currency versus an underlying currency can be calculated as the inflation factor for the presentation currency divided by the inflation factor for the underlying currency. This represents the effect of inflation on both currencies (see Exhibit 8.1).

In order to take account of real appreciation/depreciation of the presentation currency, a real devaluation factor, based on values input in the data, is calculated, with devaluation of the presentation currency represented by an increasing factor, and appreciation by a decreasing factor. The nominal devaluation factor is then multiplied by the real devaluation factor to give the overall values used by the model. It is usually worth including provision for real appreciation/depreciation in the model, even if it is assumed to be zero for most runs.

Note that for some currency pairs it may not be appropriate to assume that purchasing power parity is maintained, for example where governments artificially hold their currencies at a constant rate relative to another currency, irrespective of differential inflation. For such combinations it may be appropriate to simply assume a constant exchange rate throughout, with the option to apply devaluation as a sensitivity.

Exhibit 8.1

Illustrative basic currency calculations

Full Scheme Base Case — Input Sheet
All values without labelled units are in millions $a

Initial Exchange rates vs Sarva dollar	Currency
Euro	0.10
Sterling	0.13

Inflation Rates % p.a.	Pre timeline	until 2015	thereafter
Sarva Dollar Rate	3.00%	4.00%	3.50%
Euro Rate	2.75%	3.00%	3.50%
Sterling Rate	2.00%	2.00%	2.50%

Real Devaluation % adjustment at start of period	half year to Dec '11		half year to Dec '12	half year to Jun '13	half year to Dec '13	half year to Jun '14	
Sarva dollar vs Euro	0%	>>>	0%	20%	0%	0%	……
Sarva dollar vs Sterling	0%	>>>	0%	10%	0%	0%	……

	Price in Euros	Price in sarva dollars
Fuel Cost per litre	5.25	53

=$C$45*$D$31

Full Scheme Base Case — Worklines Sheet
All values without labelled units are in millions $a

labelled single values or Totals	pre-time line	half years >>>>>>> Jul 2011 to Dec '11		Jul 2014 to Dec '14	Jan 2015 to Jun '15	Jul 2015 to Dec '15	Jan 2016 to Jun '16	
Sarva Inflation Rate % pa. in each half year		4.00%	>>>	4.00%	4.00%	4.00%	3.50%	……
Sarva mid period Inflation Factor		1.010		1.136	1.158	1.181	1.203	……
Sarva end period Inflation Factor		1.020		1.147	1.170	1.193	1.214	……
Euro Inflation Rate % pa. in each half year		3.00%	>>>	3.00%	3.00%	3.00%	3.50%	……
Euro mid period Inflation Factor		1.007		1.101	1.117	1.134	1.152	……
Euro end period Inflation Factor		1.015		1.109	1.126	1.142	1.162	……
Sterling Inflation Rate % pa. in each half year		2.00%	>>>	2.00%	2.00%	2.00%	2.50%	……
Sterling mid period Inflation Factor		1.005		1.066	1.077	1.088	1.100	……
Sterling end period Inflation Factor		1.010		1.072	1.082	1.093	1.107	……
Sarva real devaluation factor vs Euro		1.000		1.000	1.200	1.200	1.200	……
Sarva real devaluation factor vs Sterling		1.000		1.000	1.100	1.100	1.100	……
Sarva mid pd toal devaluation factor vs Euro		1.002		1.032	1.244	1.250	1.253	……
Sarva end pd toal devaluation factor vs Euro		1.005		1.034	1.247	1.253	1.253	……
Sarva mid pd toal devaluation factor vs Sterl.		1.005		1.065	1.183	1.195	1.203	……
Sarva end pd toal devaluation factor vs Sterl.		1.000		1.070	1.189	1.200	1.206	……

=O76*(1+Input!P41)
=O77*(1+Input!P42)
=P65/P69*P76
=P66/P74*P77

Full Scheme Base Case — Operations Sheet
All values without labelled units are in millions $a

labelled single values or Totals	pre-time line	half years >>>>>>> Jul 2011 to Dec '11		Jul 2014 to Dec '14	Jan 2015 to Jun '15	Jul 2015 to Dec '15	
Fuel Price $a/litre		53.02	>>>	59.64	72.98	74.43	75.81

=Input!$F$45*Work!P69*Work!P79

8.1 Values nominally fixed in the underlying currency

In order to calculate the equivalent in the presentation currency of underlying costs that are nominally fixed – for example, fixed price construction costs – convert at the initial exchange rate and multiply by the total devaluation factor for the period in which expenditure occurs.

8.2 Values inflating in the underlying currency

To calculate values denominated in an underlying currency and inflating at the general inflation rate for that currency, convert the uninflated value at the initial exchange rate and multiply by the underlying currency inflation factor and the overall devaluation factor applicable in the period of expenditure.

8.3 Timing of adjustments

For most cost and revenue items, the factors or exchange rates used should be those applicable at the mid-point of the model period in which they are applied, reflecting average values over the period. For items that specifically arise at the beginning or end of a model period, and for loan fees, interest and balances carried forward, end of period factors or exchange rates need to be used. Start-period values can use the previous column's end-period values.

8.4 Calculation of currency adjustments for loans

For loans denominated in a currency other than the underlying currency, the presentation currency amounts representing values carried from period to period, such as loan balance, or facility size for fee calculations, must be adjusted to reflect movements between their actual currency and the currency in which they are being represented. This applies also to amounts such as loan drawings, calculated in presentation currency equivalent at the point of drawdown, which then need to be adjusted to the equivalent presentation currency amount for inclusion in the loan balance or interest calculations at the end of each half year. For details of currency adjustments for loan calculations see Section 15.3.2.

8.5 Currency adjustments for tax and accounts

The treatment of currency issues for tax and accounting purposes will vary from country to country, and possibly from deal to deal in a given country, and professional guidance should be sought to determine the handling of such issues for each project. The methods and principles detailed in this book can then be applied to allow the recommendations to be represented appropriately in the model.

8.6 Flexible currency assignment

It is not always certain in which currency a particular item will be denominated. In this situation it is helpful to be able to assign an underlying currency flexibly to individual cost, revenue or funding items, from a list of possibilities. Both the currencies included in the list, and the allocation of underlying currencies to particular cash flow items can be determined flexibly using data inputs. For simplicity and to reduce the risk of incompatible inputs, it is advisable to have a fixed presentation currency.

8.6.1 Inputs for flexible currency assignment

A given number of currency options must be set, and numbered, with the presentation currency as currency 1. For the other currencies, there must be inputs for the currency name and symbol. For each option there must also be an initial exchange rate value (the assumed exchange rate between that currency and the presentation currency at a fixed date, ideally the start of the model timeline), entered in adjacent cells in the same order as the numbered currency inputs, and macro economic information including general inflation rates and assumed real devaluation or appreciation versus the presentation currency.

For each item which requires flexible currency assignment, inputs are required for the amount in the underlying currency and the number of the currency in which the amount is denominated. The underlying currency amount is then immediately converted into a value in the presentation currency on the Data sheet. Selection of the conversion rate here, and throughout, can be made using the index function and the numeric input specifying the applicable currency. See Exhibit 8.2 for an illustration.

8.6.2 Flexible currency adjustment for simple costs and revenues

The inflation and devaluation factors (versus the presentation currency) for all currencies are calculated in grouped rows, in an order consistent with the numbering on the input sheet. For example, the

Exhibit 8.2

Flexible currency assignment for capital cost inputs

	B	C	D	E	F	G
	Full Scheme Base Case					
	Input Sheet					
	All values without labelled units are in millions $a					
	⦚					
30	**Currency number**			Currency name	Currency Symbol	Exchange rate /$a
31			Currency 1	Sarva dollar	$a	1.00
32			Currency 2	Euro	€	0.10
33			Currency 3	Sterling	£	0.13
34			Currency 4	Spare		
	⦚					=D53/INDEX($G$31:$G$34,$F53,1)
52	**Capex Inputs**			**Amount in Underlying Currency**	**Currency Selection Number**	**Amount in Presentation Currency at initial Xch Rate**
53	**Plant and Machinery**			794	3	6,352
54	**Pipeline**			498	1	498
55	**Civils**			384	2	3,840
	⦚					

mid-point inflation factors for all currencies should be calculated in consecutive rows, for currencies 1, 2, 3, etc., then all the end-point factors, and so on.

The inflation and/or devaluation factors for a given cost or revenue item (see Sections 8.1 to 8.2) can then be selected using the index function.

8.6.3 Flexible currency adjustment for loans and deposits

For more complex calculations it makes sense to set up separate rows in the worklines sheets to contain the devaluation factors which apply to a specific item, such as a loan or cash balance. Then the appropriate values can be selected into specific devaluation rows using the index function as normal, and the loan or balance calculations can use those factors without having to include any additional calculations to manage the flexible currency options (see Exhibit 8.4).

Exhibit 8.3

Application of flexible currency choice to input fuel price

	B	C	D	E	F	G	H	I	J	K	L	M
	Full Scheme Base Case											
	Input Sheet											
	All values without labelled units are in millions $a											

	Currency number		Currency name	Currency Symbol	Exchange rate /$a
30			Currency name	Currency Symbol	Exchange rate /$a
31		Currency 1	Sarva dollar	$a	1.00
32		Currency 2	Euro	€	0.10
33		Currency 3	Sterling	£	0.13
34		Currency 4	Spare		

=Input!$D32&" mid-period Inflation Factor"

	Inflation Rates % p.a.	Pre timeline	until 2015	thereafter
52			until	
53	**Inflation Rates % p.a.**	Pre timeline	2015	thereafter
54	**Sarva Dollar Rate**	3.00%	4.00%	3.50%
55	Currency 2 Rate	2.75%	3.00%	3.50%
56	Currency 3 Rate	2.00%	2.00%	2.50%
57	Currency 4 Rate	0.00%	0.00%	0.00%

=Input!$G$73*INDEX(Work!G$69:G$72,Input!$D$73,1) *INDEX(Work!G$86:G$89, Input!$D$73,1)

		Currency selector	Price in base currency	Price in sarva dollars
72		Currency selector	Price in base currency	Price in sarva dollars
73	Fuel Cost per litre	3	5.25	42

	B	C	D	E	F	G		M	N	O	P	Q
2	**Full Scheme Base Case**		labelled single		pre-	half years >>>>>>>		>>>				
3	**Worklines Sheet**		values or		time	Jul 2011	>>>	Jul 2014	Jan 2015	Jul 2015	Jan 2016	....
4	*All values without labelled units are in millions $a*		**Totals**		line	to Dec '11	>>>	to Dec '14	to Jun '15	to Dec '15	to Jun '16	....
64	Sarva Inflation Rate % pa. in each half year					4.00%	>>>	4.00%	4.00%	4.00%	3.50%	....
65	Euro Inflation Rate % pa. in each half year					3.00%	>>>	3.00%	3.00%	3.00%	3.50%	....
66	Sterling Inflation Rate % pa. in each half year					2.00%	>>>	2.00%	2.00%	2.00%	2.50%	....
67	Spare Inflation Rate % pa. in each half year					0.00%	>>>	0.00%	0.00%	0.00%	0.00%	....
68												
69	Sarva mid period Inflation Factor				1.00	1.010	>>>	1.147	1.158	1.170	1.180	....
70	Euro mid-period Inflation Factor				1.00	1.007	>>>	1.109	1.117	1.126	1.135	....
71	Sterling mid-period Inflation Factor				1.00	1.005	>>>	1.072	1.077	1.082	1.089	....
72	Spare mid-period Inflation Factor				1.00	1.000	>>>	1.000	1.000	1.000	1.000	....
86	Sarva mid period devaluation factor vs $a				1.00	1.000	>>>	1.000	1.000	1.000	1.000	....
87	$a mid period devaluation factor vs €				1.00	1.002	>>>	1.034	1.037	1.039	1.039	....
88	$a mid period devaluation factor vs £				1.00	1.005	>>>	1.070	1.076	1.081	1.083	....
89	$a mid period devaluation factor vs				1.00	1.010	>>>	1.147	1.158	1.170	1.180	....

	B	C	D	E	F	G		M	N	O	P	Q
2	**Full Scheme Base Case**		labelled single		pre-	half years >>>>>>>		>>>				
3	**Operations Sheet**		values or		time	Jul 2011	>>>	Jul 2014	Jan 2015	Jul 2015	Jan 2016	....
4	*All values without labelled units are in millions $a*		**Totals**		line	to Dec '11	>>>	to Dec '14	to Jun '15	to Dec '15	to Jun '16	....
14	Fuel Price $a/litre					42.20	>>>	44.95	45.17	45.39	45.50	....

Exhibit 8.4

Illustrative flexible loan devaluation factors

	B	C	D	E	F	G	H	I	J	K	L	M
	Full Scheme Base Case											
	Input Sheet											
	All values without labelled units are in millions $a											
	⌇⌇											
91	Loan Data		Local Loan		Foreign Loan	Sub Debt						
92	Select underlying currency for loan		1		3	2						
	⌇⌇											

=INDEX(Work!G$86:G$89,Input!$F$92,1)

=INDEX(Work!G$91:G$94,Input!$F$92,1)

	B	C	D	E	F	G	H		M	N	O	P	Q
2	Full Scheme Base Case		labelled single		pre-	half years >>>>>>		>>>					
3	Worklines Sheet		values or		time	Jul 2011	>>>		Jul 2014	Jan 2015	Jul 2015	Jan 2016	....
4	*All values without labelled units are in millions $a*		Totals		line	to Dec '11	>>>		to Dec '14	to Jun '15	to Dec '15	to Jun '16	....
	⌇⌇												
86	Sarva mid period devaluation factor vs Sa				1.00	1.000	>>>		1.000	1.000	1.000	1.000	....
87	Sa mid period devaluation factor vs €				1.00	1.002	>>>		1.034	1.037	1.039	1.039	....
88	Sa mid period devaluation factor vs £				1.00	1.005	>>>		1.070	1.076	1.081	1.083	....
89	Sa mid period devaluation factor vs				1.00	1.010	>>>		1.147	1.158	1.170	1.180	....
90													
91	Sarva end period devaluation factor vs Sa				1.00	1.000	>>>		1.000	1.000	1.000	1.000	....
92	Sa end period devaluation factor vs €				1.00	1.005	>>>		1.037	1.039	1.042	1.042	....
93	Sa end period devaluation factor vs £				1.00	1.010	>>>		1.076	1.081	1.086	1.089	....
94	Sa end period devaluation factor vs				1.00	1.020	>>>		1.158	1.170	1.181	1.192	....
	⌇⌇												
161	Foreign Loan mid period Discount Factor				1.00	1.005	>>>		1.070	1.076	1.081	1.083	....
162	Foreign Loan end period Discount Factor				1.00	1.010	>>>		1.076	1.081	1.086	1.089	....

9 Scenario and sensitivity analysis

The model generates results consistent with a set of input assumptions. One set of assumptions is selected as the 'Base Case'. These should be assumptions defined by contractual agreements, justified by historic experience or in some other way selected and agreed as defensible values on which to build a base-line set of model results. Where several options are under consideration for the structure of the project, for example regarding a physical attribute of the actual project, or planned funding or contractual arrangements, then the model needs to run a number of alternative base cases or 'scenarios'.

For any set of base case assumptions, the actual values eventually observed would be expected to deviate from base case assumptions for a number of items. A series of cases is therefore run with respect to each base case to quantify the effect of such downside variance and to test the effectiveness of any proposed mitigants. These are called sensitivity cases.

Although similar in principle, scenarios and sensitivities can have functional differences. For example, if equity is sized with respect to total base case funding, then base cases should calculate the equity amount, whilst sensitivities should test the outcome based on the equity value applicable to the relevant base case. If revenues are calculated to give a specific IRR in the base case, sensitivities must use the base case results as fixed revenue inputs. All these options can be controlled using switches in the data, but it is helpful to have the distinction clearly in mind when structuring case control tables and when switching from base case development to sensitivity analysis whilst developing the model.

During development of a deal, scenarios and associated sensitivities are often run repeatedly as data and calculations are refined and updated. Therefore, in addition to ensuring that models are written in a flexible way with full control from data, it is important to ensure that cases can be readily and accurately repeated, that the base case can reliably be restored after each sensitivity, and that all runs and associated printout can be reliably identified.

9.1 Common sensitivity cases

There are a number of commonly required sensitivities, including those listed in Box 9.1, which generate various modelling issues. Anticipation and resolution of these issues has influenced a number

Box 9.1 **Common sensitivity cases**	
Category	*Sensitivity items*
Construction	Delay Cost overrun
Finance	Interest rate Maximum term
Economic	Inflation Exchange rates

continued

Category	Sensitivity items
Operation	Product price
	Operating cost overrun
	Fuel/feedstock price
	Fuel/feedstock utilisation
	Fuel/feedstock availability
	Project 'capacity'
	Operating levels
	Market
	Combined downside case

of the elements of model design and development recommended in this book, as summarised in Box 9.2.

Box 9.2
Solutions to common issues in sensitivity analyses

Issue	Solutions
Timings	Controlled from 'Data' sheet
Rates	Entered via 'Data' sheet
	Applied via 'Worklines'
Profiles	Entered via 'Data' sheet
	Selected using switches
	Positioned using Index( ) or Sumif( ) functions
Amounts	Entered in data
	Multiplied by sensitivity factors

9.2 Use of switches

Although many sensitivities can be run simply by using alternative values for data items, some will require the implementation of different assumptions in the code. In order to maintain a single copy of the model that can run all sensitivities on a straightforward and reproducible basis, these alternatives should be modelled as options in the code, selected via a switch in the data.

As well as selecting between different calculation options, switches can be used to select between different data inputs, or different sets of data, used for the base case and various sensitivity cases. For details, see Section 5.2.

To simplify the process of running alternative base and sensitivity cases a hierarchy of switches can be used. In this case a single master switch is added to the input sheet, and the inputs for the relevant sub-switches overwritten with simple formulae giving the appropriate value for each switch according to the value set for the master switch.

The ultimate example of this process is the case control table (see Section 9.4).

9.3 Use of strings to automatically identify runs

As well as mathematical operators and functions, Excel allows strings (pieces of text) to be manipulated within the model, and processed in spreadsheet formulae. This allows sensitivity cases to generate labels that will automatically identify the case run and/or the variables changed from base case values. The assembled description of the run being performed can then be included in a header appearing on all calculation and report sheets.

9.3.1 Operators and functions useful for handling strings

Inverted commas, "…" identify characters in a formula as a string, not as part of the instructions for the formula, and they are essential when assembling strings within a formula.

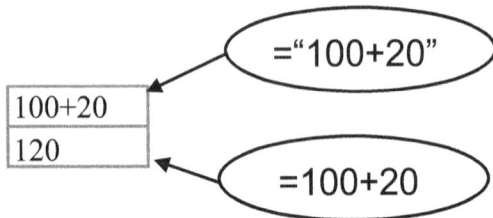

To add strings together, the **ampersand** symbol (&) is used, not the plus sign (the plus sign will work in some circumstances, but it is advisable to use & consistently).

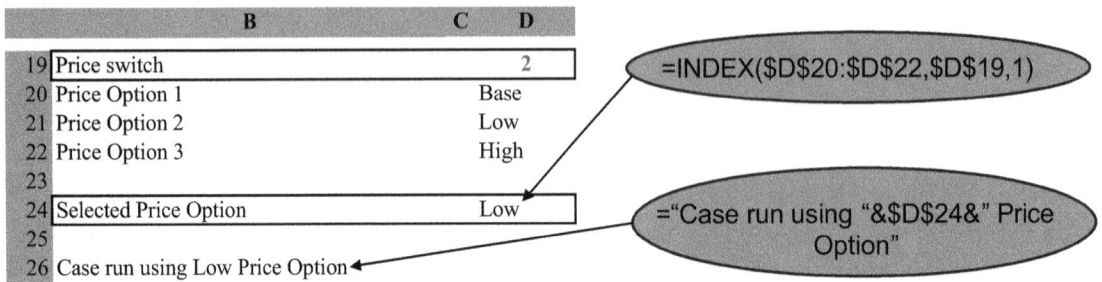

To include calculated figures in a string, values can be converted to text in a specified format using the **TEXT(*value,format*)** function. *Value* can be a directly entered value or calculation, or can pick up a value from another cell. Format is entered using the standard formatting specifiers, enclosed in inverted commas. For example, # means any character or no character if the value being represented has no digits in the specified position. Zeros before or after the decimal point specify the minimum number of decimal places to display, even if the digit is zero. Commas at the thousand position indicate that commas should be used when displaying values in thousands, and so on. If a format is followed by a semi-colon and another format, the second format will apply to negative values.

Value	Format specified as...	Result
0	###,###	
	###,###.#	.
	###,###.0	.0
	###,##0.0	0.0
12163	###,###	12,163
	###,###.#	12,163.
	###,###.#0	12,163.0
	###,###.00	12,163.00
	000,###.0	012,163.0
12163.457	###,###	12,163
	###,###.#	12,163.5
	###,##0.0	12,163.5
	###,##0.###0	12,163.457
	###,##0.0000	12,163.4570
	###,##0.0;(###,##0.0)	12,163.5
-12163.457	###,##0.0;(###,##0.0)	(12,163.5)
0.00111	###%	%
	##0%	0%
	##0.######0%	0.111%
	##0.###0000%	0.1110%

To find more format specifiers, look at the selection listed in the table for custom number formats, and experiment with them. (This is found via menu options 'Format', 'Cells', 'Number', 'Custom' in Excel 2003, and 'Home', 'Number', 'Custom' in Excel 2007.)

The TEXT(...) function can be included in the string handling formula like any other string.

	B	C	D	E	F
23			Label		$a/tonne
24	Selected Price Option		Low		28.76
25					
26	**Case run using Low Price Option at 28.76 $a per tonne**				

="Case run using "&$D$24&" Price Option at "&TEXT($F$24,"##0.00")&" $a per tonne"

9.4 Case control tables

In the process of controlling scenario and sensitivity cases with a hierarchy of master switches to make them easier to run and to preserve the base case, a 'Case Control Table' provides the ultimate master switch, with a single input value specifying all the options and parameters for a given case.

The table comprises a 'selected values' column, and a series of columns of input values for the data items which need to vary between cases. Each input column defines a set of values for a specific case. The columns are numbered, and the values picked up in the 'selected values' column are those for the case whose number is entered as the case selection input. The values in the 'selected values' column then feed into the relevant input cells in the rest of the data sheet below the table. Among the items picked up in the 'selected values' column is a case header, which then feeds directly into the run description displayed at the top of every sheet.

Cases can include non base case inputs for a single item or for multiple items.

This structure fulfils a number of functions:

- creates, documents and preserves definitive inputs for all scenario and sensitivity cases;
- ensures base case is preserved when sensitivity cases are run;
- allows a tailored heading to be associated with each specific case;
- minimises risk of inconsistency when a correlated set of sensitivity inputs is required;
- allows specific calculated values to be stored and associated with particular base or sensitivity cases; and
- allows easy comparison of assumptions between cases.

The table layout will only accept single value inputs. For variables that are input as many entries over time, however a single switch or factor can be established to control any necessary variation for the purposes of sensitivity analysis. The single controlling value can then be included in the sensitivity table.

The content of the case selection table will build and change over time. When developing the feasibility model, the Data sheet can be developed without such a table until it becomes clear which sensitivities or alternative base case scenarios will need to be run. The table can then be added, and expanded as required.

Since values may be subject to negotiation and detailed analysis at one point on the journey to financial close, and subsequently become fixed, and new items may be sensitised as more sophisticated structures are defined and agreed, it is helpful for items to be added or removed easily to/from the list included in the table. For this reason, and to reduce any potential for accidental damage to the calculation links in the model, it is preferable to keep the input cells in the data sheet in their original positions, but change their contents from an input value to a reference picking up the appropriate value from the 'selected values' column in the table.

To define a new case, simply add an extra column to the table and ensure that the index formulae in the 'Selected values' column include the new column in the selection range. Copy the current base case values for all items into the new column, then change the specific inputs relevant to the new case and add a suitable header.

To add a new variable to the table, add a new row to the table and enter (copy if possible!) a suitable label. Then enter the base case value for the new variable in all input columns in the table and ensure the selection formula is copied into the new row in the 'selected values' column. Change the original input cell for the item in the data section to pick up the value specified in the 'Selected values' column of the table.

Exhibit 9.1

Illustrative case selection table

1	**12 months completion delay case**						
2	**Input Sheet**						
3	*All values without labelled units are in millions $a*						
4							
5	Case Selection Switch	2					
6							
7	**Case Selection Table**	Selected values					
9	Case Number	**2**	**1**	**2**	**3**	**4**	>>>
10	Case Description	**Delay**	Base Case	Delay	Delay & Overrun	Production	>>>
11	Case Header	**12 months con**	Base Case	12 months co	6 months con	low case pro	>>>
13	Completion Delay (months)	**12**	0	12	6	0	....
14	Capex Sensitivity Factor	**1.00**	1.00	1.00	1.10	1.00	....
15	Production profile (1=low, 2=compliant, 3=base)	**3**	3	3	3	1.00	....
16	Initial Inflation rate % p.a.	**2.50%**	2.50%	2.50%	2.50%	2.50%	....
17	Year to (& including) which initial inflation rate applies	**2015**	2015	2015	2015	2015	....
18	Subsequent Inflation rate % p.a.	**2.40%**	2.40%	2.40%	2.40%	2.40%	....
	⅄⅄	⅄⅄	⅄⅄	⅄⅄	⅄⅄	⅄⅄	
26	Equity as % debt+equity	**20%**	20%	20%	20%	20%	....
27	Senior Debt Interest Rate % p.a.	**7.50%**	7.50%	7.50%	7.50%	7.50%	....
28	Target Senior Debt ADSCR	**1.40**	1.40	1.40	1.40	1.40	....
29	Use calculated (0) or stored (1) sculpted repayment profile?	**1**	0	1	1	1	....
	⅄⅄						
41	Months from Financial Close to scheduled completion	36					
42	Months of Completion delay	12	*value taken from case selection table*				
	⅄⅄						
56	Construction Costs Sensitivity Factor	1.00	*value taken from case selection table*				
	⅄⅄						
118	Production Profile switch (1=low, 2=compliant, 3=base)	3	*value taken from case selection table*				
119			Half years from start of operation>>>>				
120			1st half yr 1	2nd half yr 1	1st half yr 2	2nd half yr 2	......
121	Low Production Case Profile /tonnes		32.00	54.00	76.00	76.00	....
122	Compliant Production Case Profile /tonnes		32.00	66.00	82.00	94.00	....
123	Base Case Production Profile /tonnes		34.00	62.00	84.00	98.00	....
124							
125	Selected Production Profile		34.00	62.00	84.00	98.00	....

Callouts:

=TEXT(H13,"##0")&" months completion delay case"

=INDEX($F30:$AA30,1,$D$5)

=$D$14

=$D$13

=$D$15

=INDEX(H$121:H$123, $D$118,1)

To remove a variable, simply copy the base case input into the original input cell in the data, and delete the relevant row from the case selection table.

Input cells changed to pick up values from the table should be labelled and formatted to make this clear, to reduce the risk of accidental overwriting of the formula by directly inputting data into the cell, rather than into the input sections of the data table. Data validation can also be used to prevent overwriting of these and other formula cells on the Data sheet (see Section 12.5).

If a project has a number of defined scenarios, to all of which a set of sensitivity cases must be applied, it can be helpful to include scenario management tables, which include the data options for different scenarios, and enter the value for the scenario selection switch as an input in the main Case Control Table, then any combination of scenario and sensitivity can be run easily and simply.

9.5 Creating a stored library of key values for scenarios and sensitivities

It is relatively easy to store a column of selected inputs and results for the current case, building a library of such sets of results for a range of scenario and sensitivity cases. Such a record can also track changes to model code and data, and record the incremental effects of each change on key results.

The results will be stored with a simple macro, so for safety and convenience the spreadsheet part of this option should be set up on a new sheet, with the standard column layout. Select the key inputs defining the cases being run, and the key results generated and copy their row headings or descriptions into column B, and pick up their values into column D (see Exhibit 9.2). An easy way to store a range

Exhibit 9.2

Result store sheet

	B	C	D	E F	G	H	I	J	J	M
1	Full Scheme Base Case									
2	Results Store Sheet									
3	*All values without labelled units are in millions $a*									
4										
5	Notes									
6										
7	=Data!$D$11		Key Values							
8										
9	Run Description		Full Sch Delay			Partial Sch Del	Full Sch	Partial Sch		
	=TODAY()		Full Scheme with 3 months completion Delay			Partial Scheme with 3 months completion Delay				
10	Run Header =Ret!D43						Full Scheme	Partial Scheme		
11	Date stored		26/08/09			26/08/09	26/08/09	26/08/09		
12	Time stored		16:41			16:38	16:26	16:22		
13	Financial Close Date		01/04/14			01/04/14	01/04/14	01/04/14		
14	Project Nominal IRR % p.a.		14.02%			12.90%	14.40%	13.40%		
15	Nominal Investor IRR % p.a.		21.04%			20.65%	22.86%	22.41%		
16	Real Investor IRR % p.a.		17.79%			17.21%	18.34%	17.83%		
17	Product Sale Price $a per tonne		53.20			53.20	53.20	53.20		
	⁑			=NCF!D68						
53	Total Interest Earned on Deposits $a million		2,813			2,813	4,012	2,514		
54	Net Cash Flow to Investors $a million		98,795			79,671	109,784	85,632		
55	Pure equity as Paid In $a million		938			815	998	838		
56	Calculated Dividends $a million		99,733			80,486	110,782	86,470		
57										

Range Storesults

Pasted values

of useful information is to include the nominal totals from the net cash flow summary, and this is most easily done simply by copying all the net cash flow (NCF) row headings into the new sheet, copying into the appropriate rows of column D a formula picking up the corresponding values from the 'totals' column of the NCF, and then simply deleting, on the new 'results' sheet, rows corresponding to blank or irrelevant rows on the NCF.

Name the range in column D which contains the selected input and result values.

A macro is then needed to store the current set of results and make space in the table for further additions. This macro can be created entirely by recording, no editing of visual basic should be required. See Section 6.5.1 for the methodology of recording a macro. The macro needs to:

1   select the current inputs and results;
2   copy the current selection;
3   paste as values into the same rows of column G;
4   paste formatting; and
5   insert a new column to the left of the stored results.

Having switched on macro record and allocated a name and a shortcut to the new macro, the required steps can be recorded by:

1   use 'goto' by pressing F5, select the range containing the results to be stored;
2   copy the selected range;
3   move the cursor to column G, in the same row as the top of the results range (for example, G9 in Exhibit 9.2). This must be done with a cell address not a range name, as the range name would move with the data, and the macro would simply overwrite the previous figures;
4   paste as values;
5   paste formats;
6   insert column; and
7   stop recording.

The macro can be used whenever a definitive case has been run, and this builds a library of results for all the key base and sensitivity cases.

When critical updates or corrections are made to model code or data, the 'Store' sheet can be manually annotated to mark the points at which changes have been made, and summarise the source of the changes, see Exhibit 9.3. Notes entered above the rows into which values are pasted will not be overwritten.

9.6 Creating tables of results for specific sensitivities

In addition to the review of detailed results for a limited number of base and sensitivity cases, it is sometimes required to examine the effect on a limited set of outputs of variation in one or more input values. The data tables facility in Excel supports the production of such tables of results, but without the facility to calculate figures which require macro operation (or Excel built-in options such as goal-seek). It is possible to create a combination of spreadsheet elements and VBA code which can produce results tables in a very flexible and reasonably straightforward way.

Following rules of good practice for the use of macros, all calculations should be transparently carried out on the spreadsheet, the macro should ideally be just another copy-paste process, albeit more sophisticated than the recalc macro. Also, it is extremely helpful if things like the size of tables,

Exhibit 9.3

Annotated store sheet

	B	C	D	E	F	G	H	I	J	J	M
1	**Full Scheme Base Case**										
2	**Results Store Sheet**										
3	*All values without labelled units are in millions $a*										
4											
5	Notes						**Loan repayment method revised**				
6											
7			Key Values								
8											
9	Run Description		Full Scheme				Partial Scheme	Full Sch Delay	Partial Sch Dela	Full Sch	Partial Sch
10	Run Header		Full Scheme Ba				Partial Scheme Base Case	Full Scheme with 3 months completion Delay	Partial Scheme with 3 months completion Delay	Full Scheme	Partial Scheme
11	Date stored		30/09/09				30/09/09	26/08/09	26/08/09	26/08/09	26/08/09
12	Time stored		14:35				14:06	16:41	16:38	16:26	16:22
13	Financial Close Date		01/04/14				01/04/14	01/04/14	01/04/14	01/04/14	01/04/14
14	Project Nominal IRR % p.a.		14.60%				13.80%	14.02%	12.90%	14.40%	13.40%
15	Nominal Investor IRR % p.a.		25.00%				22.82%	21.04%	20.65%	22.86%	22.41%
16	Real Investor IRR % p.a.		21.70%				19.64%	17.79%	17.21%	18.34%	17.83%
17	Product Sale Price $a per tonne		53.20				53.20	53.20	53.20	53.20	53.20
	⁓⁓										
53	Total Interest Earned on Deposits *$a million*		4,226				2,813	2,813	2,813	4,012	2,514
54	Net Cash Flow to Investors *$a million*		119,420				87,632	98,795	79,671	109,784	85,632
55	Pure equity as Paid In *$a million*		1,016				842	938	815	998	838
56	Calculated Dividends *$a million*		120,435				88,474	99,733	80,486	110,782	86,470
57											

or the number of result values recorded can be amended by making simple changes to the spreadsheet, rather than by repeatedly changing the VBA code.

A simple means of stepping through a table to store results is required. If we do this by positioning the point at which the macro pastes items, then adding additional tables for extra results will require duplication of parts of the VBA code, and the code itself will be more complex and require more non-recordable elements. A simple means of completing a table via spreadsheet code only is therefore required. This can be achieved by using twin sets of tables to generate the tables of results, the completed tables can then be stored below the result generating tables, to give a library of stored results.

The twin result generating tables should be identically sized. One (let us call it 'Restable') will be set to zero throughout when initiating the macro, and will then be updated with pasted results from the formula-based twin table ('Rescalc') as each case is run. The tables will include one row for each tested value of one input variable. The table layout for each result item will include one column per tested value for the other input variable. The rows and columns will be numbered. See Exhibit 9.4.

The macro will step through the values for each variable using two counters. The formula in each of the results cells of Rescalc will check the table row and column numbers corresponding to that cell, and if they match the current values for the counters, will pick up the current value for the applicable result item. Otherwise the formula picks up the value in the corresponding cell of Restable. Thus, initially all cells are set to zero. The counters start at 1,1, and the cells corresponding to the first result row and column in the tables pick up the current result values. As each case is solved, Rescalc is pasted as values onto Restable, storing the results for the current case as values. The counters are increased, and Rescalc picks up the stored results for previous cases from Restable, and the current result in the

Exhibit 9.4

Key elements of sensitivity results table

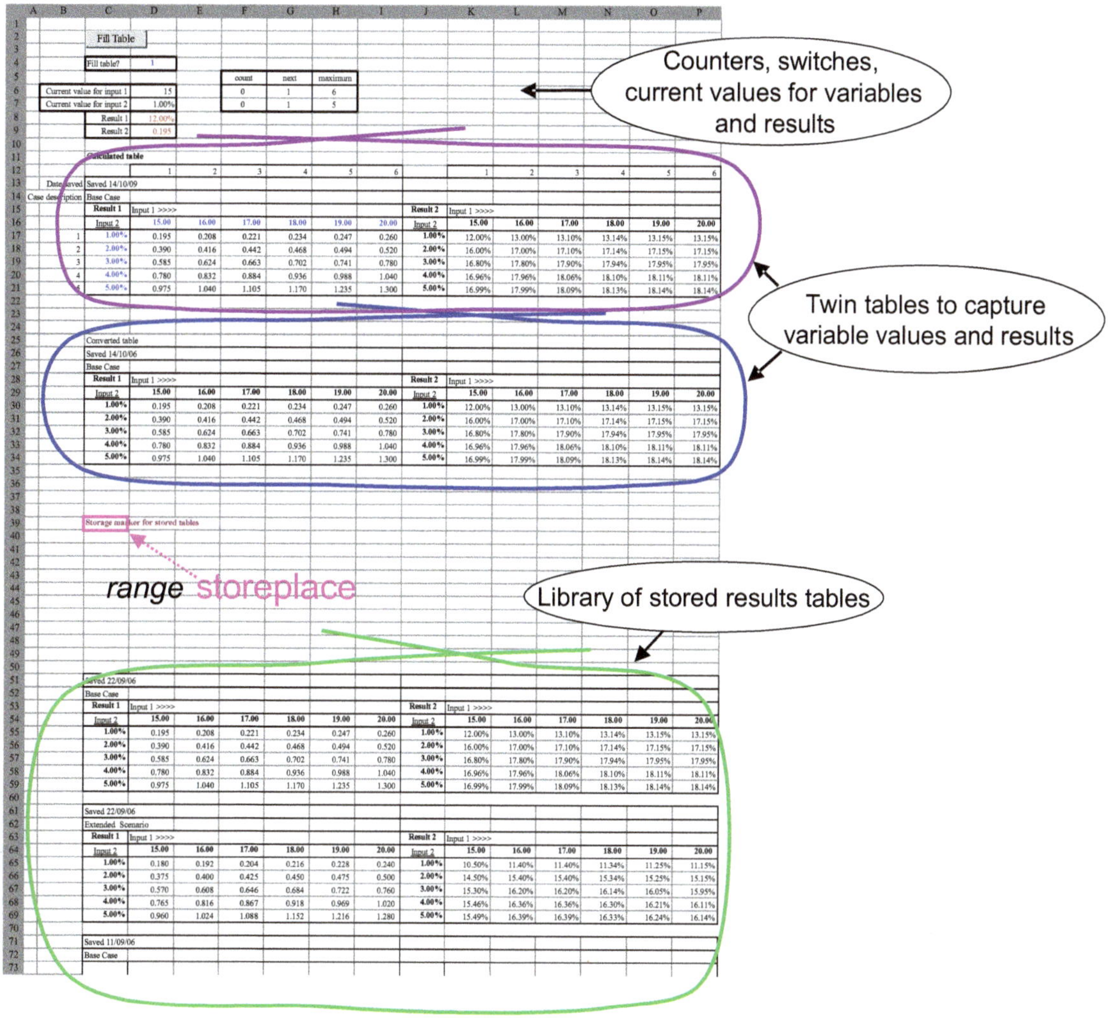

continued

Callout formulas:
- =INDEX($D$16:$I$16,1,$F$6)
- =INDEX($C$17:$C$21,$F$7,1)
- =F6+1
- =F7+1
- =MAX($D$12:$I$12)
- =MAX($D$12:$I$12)
- *Pasted values*
- *Calculated values picked up from elsewhere in model*
- =D16
- =E12
- =IF(AND(E$12=$F$6,$B20=$F$7),$D$8,E33)
- =IF(AND(L$12=$F$6,$B20=$F$7),$D$9,L33)
- Rescalc
- Restable

Top table

	Fill Table			count	next	maximum	
Fill table?	1						
Current value for input 1	16		2	3	6		
Current value for input 2	4.00%		4	5	5		
Result 1	0.832						
Result 2	17.96%						

Calculated table

		1	2	3	4	5	6		1	2	3	4	5	6
Date saved	Saved 14/10/09													
Case description	Base Case													
	Result 1	Input 1 >>>>						Result 2	Input 1 >>>>					
	Input 2	15.00	16.00	17.00	18.00	19.00	20.00	Input 2	15.00	16.00	17.00	18.00	19.00	20.00
1	1.00%	0.195	0.208	0.000	0.000	0.000	0.000	1.00%	12.00%	13.00%	0.00%	0.00%	0.00%	0.00%
2	2.00%	0.390	0.416	0.000	0.000	0.000	0.000	2.00%	16.00%	17.00%	0.00%	0.00%	0.00%	0.00%
3	3.00%	0.585	0.624	0.000	0.000	0.000	0.000	3.00%	16.80%	17.80%	0.00%	0.00%	0.00%	0.00%
4	4.00%	0.780	0.832	0.000	0.000	0.000	0.000	4.00%	16.96%	17.96%	0.00%	0.00%	0.00%	0.00%
5	5.00%	0.975	0.000	0.000	0.000	0.000	0.000	5.00%	16.99%	0.00%	0.00%	0.00%	0.00%	0.00%

Converted table (*Pasted values*)

	1	2	3	4	5	6		1	2	3	4	5	6
Saved 14/10/06													
Base Case													
Result 1	Input 1 >>>>						Result 2	Input 1 >>>>					
Input 2	15.00	16.00	17.00	18.00	19.00	20.00	Input 2	15.00	16.00	17.00	18.00	19.00	20.00
1.00%	0.195	0.208	0.000	0.000	0.000	0.000	1.00%	12.00%	13.00%	0.00%	0.00%	0.00%	0.00%
2.00%	0.390	0.416	0.000	0.000	0.000	0.000	2.00%	16.00%	17.00%	0.00%	0.00%	0.00%	0.00%
3.00%	0.585	0.624	0.000	0.000	0.000	0.000	3.00%	16.80%	17.80%	0.00%	0.00%	0.00%	0.00%
4.00%	0.780	0.000	0.000	0.000	0.000	0.000	4.00%	16.96%	0.00%	0.00%	0.00%	0.00%	0.00%
5.00%	0.975	0.000	0.000	0.000	0.000	0.000	5.00%	16.99%	0.00%	0.00%	0.00%	0.00%	0.00%

Button to run macro which fills and stores result table

				count	next	maximum
	Fill Table					
	Fill table?	1				
			range incount1	*range incnext1*	*range maxicount1*	
	Current value for input 1	16		2	3	6
	Current value for input 2	4.00%		4	5	5
	Result 1	0.832	*range incount2*		*range maxicount2*	
	Result 2	17.96%		*range incnext2*		

Pasted values

appropriate cell. In this way the table is populated sequentially with the results for each case. When complete, the table is pasted into a specified space in the spreadsheet, and a set of blank rows inserted above it, ready for the next set of results.

Exhibit 9.1

Example VBA code for result table macro

```vba
Sub resulttable()
'
' resulttable Macro
' Macro recorded 23/09/2006 by P.A.Lynch
'
'Reset counters to 1
    Application.Goto Reference:="incount1"
    ActiveCell.FormulaR1C1 = "0"
    Application.Goto Reference:="incount2"
    ActiveCell.FormulaR1C1 = "0"
'reset results table
    Application.Goto Reference:="restable"
    Selection.ClearContents
'calculate model
    Calculate
'for each input1 value, cycle through input 2 values and store results
    While Range("incnext1") <= Range("maxicount1")
        'increase input 1 counter by 1, by copy-pasting the incremented value
        Application.Goto Reference:="incnext1"
        Selection.Copy
        Application.Goto Reference:="incount1"
        Selection.PasteSpecial Paste:=xlPasteValues, Operation:=xlNone, SkipBlanks _
        :=False, Transpose:=False
        Application.CutCopyMode = False
        'cycle through input 2 values
        While Range("incnext2") <= Range("maxicount2")
            'increase input 2 counter by 1
            Application.Goto Reference:="incnext2"
            Selection.Copy
            Application.Goto Reference:="incount2"
            Selection.PasteSpecial Paste:=xlPasteValues, Operation:=xlNone, SkipBlanks _
            :=False, Transpose:=False
            Application.CutCopyMode = False
            'calculate result with current inputs, using recalc macro
            Application.Run "Recalc"
            'store table updated with latest result
            Application.Goto Reference:="rescalc"
            Selection.Copy
```

continued

```
        Application.Goto Reference:="restable"
        Selection.PasteSpecial Paste:=xlPasteValues, Operation:=xlNone, SkipBlanks _
            :=False, Transpose:=False
        Selection.PasteSpecial Paste:=xlPasteFormats, Operation:=xlNone, _
        SkipBlanks:=False, Transpose:=False
    Wend
  'Reset input 2 counter
  Application.Goto Reference:="incount2"
  ActiveCell.FormulaR1C1 = "0"
  Calculate
  Wend
'Store completed table of results
'Copy restable
Application.Goto Reference:="restable"
  Selection.Copy
  'Paste restable as values into cell below range 'storeplace'
  Application.Goto Reference:="storeplace"
  ActiveCell.Offset(1, 0).Activate
  Selection.PasteSpecial Paste:=xlPasteValues, Operation:=xlNone, SkipBlanks _
      :=False, Transpose:=False
  Selection.PasteSpecial Paste:=xlPasteFormats, Operation:=xlNone, _
    SkipBlanks:=False, Transpose:=False
  Application.CutCopyMode = False
  ActiveCell.Offset(0, -1).Activate
'Insert blank rows above stored table, ready to store next table
  For I = 0 To Range("maxicount2") + 5
      Selection.EntireRow.Insert
  Next
End Sub
```

Exhibit 9.5 shows example VBA code for a macro to populate the sensitivity tables. With care, the size of tables can be adjusted without requiring any changes to the VBA, by ensuring that new rows or columns are consistently inserted within the existing named ranges. Once created, the macro and supporting sheets can be copied into new models as described in Section 6.5.3.

10 Cover factors

A key part of the role of a financial model is to establish the amount of debt supportable by the project and the robustness of the project in terms of its ability to service and repay debt under a range of downside assumptions. The debt cover factors provide a simple way of reviewing this information.

The standard project finance cover factors are the annual and semi-annual debt service cover factors (ADSCR and SADSCR) and the NPV cover factors, the loan life cover ratio (LLCR) and project life cover ratios (PLCR). Note that the terms 'cover ratio' and 'cover factor' are used interchangeably, and values are almost invariably expressed as factors, irrespective of the term used.

In combination, the cover factors give guidance as to a project's ability, under a range of assumptions:

- to repay debt according to the scheduled profile (ADSCR and SADSCR);
- to make repayment in full over the specified (LLCR); and
- to ultimately repay debt in full during the projected (PLCR).

The required values for the base case cover factors will depend upon the perceived risk inherent in the project. The values achieved for the cover factors in various downside sensitivity cases are therefore generally a more important guide to the acceptability of cover than a simple review of the base case values.

10.1 CFADS

Cash flows available for debt service (CFADS) form a key part of the calculation of all cover factors. As with many aspects of the cover factor calculations, an apparently clearly-defined concept is in fact open to varying interpretation. Based on post-tax net operating cash flows, the CFADS may include (or deduct) various cash inflows and outflows, for example:

- loan drawings to fund interest;
- interest earned on debt service reserve account (DSRA), maintenance reserve account (MRA), cash at bank;
- transfers to or from MRA;
- transfers to or from DSRA;
- major maintenance costs; and
- balance on deposit in MRA, DSRA, cash at bank.

As for so many aspects of modelling, the key is to be clear what question the model should be answering. The cover factor calculations, including the CFADS, can then be made consistent with provision of a meaningful answer to that question.

Among the principles which should apply in all cases, however, is the avoidance of any double-counting. Cash flows should certainly only be counted once in any given cover factor. This can create the requirement for different CFAD definitions for the ADSCRs and the PLCR or LLCR.

10.2 Debt service cover ratios

These are the simplest of the cover factors, and are basically a measure of the extent to which **available cash flow in each period covers the scheduled loan repayments plus interest in that period** during the scheduled loan life post-completion. The **SADSCR** is the semi-annual debt service cover ratio, the value for a six month period, the **ADSCR** is the annual debt service cover ratio, the value for a one-year period.

A minimum SADSCR or ADSCR of 1.00 or above shows that the scheduled interest and repayments can be met directly, when due, from the projected available cash flows during every half year or every year of the repayment period.

$$\text{ADSCR} = \frac{\text{Cash flow available for debt service during year}}{\text{Scheduled debt service during year}}$$

Note that for projects with large intermittent maintenance costs, it may be impossible to calculate meaningful DSCRs without reflecting transfers to/from the maintenance reserve account, since values may otherwise be below 1.00 or negative in maintenance periods, even in a strong base-case.

10.2.1 Average debt service cover factors

The average debt service cover factor is now a commonly seen measure, regularly appearing in loan and project agreements. Unlike the other cover factors discussed here, it does not have a precise meaning with respect to the relationship between cash and debt, and at most gives an indication as to whether the DSCR ever exceeds the minimum DSCR value during the loan life. Clearly this information, and much more besides could be gained by considering the LLCR (see below) alongside the DSCR.

The origins of this abominable metric are unclear. It may have been a simplistic attempt by lenders to avoid very tight optimisations which use the minimum ADSCR as the target in every period, although, again, the LLCR provides a better way to do this. Alternatively it may have been a crude attempt to ensure compliance with a rating agency requirement that project finance portfolios maintain an average minimum ADSCR at least equal to a particular target value, by applying the requirement directly to each project.

Whatever its origin, it has somehow become a standard measure and it is often necessary to model this meaningless figure, and indeed to present it as a key output. When it is specified as an input, for example as a target for repayment sculpting, debt sizing or revenue optimisation, mathematical necessity intervenes and it either has to be interpreted as simply a target constant ADSCR value, or negotiated into an LLCR instead.

10.3 NPV loan and project life cover factors

NPV cover factors show the relationship at a specific point in time between debt outstanding and projected cash flows available for debt service. The LLCR gives the precise multiple of the debt outstanding at a specified point in time which could be serviced and repaid from available cash over the remaining scheduled loan life. The PLCR gives the precise multiple of the debt outstanding which could be serviced and repaid over the remaining project life. These ratios do not, however, indicate when during the loan life the loan could be repaid, nor whether, for example, interest could be paid in full, when due, in all periods. These ratios thus need to be used alongside the DSCRs to give the full story.

The LLCR and PLCR are calculated by discounting future available cash back to a given date, using the loan interest rate as the discount rate, so that the calculated NPV properly reflects the value of future cash with respect to the debt outstanding at the NPV date. The NPV is divided by the debt outstanding at the NPV date. For modelling, the calculation dates should be at the start or end of the model half-years during the loan life.

10.4 Including deposits in cover factors

As for CFADS, the appropriateness of including cash on deposit in cover factor calculations depends on the question the cover factors have to answer.

In general, cash balances should not be included in DSCR calculations. The DSCRs represent the relationship between the available cash flows and the debt service, i.e., the project's ability to service debt, in a given time period. A quick thought experiment shows how this result would be distorted if, for example, the DSRA balance were to be included in the calculation. A fully funded DSRA, for six months debt service, would add 1.00 to the SADSCR in every half year, but the relevant cash could only be used once. A project unable to meet debt service in virtually all periods might therefore be given ADSCRs > 1.00 throughout the loan life by such a calculation. This would clearly be a meaningless and misleading result.

The LLCR and PLCR calculations give a picture of the relationship between debt and cash flows over the whole remaining loan life from a given point in time. Inclusion of cash on deposit at the point of calculation is thus consistent with the information given by these cover factors. In practice it is common to calculate several of these cover factors, for example, without deposits, with MRA, with MRA and DSRA, etc.

Note that, if the CFADS for DSCRs reflect transfers to and from an account, then there is the risk of double counting if using the same CFADS to calculate PV cover factors with cash deposits since cash may be included in the calculation via a cash balance, and again when released from deposit in a later period. For this reason it is often helpful to calculate separate CFADS for DSCFs and for PV cover factors.

For details of cover factor calculations in the model, see Section 22.

11 Optimisation

11.1 Introduction

Optimisation is the process of using the model to identify the optimum value for a particular item, such as an annual revenue figure, or a debt repayment profile. It is an almost universal feature of PFI/PPP bid models, but also has a place in more classic project finance or discounted cash flow (DCF) valuation models.

11.2 The theory behind the modelling

Optimisation applies a set of targets and constraints and seeks to maximise or minimise a particular output. For example, in a classic PFI with bid assessment based on the NPV of annual payments to the project, the bidder's model must seek the annual payment (AP) giving the minimum NPV, whilst complying with a set of constraints such as required levels of cover factor and equity return. A range of calculations may be adjusted to achieve this, such as loan life, minimum repayment required in each period, restrictions on the rate at which equity returns are paid, etc. In order to model optimisation effectively, it is important to think through the concepts involved.

For example, when trying to minimise the NPV of revenues, in the absence of other constraints, items which accrue costs faster than the NPV discount rate should be repaid as quickly as possible, giving the smallest NPV. Items which accrue costs more slowly than the NPV discount rate should be paid as late as possible, again, giving the smallest possible NPV.

In the absence of all other constraints, therefore, the ideal revenue profile for a project seeking to minimise the NPV of its revenues is an immediate payment from the first AP of all amounts due to lenders or investors with interest rates or target returns higher than the discount rate, sufficient to provide repayment or target return in full, with a single repayment from the final AP of all funding sources with interest rates below the NPV discount rate. Any required deposits with interest rates less than the discount rate should be funded as late as possible, and any deposits with interest rates better than the discount rate, as early as possible. Revenues should then match these calculated values. In practice, however, many constraints apply which prevent such extreme solutions being offered. Constraints are often set by the project initiators to limit, for example, the permitted annual variation in revenue amounts, and the speed at which equity returns may be achieved. Lenders likewise may constrain equity payments whilst debt remains outstanding, and historically have seemed reluctant to accept 100% final period debt repayment (!). What is required, then is to find the optimum achievable **subject to the given constraints**. Establishing and understanding what the constraints are and how they interact with our targets and ideals is a key part of successfully modelling an optimisation.

11.3 Iteration and damping factors

Many of the results targeted in the optimisation process cannot be calculated directly, but must depend on an iterative process to find an acceptable solution. Iteration can be applied, even where a direct process of successive approximation (see Section 7.4.1) does not seem to apply. Iteration to a solution can often be achieved in such cases by calculating an estimate of the proportionate *change* required, rather than simply cycling through a series of different incorrect results.

Exhibit 11.1

The cost of debt and equity (a) in simple monetary terms and (b) and (c) in NPV terms. In all figures the interest rate is assumed to be 7% p.a. and the required equity IRR 18% pa. In figure (b) the NPV discount rate is 9% p.a. and in figure (c) 5% p.a.

a

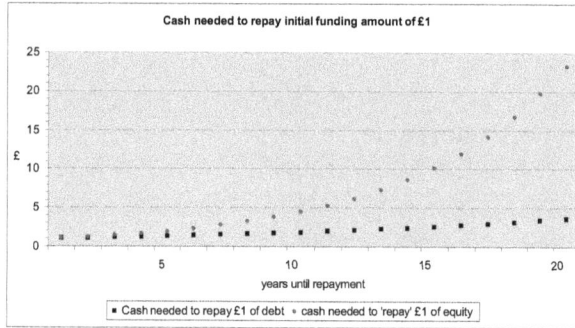

Cash needed to repay initial funding amount of £1

■ Cash needed to repay £1 of debt · cash needed to 'repay' £1 of equity

b

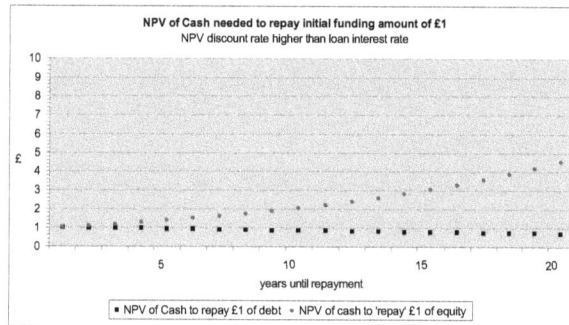

NPV of Cash needed to repay initial funding amount of £1
NPV discount rate higher than loan interest rate

■ NPV of Cash to repay £1 of debt · NPV of cash to 'repay' £1 of equity

c

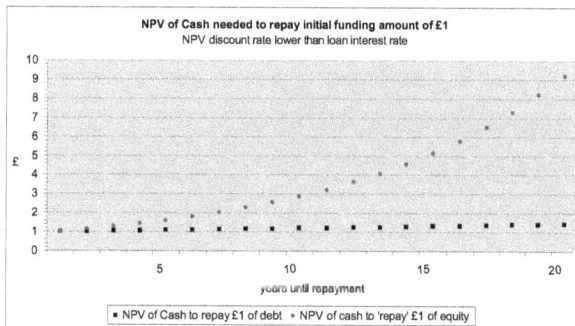

NPV of Cash needed to repay initial funding amount of £1
NPV discount rate lower than loan interest rate

■ NPV of Cash to repay £1 of debt · NPV of cash to 'repay' £1 of equity

To diminish the probability of oscillating away from a stable solution, 'damping factors' can be applied. This simply means that, rather than applying the estimated adjustment (positive or negative) in full, only a percentage of the calculated change is used.

There is an obvious trade-off between stability and efficiency here. The smaller the damping factor, and hence the smaller the adjustment applied at each iteration, the more security is provided against unstable calculations failing to reach a solution but the longer the iterative process will take. The precise values of damping factors are something, therefore, which needs to be judged based on trial and error for each project.

11.4 Optimising revenues

The calculation of the minimum revenue level which meets certain criteria is commonplace and critical for many PFI deals, but is also relevant in classic project finance deals, where it may be necessary, for example, to examine the threshold revenue level which makes a project viable, or to define a minimum workable value for contract negotiations.

Whether revenues are to be generated as a simple inflating annual payment, or as a per unit price, provided the revenue profile is predetermined, then the re-calc macro (see Section 7.4.2) can be used to set the revenue amounts based on a single, iterated figure.

Complexities in tax and distributable profit calculations generally mean that the correct revenue figure cannot be calculated directly in the model (irrespective of circularity issues). Rather than cycling through a series of incorrect values, therefore, the model should estimate the proportionate change in revenue which will meet the required targets and constraints. Applying the calculated change, usually with a damping factor (see Section 11.3) then allows iteration towards a solution.

The adjustment can be applied simply on the macro support sheet, where the current revenue value is calculated as the last stored value adjusted by the estimated proportionate change.

11.4.1 Applying LLCR constraints

Implicit in the LLCR target is the requirement to repay the loan over a given repayment period. The NPV at completion of available cash over the scheduled loan life, calculated as for the LLCR (see Section 22.2), must be at least equal to the outstanding debt at completion multiplied by the target LLCR. Any excess or shortfall gives the NPV of the possible revenue reduction or required revenue increase with respect to the LLCR target.

In order to calculate an estimate for the percentage revenue adjustment required to meet the LLCR target, the NPV surplus or shortfall should be compared with the NPV at completion of gross revenues, also discounted at the loan interest rate.

Box 11.1

Example: Calculation of revenue adjustment to target specific LLCR

Target LLCR = 1.5

Outstanding debt at completion = 120
Outstanding debt at completion × target LLCR = 180

NPV (at completion) of available cash = 150

Shortfall in NPV of available cash = 180 − 150 = **30**

NPV (at completion) of gross revenues = **300**

Estimate of required change in revenues = 30/300 = **+10%**

Revenue value for next iteration = current pasted value * (1 + 10% * damping factor)

This method works whatever the revenue base, i.e., whether revenue is defined as a per-annum figure or a per-unit figure.

11.4.2 Applying ADSCR constraints

The ADSCR relates to a fixed repayment profile, as well as a specified repayment term. With a fixed revenue profile and fixed repayment profile, meeting the ADSCR in every period can give revenues very much higher than would otherwise be needed. If the lender will permit it, therefore, it is often very helpful to 'sculpt' repayments, allowing ADSCR to be met by reducing debt service in some periods rather than by increasing revenues (see Section 15.3.2.7). If such sculpting is permitted, and if project cash flows reliably provide more than the minimum ADSCR for interest only, then the revenue optimisation calculation need not specifically address ADSCR.

11.4.3 Applying IRR constraints

IRR is the outcome of all project cash movements, and does not require specific payments in specific periods, it is therefore an ideal metric with which to adjust the revenue level. Depending on the required LLCR and the debt:equity ratio, achieving the required IRR may automatically give an adequate LLCR, in which case, if repayments can be sculpted to meet ADSCR, solving for the target IRR may prove a sufficient means of finding the required revenue values.

Since, mathematically, the IRR of a sequence of cash flows is the discount rate which produces an NPV of zero, any non-zero NPV, discounting at the target IRR, indicates the required change in the NPV of cash flows to equity in order to exactly achieve the target IRR. As for the LLCR calculation, calculating this amount as a proportion of the NPV of gross revenues, discounted to the same date (easiest date is start of the model timeline) also using the target IRR, gives an estimate of the required change in revenues.

Box 11.2
Example: Calculation of revenue adjustment to target specific LLCR

Target nominal Equity IRR = 15% per annum

NPV of cash flows to/from investors, discounting at 15% per annum = 50
NPV of gross revenues, discounting at 15% per annum = 500

Estimate of required change in revenues = -50/500 = **–10%**

Revenue value for next iteration = current pasted value *(1 – 10%*damping factor)

11.4.4 Combining targets

When targetting both LLCR and equity IRR, the applied adjustment should be the greater of the two implied adjustments, thus:

- if one is positive and one negative, the positive value will be used;
- if both are negative, the smaller reduction will be applied; or
- if both are positive, the larger increase will be applied.

Thus, the calculation will seek to *at least* meet both targets. This principle can generally be extended to include multiple targets, not just LLCR and IRR.

11.4.5 Optimising the debt:equity ratio

When solving for both LLCR and IRR it will usually be the case that one target is met exactly, and one exceeded. This means that, although there is no 'spare' cash in the project, nonetheless, revenues can be reduced if lenders and investors can be flexible about the debt:equity ratio.

Box 11.3

Example

Target nominal Equity IRR = 16% per annum
Target nominal LLCR = 1.40

(a) IRR exceeds target

Nominal Equity IRR = 17.5% per annum
LLCR = 1.40

Since the IRR is greater than needed, no extra revenue would be needed to support some undefined extra amount of equity at the target return.
   The extra equity could replace some debt, and less revenue would be needed to meet the LLCR target
   (*this would reduce the spare cash for equity, and iteration would be needed to find the solution*)

(b) LLCR exceeds target

Nominal Equity IRR = 16% per annum
LLCR = 1.45

Since the LLCR is greater than needed, no extra revenue would be needed to support some undefined extra amount of debt within the target LLCR.
   The extra debt could replace some equity, and less revenue would be needed to meet the IRR target
   (*this would reduce the spare cash for debt, and iteration would be needed to find the solution*)

To calculate this adjustment, use

$$\text{Supportable Debt} = \frac{\text{NPV of available cash at completion}}{\text{target LLCR}}$$

Iterating the NPV figure via the re-calc macro (see Section 7.4.2). The ratio of debt:equity can then be calculated based on a supportable equity figure, calculated as the NPV at completion of cash flows to investors, discounted at the target IRR. The implied percentage funding from debt can then be calculated as:

$$\text{Implied \% funding from debt} = 1 - \frac{\text{Supportable equity}}{\text{total funding}}$$

The percentage funding from debt can then be calculated via the recalc macro for the next iteration as:

$$\text{revised \% funding from debt} = \text{Stored \% funding from debt} \times (1\text{-damping factor}) + \text{implied \% funding from debt} \times \text{damping factor}$$

Revenues then target the required IRR. With appropriate damping factors, this calculation should iterate to a satisfactory solution, with IRR and LLCR both equal to the target values.

11.5 Cost-based tariff calculations

Historically, many projects, particularly build-own-operate (BOO) or build-own-transfer (BOT) deals, were built around a 'cost-based' revenue structure, with revenues designed to meet all agreed costs as paid, including debt service, tax and a given equity return. Perhaps because it is not seen to offer sufficient transfer of risk to the project sponsors, and can result in very variable payment streams, this method of revenue sculpting seems to have become less common.

To the extent that such revenues must be calculated to take account of any receivables delay, and to cover tax payments based upon the revenues from which they are paid, cost-based tariff calculations have great scope for circularity. If care is taken, however, it should be possible to resolve the issues and avoid any circular code.

When putting together such a tariff calculation, start by considering which values in each period are independent of the final tariff figure, and hence present no problems with circularity. Providing debt service is defined independently of revenues, this should be most values other than the receivables adjustment in the period and any tax paid in the period for which it is calculated. If all values in any period are independent of the final tariff figure in that period, then no potential circularity arises, and no special adjustments are required.

When adjustments are needed, a basic tariff can be calculated equal to the revenues required to meet all allowed costs, net of any revenue that should be offset in the tariff calculation (for example, earned interest and receivables from a previous period). This figure can then be used as a basis to calculate the additional elements to be included in the total tariff in a way that avoids simply using circular code (the disadvantages of which are discussed in Section 7.2).

Using the basic tariff estimate, first calculate any working capital adjustment to be reflected in the tariff. So, for example, in a semi-annual tariff calculation with two months receivables delay, the basic tariff needs to be increased to allow for 2/6 of the calculated tariff not being received in the current half-year. (In such a case the revenues brought forward from the previous period should have been deducted from the base tariff calculation.) This can be achieved simply, by dividing the basic tariff by 2/3 to give the total adjusted figure.

Once the basic tariff has been adjusted to include the estimated receivable adjustment, the result can be used as an estimated revenue figure for calculating any tax costs to be paid in the current period which are based on revenues in the period and are to be included in the total tariff. Using the estimated revenue, together with actual costs, capital allowance and losses carried forward figures, an estimated tax basis is calculated. Using this, the tax element can be calculated for the tariff, simply taking the tax basis multiplied by the applicable tax rate and any percentage adjustment if part of the tax is paid in this, and part in later periods. To allow for the fact that tax will have to be paid on the additional revenues included to cover tax payments, the calculated tax element of the tariff should then be grossed-up by dividing by 1 minus the tax rate.

This calculation becomes much more complicated when tax is paid on revenues in the period, and the receivables adjustment is to be covered by the tariff. This is because the revenues added to pay tax must be increased to cover the receivables delay on the additional revenues, the increase, in turn having to be adjusted for tax, then for receivables, etc. It is not possible ultimately to resolve this calculation, but because the increments being made steadily reduce with iteration, it is possible to input a calculation that will estimate the result to an acceptable level of accuracy. The required formula basically takes the increment each time, and grosses up alternately for tax and receivables. For example, see Box 11.4.

Box 11.4

Given:
'Tax adj' = 1 / (1 – tax rate) – 1
'W.Cap adj' = 1 / (1 – receivables period as percentage model period) – 1
Tax estimate = estimated tax basis x tax rate / (1 – tax rate)

The basic formula required is;

Tax estimate x (1 + 'W.Cap adj' x (1 + 'Tax adj' x (1 + 'W.Cap adj' x (1 + 'Taxadj'))))

The underlined section gives the repeating unit within the formula. The formula should be input, and the number of repeating units increased until a satisfactory level of correspondence is achieved between the total tariff figure and the calculated actual costs and working capital adjustment.

Once the tariff has been calculated, tax and receivables values should be calculated based on the resultant revenues in the normal way. If the tariff is intended to exactly match costs for the period, the output from these calculations can be used, in turn, to check the tariff calculations.

Although it is very satisfying to produce a tariff that exactly matches the calculated cost and return values, before embarking upon complicated adjustments such as those detailed above it is worth ensuring that they are appropriate. If the tariff is to be based in some way on the figures calculated by the model, then such accuracy may be necessary. If, on the other hand, the model is trying to reflect the projected application of a formulaic tariff calculation, consider the details of the formula as it is to be applied, bearing in mind the information that will realistically be available at the time when each calculation is made. It may be more realistic in this case to include a reasonable estimate for some tariff elements, together with an adjustment mechanism in the next or subsequent periods, to redress any excess or shortfall apparent in comparison with the actual values.

Exhibit 11.2 shows an example of a tariff tax calculation involving the following elements.

- Operating Costs: the total of all operating costs calculated for the period.
- Debt Service: the total of all fees, interest payments and repayments in the period.
- Intermittent Maintenance Costs: any repair or maintenance costs included in the tariff agreement. This may be represented by agreed funding for a maintenance reserve fund, spreading out what may be quite large costs in intermittent periods which would otherwise give a very uneven tariff profile.
- Calculated Equity Returns: if the tariff is to include a specific provision for equity return, provision for the return must be calculated on some basis, and included in the tariff figure for each period.
- Payables From Previous Period: if the tariff is to include adjustment for payables/receivables, then the delayed costs from the previous period must be included in the costs to be covered by the tariff in each period.

- Tax From Previous Period/Catch-up: if the tariff is matching costs exactly, then any tax calculated based on the previous period's revenues, but payable in this period, must be added to the costs to be covered by the tariff in this period. Alternatively, if the tariff is based on an estimate of some values, with subsequent adjustments to correct for underestimates or overestimates, then the calculation needs to include a catch-up adjustment, correcting for estimating errors in the tariff tax calculations for previous periods.
- Total Costs to be Met by Tariff: the total of the basic costs to be met from the tariff in the period.

Less

- Delayed Revenue From Last Period: if the tariff is being adjusted for payables/receivables, then the costs to be met from the tariff in each period should be reduced by the delayed revenues from the previous period.
- Payables in Period: if the tariff is being adjusted for payables/receivables, then the costs to be met from the tariff in the period should be reduced by the delayed payables for the period.
- Earned Interest: if interest on cash deposits is to be taken into account for the tariff calculation, then it should be deducted from the costs to be covered by the tariff in each period.
- Net Costs to be Met by Tariff: total costs to be met by tariff less delayed revenue from last period, less payables in the period, less earned interest.
- Tariff Adjusted for Working Capital Delay: first estimate of tariff (equal to net costs to be met by tariff) grossed up to allow for receivables adjustment, if receivables/payables are to be covered by the tariff.
- Tariff Tax Calculation: if all or part of the calculated tax in a period is paid in the same period as the revenues upon which it is charged, then, if the tariff is intended to exactly match tax costs in each period, a tax figure must be calculated for use in the tariff.
- Estimated Net Operating Revenues: Tariff adjusted for Working Capital Delay as calculated above, less operating costs.
- Earned Interest: additional revenues must be added to tariff revenues for the tax calculation.
- Loan Interest: loan interest and fees to be expensed for tax purposes.
- Capital Allowances: calculated capital allowances for tax.
- Taxable Profits: estimated taxable profits calculated as revenues pre-tax adjustment less operating costs, loan interest and capital allowances.
- Losses Brought Forward: where tax calculations allow the carry forward of losses from period to period, the losses carried forward from previous periods should be picked up from the actual tax calculation section. Taking the losses from the actual tax section avoids estimating inaccuracies in the tariff tax calculation being compounded from period to period via carried forward values.
- Tax Basis: taxable profits less losses brought forward, giving the estimated figure upon which tax can be calculated. Values may be grouped into, for example, annual periods as required for the tax calculation.
- Estimated Tax Paid: tax basis in each period multiplied by the tax rate.
- Revenue Increase for Tax Payment: takes the portion of the calculated tax that is payable in the period of calculation, multiplied by first estimate tax for tariff, adjusted, if necessary, for receivables delay in payments, as detailed above.

● Total Tariff: the tariff adjusted for working capital delay as calculated above, plus the tax element of the tariff.

Exhibit 11.2

Illustrative cost-based revenue calculation sheet

	A	B	C	D		K	L	M	N
						Jul-14	Jan-15	Jul-15	Jan-
4					Pre	to	to	to	to
5	**Tariff Calculation**		**Totals**		Co	Dec-14	Jun-15	Dec-15	Jun-
6	*All values in millions Zgs*								
7									
8									
9	Cost-based widget price calculation								
10									
11	Total Operating Costs		608.13			0.00	8.15	8.39	
12	Total Debt Service		18,804.63			0.00	629.17	639.73	6
13	Intermittent maintenance costs		3,427.00			0.00	0.00	0.00	
14	Tax paid (re. Previous period)		12,220.55			0.00	0.00	0.00	1
15	Payables recievables adjustment		(10,862.29)			0.00	(0.43)	(195.43)	(1
16	Equity Return		25,398.29			0.00	340.19	350.25	3
17									
18	less Earned Interest		0.00			0.00	0.00	0.00	
19	First estimated net costs to be met by tariff		49,596.30			0.00	977.08	802.94	1,0
20									
21	**First estimate adjusted for w/cap delay**		58,889.47			0.00	1,172.50	963.53	1,2
22									
23	Tax for Tarrif calculation								
25	Estimated net op revenues		58,281.34			0	1,164	955	
27	Senior Debt Interest & Fees		6,046.13			0.00	312.30	316.67	3
29	Capital Allowances		8,686.12			0.00	0.00	854.92	8
31	Estimated Net Taxable Profits		43,549.10			0.00	852.05	(216.45)	
32	Annual Estimated Net taxable profits		43,549.10			0.00	0.00	635.61	
34	Earned Interest		0.00			0.00	0.00	0.00	
36	Losses Carried forward					0.00	0.00	0.00	
38	Estimated Tax Basis		43,595.49			0.00	0.00	635.61	
40	Estimated Tax Payable		15,258.42			0.00	0.00	222.46	
41	Estimated Tax Paid		4,577.53			0.00	0.00	66.74	
42									
43	**Revenue increase for tax payment**		6,284.29			0.00	0.00	91.62	
44									
45	**Total Tariff**					0.00	1,172.50	1,055.15	1,2

Once calculated, the tariff figure should feed back into the operating calculations and provide the basis for the revenue calculations. The calculated revenue figures then feed into the actual tax calculation, allowing cross-checks, where appropriate, between the actual figures and the estimated values in the tariff calculation.

12 The data sheet

The data section should contain all numeric inputs for the model, as well as all switches controlling data and calculation options.

12.1 Benefits of keeping input values in one area

Anyone who has ever had to work with a model not conforming to this structure will have some idea why a discrete data section is to be preferred. In order to properly control and run a model, it is extremely important to keep track of the assumptions upon which any given run is based, and to be able to access and change assumptions with confidence that this will be logically and comprehensively reflected throughout the model. This requirement is obviously much better supported by having all data items entered in one area where they can be easily located, reviewed and changed.

The data section in itself automatically produces part of the documentation for the model. Review of the data will give a full picture of the numeric, and a partial picture of the calculation assumptions in the model.

Values entered as labelled items scattered through the model or, worst of all, as figures included directly in formulae in the code, are difficult to find, check, review and change. They are easily forgotten or overlooked, and can give rise to the production of invalid and misleading results.

Make life simple for yourself, and anyone else who may need to use a model you have developed, and keep the data in one place! Try in this, as in all the techniques described here, to minimise the stress involved in using the model, and minimise the risk of producing incorrect or misleading figures.

12.2 Format and layout within the data sheet

There is a widespread convention that input items are formatted in blue. This is a fairly helpful idea, and one that is easy to conform to. The information conveyed by this means is lost when printing in black and white, but generally, provided inputs are confined to the data sheet, it is only crucial when working on-screen, not when reviewing print-outs.

Other colour and shading conventions can be applied within the data sheet. Where formulae are required on the data sheet, they can be distinguished from inputs by *not* being formatted in blue, and, for extra clarity, by background shading in grey. Test data, that is values used as test inputs during model development before actual data values are known, can be distinguished with a bright yellow background. This helps draw attention to the invalid items when viewing on screen, and the use of background shading rather than font colour means that the cells will also be highlighted in print-out.

Just as for the model as a whole, it is helpful to follow a logical layout for the data sheet making it easier to find given data items. This is particularly true once the data section reaches the considerable size common in the later stages of complex deals. Data items should be grouped into sensible categories, and it makes sense to roughly reflect the layout of the calculation sections of the model, with some specific additions. Suggested categories, in order, are given below:

- timing data;
- macroeconomic data;
- capital cost data;
- finance data;

- operating data; and
- tax and accounting data.

Data can take the form of single values, 'sets' of related values, and values which vary with time and need to be entered across a row.

Single values can be entered on separate rows, with values placed in column 'D' of the suggested page layout (see Section 2.5) and sets of inputs can be entered as tables.

When entering time-variant items ensure that the applicable timeline is made very clear, for example, the model timeline, half years from Financial Close or from Completion, etc. Ideally maintain consistency with the model timeline at least with respect to period length, for example, where possible maintain the assumption that columns represent half years, but even for annual data, try to remain consistent with the concept of horizontal rather than vertical timelines, as this will make some calculations easier, and will allow a more compact input format.

For all data items, enter row titles or single item titles in columns A or B, as for other sheets. Resist the temptation to fill in blank space by floating isolated inputs or tables of inputs in later columns. Aligning all inputs or tables of inputs with the left hand edge of the worksheet ensures that all items can readily be seen when scanning through the data section on the screen. Avoiding overlaps of different blocks of data input in different columns of the same rows avoids unnecessary problems when new items need to be inserted.

The recommended data layout will usually result in a lot of white space when printing. This can be dealt with by preparing a summary report that picks up key values from the data section and arranges them in a format that fits efficiently on the page for printing.

12.3 Contents of data section

Basically, any **numeric input** for the model belongs in the data sheet(s), not in a calculation sheet, and definitely not buried in a formula somewhere. Note that this does not mean that *every numeric item* should be entered via a labelled input. There are a number of intrinsic model assumptions which may be represented by numeric values but would be completely inappropriate as input items, for example, the number of months in a calendar year, the number of hours in a day, etc. Standard spreadsheet checking tools will often highlight the presence of such numeric values in formulae, and it is a clear sign of laziness or ignorance when such warnings are glibly reproduced in a model audit report, without the apparent application of any intervening human intelligence.

Timing data such as financial close, start of operations, last loan drawdown, etc., should be specified as input items in the data, not simply 'hard-wired' into the code (see Section 2.2.1). Timing data entered as absolute (for example, date of financial close) or relative values (for example, months from Fin.Close to start of operations) should be used to control all timings within the model, maintaining flexibility and allowing timing assumptions to be reviewed from the data section. The data values can control calculations via masks in the worklines section or directly in specific formulae.

Switches controlling the choice of data assumptions or the operation of the calculation sections of the model also belong in the data section, labelled to indicate their function and the meaning of each possible value for the switch.

Calculations should be kept to a minimum in the data section, and should be formatted to make it very clear that they are not inputs and should not be overwritten with input data.

Data items should be values which, if changed, will produce appropriate changes in the model. They should be clearly labelled, with units where relevant. **All data items should be what their label says they are.**

In so far as possible, the data section should not allow entry of incompatible input values. For example, if a calculation needs to divide a given item between two categories on a percentage basis, the data section should have an input item for one of the percentages only. The code can then easily calculate the other item as the remainder. If both categories have a data item for percentage split, then no useful additional information is provided, but scope for error is introduced since values may be entered which do not total 100%.

Unless defining an amount fixed in nominal terms (for example, a loan facility amount), input monetary values should be in real terms – i.e., even for values entered over a number of time periods, all values should be as at a single specified value date (see Section 4.1). Inflation and currency assumptions will be specified as part of the model data, and may well be varied as part of the sensitivity analyses.

The model needs input at a sufficiently fine level of detail to ensure that required sensitivities can be run based the selected data items. This must be balanced against the downsides of trying to model complex engineering or operating parameters directly in the financial model (assuming these can instead be supplied from other sources). Where relationships between input values are not captured in the model, linked items can be entered as sets, with switches allowing selection between sets of inputs. For example, in a transport project the relationship between forecast price and passenger numbers is very complex, and part of a specialist modelling field in its own right. It is not realistic to include these calculations in the financial model, but nor is it appropriate to sensitise either price or passenger numbers independently. A workable solution might therefore be to have the traffic consultants define several cases, for example, low, medium and high, enter the appropriate sets of passenger and price values for each, and select the required case with a switch.

12.4 Input categories

The data entries required to control most model calculations are indicated in the sections describing those calculations. Some data items, however, deserve specific mention here.

12.4.1 Macroeconomic data

Macroeconomic data will include assumptions about inflation rates and currency issues.

The model requires a 'general' inflation value for each currency, to be used for such calculations as real IRRs or currency devaluation, but may also need specific rates for different categories of cost. Generally the model can be constructed around a single general inflation rate per currency, with alternative rates and factors for specific items added during model development as required.

Inflation rates should be input as per annum rates, either as a single value applicable over the whole analysis period, as several rates applicable over specific sections of the timeline, or as varying per annum rates input directly into the time periods to which they apply.

Timing is key with regard to inflation calculations. Given that data may be provided in values for a date prior to the start of the model, it is useful to include a provision for a per annum rate or a flat adjustment to be used to convert input values to values as at the start of the first period of the model (see Section 4.1).

For projects with values denominated in more than one **currency**, a number of specific data entries are required, see Section 8. Generally, an inflation rate should be included for each currency, together with an initial exchange rate and provision for real depreciation/appreciation.

12.4.2 Tax and accounting data

Unless the required tax and accounting treatments for the project are clearly defined and understood from the early stages of model development, and it is clear that the capital amounts deducted to calculate taxable profits will be equal to depreciation calculated for accounting purposes, it is probably advisable that the model includes provision for depreciation parameters to be entered separately for tax and accounting calculations.

12.4.3 Legal fees

Legal fees associated with arranging funding are often forgotten in the early stages of model development. They are, however, a substantial up-front cost and should be included as a data item unless already included in the construction costs. They can then form a row in the capital cost or finance sections of the model.

12.5 The data validation menu

Although the 'Data' menu is generally not useful for project finance modelling, the 'Validation' item is the exception. This option allows restrictions to be placed on the inputs for a given cell or set of cells, and a suitable message to be displayed if unsuitable inputs are attempted.

Exhibit 12.1

Example of protection of a calculation cell on the input sheet using Data Validation

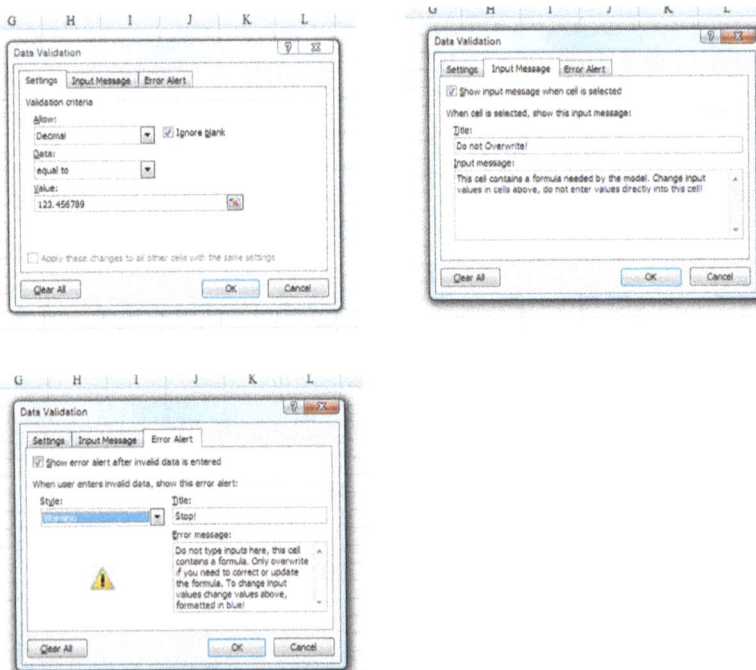

12.5.1 Protecting formulae on the data sheet

Validation can be used as a simple way of preventing accidental overwriting of formulae on the data sheet. From the Data Validation menu, on the 'Settings' tab, Select 'Decimal' for 'Allow:'. Next choose 'equal to' under 'Data:', and enter a reasonably complex decimal.

If you want a message to be displayed whenever the cell is selected, use the 'Input Message' tab.

Finally, use the 'Error Alert' tab to set the message displayed if an attempt is made to input an invalid entry into the cell, and whether the message will simply give a warning, prompt before accepting the entry, or refuse invalid inputs (see Exhibit 12.1).

12.5.2 Restricting input values

Sometimes only a limited range of inputs is valid for a particular data item. Sometimes this is self-evident, for example, an entry labelled 'number of operating months per year' needs values between 0 and 12. However, the model may require whole numbers only, or the formulae may only work for inputs below a certain value. The expected inputs should fall within the range of values which will work, but this is not guaranteed. An example is the period of delay for payables and receivables. Values up to six months can be modelled easily, but more than a half year of delay requires a much more complex formula. Rather than add complexity and spend a lot of time on a calculation unlikely to be used, the model can be made consistent simply by restricting the permitted range of input values.

In this case it is probably only necessary to generate a warning message if an attempt is made to enter an inappropriate value, not to display a message every time the cell is selected (see Exhibit 12.2).

Exhibit 12.2

Example of restriction of possible input values using Data Validation

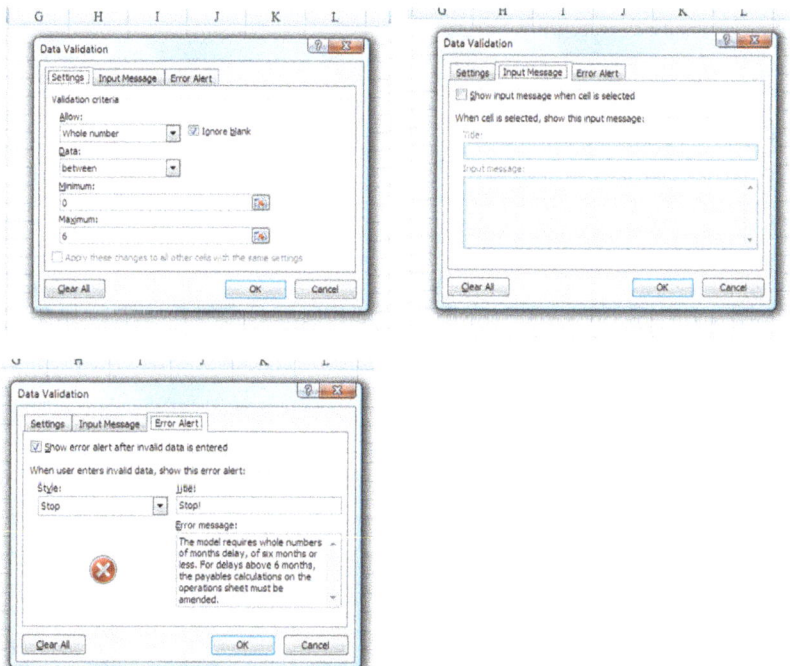

12.6 Format of supplied data

Data may be provided in a wide variety of formats and it is sometimes necessary to pre-process supplied data into a suitable format for the model.

In attempting to secure a supply of data in a convenient format, a good first step is to provide a pro-forma of the data sheet. This requires a detailed analysis of the data items which the model will require and the best format in which to enter them. The rather organic process of extending and refining the data sheet as the model is built can change and expand the initial outline, but at least you can provide a clear indication of the values you need, and the units and format you need them in.

The pro forma should indicate the items required, the units in which they are to be specified, an ideal value date for monetary values (or at least a requirement that value date and/or built-in inflation assumptions be given for supplied values), and the time periods for which values are required (for example, monthly, quarterly, semi-annual). It is important to remember that timing data must also be supplied, including expenditure profiles for costs, timing for start of operations, build-up of operating values and timings for finance structure.

Given that a data 'wish list' has been prepared and distributed, it would be overly optimistic to assume that the data provided to the modeller will be presented in the requested form, and for the listed items. So what sorts of problems are likely to arise?

Exhibit 12.3

Simple processing of supplied data into the required format for the model, using formulae designed for easy copying for multiple data items

				Expenditure Profiles from start of construction >>>>>>								
1 Monthly Capex expenditure profiles												
2					Month	Month	Month	Month	Month	Month	Month	Month	Mo
3					1	2	3	4	5	6	7	8	9
4													
6 Engineers and Consultants				12.00%	4.00%	3.00%	3.00%	3.00%	3.00%	3.00%	3.00%	3.(
8 Civil Works				20.00%	5.00%	5.00%	4.00%	6.00%	4.00%	2.00%	2.00%	3.(
9 Start-up Costs												
10 Plant and Machinery				25.00%						10.00%		
12 Engineers and Consultants				12.00%	4.00%	3.00%	3.00%	3.00%	3.00%	3.00%	3.00%	3.(

16 Simple counter										
17	month1	1		1	7	13	19	25	31	37
18	month2	2		2	8	14	20	26	32	38
19	month3	3		3	9	15	21	27	33	39
20	month4	4		4	10	16	22	28	34	40
21	month5	5		5	11	17	23	29	35	41
22	month6	6		6	12	18	24	30	36	42

				=INDEX($E$6:$CC$12,$D27,E$17+$C27-1)						
25 Engineers and Consultants										
27	month1	1	1	12%	3%	3%	3%	3%	0%	0%
28	month2	2	1	4%	3%	3%	3%	3%	0%	0%
29 =D27	month3	3	1	3%	3%	3%	3%	3%	0%	0%
30	month4	4	1	3%	3%	3%	3%	3%	0%	0%
31	month5	5	1	3%	3%	3%	3%	3%	0%	0%
32	month6	6	1	3%	3%	3%	3%	3%	0%	0%

				=INDEX($E$6:$BC$12,$D37,E$17+$C37-1)						
35 Civil Works										
37	month1	1	3	20%	2%	3%	3%	1%	0%	0%
38	month2	2	3	5%	2%	3%	3%	1%	0%	0%

12.6.1 Wrong frequency

As discussed earlier, it is generally ideal to prepare the model with an overall semi-annual timeline. This being so, annual data may need to be adjusted for use on a semi-annual basis. This will generally be required for values input over several periods (for example, the expenditure profile for capital costs or traffic forecasts varying over time), but need not apply to single input values that might appropriately be input on a per annum basis and adjusted to semi-annual values in the calculations – for example, fixed operating costs per annum.

To convert from annual to semi-annual values, it is often initially sufficient simply to divide the given values by two. This can be done directly in the data input cells, which is quick and simple and offers the benefit that the original data values can be seen and checked in the input cells.

For values at a greater than semi-annual frequency, values can generally either be added together to give semi-annual totals (entering values directly into the cells, as for annual values, to make it easier to check input values against original data), or entered into semi-annual columns as quarterly or monthly data (see Section 3.2). The appropriate treatment should be selected based upon the anticipated final frequency for the data items being considered.

If data is provided in Excel but not in the required format, initial processing (using counters with Index(...) or SUMIF(...) (see Section 3.4)) can be carried out to arrange the figures into the required format before pasting into the model data sheet (see Exhibit 12.3).

Care must be taken with values representing something other than a total over a given period. Annual average values, or end of period values, flow rates or production rates cannot necessarily be converted to simple semi-annual equivalents by simple division or addition. The issue generally arises with values that are changing over time and that represent non-additive units – for example, a build-up of water flow specified in M^3 per second. For average values, annual averages can (for a 'quick and dirty' adjustment) simply be repeated in both the half years to which they apply. If the model is at a more detailed stage, then some intricate calculations may be required, taking account of the values in surrounding periods and any information available from the original data source to convert the average annual balance into corresponding average semi-annual values. The result of this processing should be that calculation based upon the semi-annual values gives the same total number of units (for example, M^3) for the year as would be the case for an annual calculation using the annual average. A similar calculation in reverse is required to convert quarterly averages to annual values. The ideal treatment of such data is, of course, to go back to its source and have it resupplied in a more useable format.

12.6.2 Nominal values

If data is supplied in nominal values (i.e., in inflated terms), then it is important to establish the inflation assumptions that have been used, unless the given values are quoted prices that are to be fixed in nominal terms – for example, the figures for a fixed price construction contract.

Assuming that the figures are not nominally fixed, then the inherent inflation must be removed, to allow the explicit inflation assumptions applied in the model to be used to recalculate nominal values for the given item.

12.6.3 Too complex

If data is supplied with a great deal of complex detail, it is worth considering to what extent it is needed for the model. If eight different items are processed to give values for a single required item, then it is probably simplest to enter the final value in the model, and require that any alternative sets of data be provided in the form of the final value only. But this would not be appropriate if one of the underlying values was likely to form a key item in negotiations, requiring model runs varying the item at short notice. The need to seek updates via the original source would probably prove an unacceptable constraint in such a case.

12.6.4 Too simple

If data is supplied in too processed a form (for example, fuel costs as monetary amounts rather than as fuel price per unit of fuel with number of fuel units utilised per unit of production), then the underlying data items should be requested from the source. It is sometimes assumed that the more processing done before including values in the model, the more helpful to the modeller. Explaining that this is not the case, and why, may be sufficient to ensure that the required values are forthcoming. If the correct values are, none the less, not immediately available, then calculate the fuel cost per unit of production from the figures given, and use this in the model. When such approximation cannot be made, then the data source must either supply the basic data required, or must supply the given item based on a range of alternative values for the underlying data, as needed for sensitivity cases.

12.6.5 From documentation

Some data, of course, is not supplied by partners, clients or advisers to a project, but must be extracted from documentation, without the option of seeking further information from the source of the data. In such cases the document, for example, a feasibility study or an invitation to bid, has not generally been prepared specifically to support the preparation of a financial model, or even a finance structure. The relevant data must therefore be extracted with care and, almost as importantly, irrelevant data must be excluded from the model. Complex provisions for various exceptional circumstances may well not have any contribution to make to the model. Other detailed specifications may, on the other hand, be essential to valid operation of the model.

The process of developing a model based upon such documentation, particularly in the case of bid documents, can be a very useful way of exploring the structures proposed and finding any apparent gaps in the project specification, which may represent an oversight, or may be the key to adapting the terms of the document to fit the needs of the bidder. It is useful, therefore, when working on this basis to prepare a note detailing the assumptions and data drawn from the document, with references to the precise source of each assumption, together with any unresolved issues or further data requirements arising from the application of the listed information. This has the added benefit of providing a clear list of extracted information that can be circulated and cross-checked by others reviewing the document.

12.7 Confirmation of data values

In all cases, it is worth sending a printout and accompanying note to individuals providing model data, showing their information *in situ* in the data section, and explaining how each item is applied to the calculations. This allows review and confirmation that their information has been correctly reflected in the model. In a situation where the availability of data is limited, necessitating the use of reasonable assumptions to support a working model, ensure that the basis for such assumptions is known to those involved in the deal and the model, preferably via written documentation.

12.8 Documentation of input data

For data items, both as part of a double-checking process as items are entered and as an inherently useful process for future reference, it can be helpful to enter a brief note regarding the source and nature of each item. This can usefully be done by entering hidden text in the spare column to the left of the 'Totals' column. Reformatting as visible text and temporarily adjusting the width of the column can provide a printout showing the source of each data item next to its label in the Data sheet. This provides useful documentation of the sources of input values, and is easy to update when new values are entered.

13 The 'Work' sheet

This section of the model is intended to hold all the items that are not in themselves interesting or appropriate for inclusion in any of the other main model sections, but which are useful or necessary as distinct values for use in other sections.

Period start and end dates, two rows providing the basis for all date-related timings in the model, specifying the dates of the first and last days in each column of the timeline.

Worklines, in general, are rows or single items that form intermediate steps in one or more other calculations and which are not of direct interest in their own right.

Masks are rows that in some way reflect timing assumptions and allow such assumptions to be readily applied to the appropriate calculations in the model.

Factors are calculated values providing proportionate adjustments to specific calculations, for example adjustments arising from inflation, exchange rate movements, or growth rates.

Counters are simply progressive number series used in various calculations.

13.1 Purpose of worklines

These calculations provide background values necessary to other calculations, but not necessarily of interest in themselves, in an accessible and checkable format.

Values calculated in worklines may be used in several calculations and so eliminate the need for repetition of the same calculation in several different formulae.

Placing the worklines in a specific sheet in of the model means that they do not confuse the calculation sections by showing intermediate values (which may be difficult to label meaningfully), but avoids the inconvenience and risk of having hidden values in the calculation section that are easy to erase or overwrite accidentally, and hard to check.

13.2 Purpose of masks

Masks allow timing assumptions, specified via data input, to be applied easily to the appropriate calculations. Many timing assumptions apply to more than one calculation, and it is obviously efficient to convert the relevant inputs to values on the timeline once, saving time, simplifying the formulae using the information, and needing to be checked only once. The calculated values can then simply be applied as a single item in any formula to which the timing data applies.

Collection of the masks in this sheet avoids cluttering calculation sheets with background calculations. More usefully, it ensures that masks can easily be found when developing the model, even if a given mask is used in calculations in several sheets, or several calculations in one section of the model. Once prepared and checked, the timing calculation can be picked up correctly in all formulae where it is needed, rather than being re-entered in each formula that uses it, giving scope for error. As for worklines, although not shown in the calculation sections, inclusion of masks in the worklines means that they can easily be found and reviewed when checking the model.

13.3 Purpose of factors

These allow various multiplying factors to be calculated based upon input data values (for example, inflation rates) that can then simply be applied to a number of items in the model, as required. The benefits are as for masks, with the additional advantage that if changes are made to the basis for processing data applied via a factor, the change can be made once to the factor calculation, and will automatically be applied to all calculations in which the factor is used.

13.4 Purpose of counters

Counters of various kinds may be used to support calculations – usually those reflecting timing issues in some way. They provide a simple reference, for example, for comparison with periods specified in the input data.

13.5 Uses and calculation of period start and end dates

The start and end date rows provide the information needed to locate any timepoint along the model timeline.

The 'Start date' row begins with a directly entered date (the period of the timeline is treated as an inherent model feature, not a changeable input) and thereafter is calculated (as the previous period's 'End Date' plus 1). The end date in each period is calculated from the start date using the EDATE(...) function. For a semi annual model, the period end date is EDATE(*start date*,5), i.e., the last day of the fifth month after the start date month. Note that to use EDATE(...) and EOMONTH(...) functions the Analysis Toolpak add-in supplied with Excel must be installed and activated.

13.6 Uses and calculation of masks

Masks are used to transfer timing data into calculations, usually via straightforward multiplication. To fulfil this role they often simply comprise a series of zeros and ones, turning values 'off' outside a specified time range. They may also include a fraction representing a time period that covers less than one whole model period: for example, an operating period mask might reflect a start of operations mid-way through a six-month operating period, by taking a value of 0.5 in the half year in which operation commences, and a value of 1 thereafter. In some cases the mask may incorporate more complex information, such as the number of remaining repayment periods in a loan repayment mask.

A simple mask is calculated with reference to input timing data, generally in comparison with a counter of some sort.

Standard masks required in most models would include the following.

- Simple annual mask ~ alternating 1s and 0s across the timeline, providing a simple basis for restricting calculations to first or second half year only. Calculated as 1-previous period's value.
- Financial Close Mask ~ zeros in all periods except the period of Financial Close, when the value is 1. Used as a basis for the calculation of a counter from financial close, and a multiplier for all cost and other items occurring at Financial Close. Calculated from an input Date of Financial Close and the start and end dates in each period. One possible formula for calculating this mask is IF(AND(*date of Fin Close* >= *period start date*, *date of Fin Close* <= *period end date*),1,0).
- Construction Period Mask ~ '1's in all periods which include time on or after financial close and on or before the completion date.
- Operating Period Mask ~ '1's in all periods which include time between the completion date and the end of the analysis period.

Details of specific masks are given throughout this text in association with the calculations they support.

13.7 Uses and calculation of factors

Factors convert input assumptions into period-by-period values by which relevant rows can simply be multiplied. Generally speaking, factors are used to apply input inflation assumptions (see Section 4.2) and currency adjustments (see Section 8), as well as growth rates of various kinds.

13.8 Uses and calculation of counters

Counters are simple number progressions, often entered into the worklines section directly, with no requirement for data input. A simple numeric counter can be used as a reference when using INDEX(...) or SUMIF(...) functions.

A year counter indicates the calendar year allocated to each half year, easily calculated from the start or end date values, using the YEAR(...) function.

14 Construction period costs

The capital costs section of the model takes input data relating to construction and other non-finance based capital costs, and presents them as nominal values in the correct periods of expenditure, with useful sub-totals as required. This may be a very short, simple section, or a long, complex section, depending upon the number of currencies, the level of detail as to categories of cost and the format of capital cost input.

The capital costs should ideally be defined in the data as nominally fixed or uninflated values, given as total values for each category of cost, with spend profiles specified as percentages over time, and with specified value dates for inflating amounts. The expenditure profiles should be input on a timeline from Financial Close, then positioned as required using appropriate counters with the INDEX(...) or SUMIF(...) functions (see Section 3.1.3 and Exhibit 3.1).

If care is taken to maintain a consistent layout for the input values and the corresponding rows in the 'Capex' sheet, then one formula can often be copied for all cost items. For monthly figures, it may be preferable to create a formula which can be copied for all six months for a given cost, but requires some editing for each separate cost category (see Section 3.2 and Exhibit 14.1).

Costs should be broken down into types of expenditure using the minimum number of categories that will provide all required information, allow depreciation and so on to be calculated conveniently, and accommodate sensibly the format in which the data is likely to be provided and updated.

Separate categories, a specified percentage breakdown, or an allocated currency number (see Section 8) should be provided for costs denominated in different underlying currencies.

The values in the calculation section should reflect the categories defined in the data section, unless an excessively detailed breakdown is included in the Data sheet in order to accommodate the format of supplied data.

The construction costs should be shown in the presentation currency, at the values and in the periods in which expenditure would be made according to the assumptions in the model. Sub-totals can be included for, for example, all costs denominated in each currency, or costs included in the general categories upon which depreciation might be based.

Exhibit 14.1

Input and positioning of monthly capital expenditure

	B	C	D	E	F	G	H	I	J	K
8	**Timing Inputs**									
9										
10	Scheduled Financial Close			01/07/2011						
74	**Capital Cost Data**									
75						1/2 Years following Financial Close >>>>>>>>>>>>>				
76						1st half	2nd half	1st half	2nd half	1st half	2n
77						Year 1	Year 1	Year 2	Year 2	Year 3	Y
78	Construction Costs			Total Value		Expenditure Profiles >>>>>>>>					
79	Site & Civils			500,500,000							
80	Civils expenditure in month 1 of half year period					5.00%	5.00%	5.00%	5.00%		
81	Civils expenditure in month 2 of half year period					5.00%	5.00%	5.00%	5.00%		
82	Civils expenditure in month 3 of half year period					5.00%	5.00%	5.00%	0.00%		
83	Civils expenditure in month 4 of half year period					5.00%	5.00%	5.00%	0.00%		
84	Civils expenditure in month 5 of half year period					5.00%	5.00%	5.00%	0.00%		
85	Civils expenditure in month 6 of half year period					5.00%	5.00%	5.00%	0.00%		
86											
87	Plant & Machinery			200,000,000							
88	P&M expenditure in month 1 of half year period					0.00%	0.00%	5.00%	3.00%	4.50%	
89	P&M expenditure in month 2 of half year period					0.00%	0.00%	5.10%	3.00%	5.00%	
90	P&M expenditure in month 3 of half year period					0.00%	4.25%	5.20%	6.30%	5.00%	

\ **Inputs** /

	B	C	D	E	F	G	H	I	J	K	L	M	N	O
11														
12	Period start date					01/04/2011	01/10/2011	01/04/2012	01/10/2012	01/04/2013	01/10/2013	01/04/2014	01/10/2014	01/04
13	Period end date					30/09/2011	31/03/2012	30/09/2012	31/03/2013	30/09/2013	31/03/2014	30/09/2014	31/03/2015	30/09
14														
27	Simple Monthly counter in month 1 of half year period				=F27+1	1	7	13	19	25	31	37	43	49
28	" month 2 of half year period					2	8	14	20	26	32	38	44	50
29	" " month 3 of half year period					3	9	15	21	27	33	39	45	51
30	" " month 4 of half year period					4	10	16	22	28	34	40	46	52
31	" " month 5 of half year period					5	11	17	23	29	35	41	47	53
32	" " month 6 of half year period					6	12	18	24	30	36	42	48	54

	B		C	D	E	F	G	H	I	J
17							Months in 1st	Months in 2nd	Financial Close	Proportions for average interest Balance
18	**Monthly work items**					Months	half of year	half of year	months mask	
19						0	3			
20	month 1 of half year period					1	4	10	0	0.9167
21	month 2 of half year period					2	5	11	0	0.7500
22	month 3 of half year period					3	6	12	0	0.5833
23	month 4 of half year period					4	7	1	1	0.4167
24	month 5 of half year period					5	8	2	0	0.2500
25	month 6 of half year period					6	9	3	0	0.0833

=(MONTH(G12)-1)

=MOD(F20,12)+1

=SUMIF(F20:F25,MONTH(Inputs!D10),Work!D20:D25)+SUMIF(G20:G25,MONTH(Inputs!D10),Work!D20:D25)

	B		C	D	E	F	G	H	I	J	K	L	M	N	O
53	Month of Financial Close				4										
54	Month of Completion				1 post		5								
55															
56	Financial Close Mask						1	0	0	0	0	0	0	0	0
57															
58	Monthly counter from fin close in month 1 of half year period						0	4	10	16	22	28	34	40	4
59	" month 2 of half year period						0	5	11	17	23	29	35	41	4
60	" " month 3 of half year period						0	6	12	18	24	30	36	42	4
61	" " month 4 of half year period						1	7	13	19	25	31	37	43	4
62	" " month 5 of half year period		0				2	8	14	20	26	32	38	44	5
63	" " month 6 of half year period					0	3	9	15	21	27	33	39	45	5

\ **Work** /

=IF($D20=$D$53,1,0)*G$56+F63+MIN(1,F63)

=SUMIF(Work!$F$27:$BV$32,Work!G58,Inputs!$F$80:$BV$85)*Inputs!$D$79

	B	C	D	E	F	G	H	I	J	K	L
8											
9	Site & Civils										
10	Civils expenditure in month 1 of half year period					0	25,025,000	25,025,000	25,025,000	0	0
11	Civils expenditure in month 2 of half year period					0	25,025,000	25,025,000	25,025,000	0	0
12	Civils expenditure in month 3 of half year period					0	25,025,000	25,025,000	25,025,000	0	0
13	Civils expenditure in month 4 of half year period					25,025,000	25,025,000	25,025,000	25,025,000	0	0
14	Civils expenditure in month 5 of half year period					25,025,000	25,025,000	25,025,000	25,025,000	0	0
15	Civils expenditure in month 6 of half year period					25,025,000	25,025,000	25,025,000	0	0	0
16	Total Civils		500,500,000			75,075,000	150,150,000	150,150,000	125,125,000	0	0
17	Plant & Machinery										
18	E&M expenditure in month 1 of half year period					0	0	8,499,999	6,000,000	6,000,000	22,000,000

k \ **Capex** / F

15 Funding

15.1 Laying out funding calculations on a 'cascade' basis

For a project finance deal, the use of funds, and usually the drawdown of funds, will be matched to the construction period funding requirement. In practice, this generally means that in each period (whether monthly, quarterly, half-yearly, etc.,) certain funding amounts may be fixed, with the balance of costs for that period being funded as required from a combination of other sources. It is generally most appropriate, therefore, to structure the funding calculations on a 'cascade' basis, whereby the net funding requirement is calculated as each funding source is taken into account, and funding sources are considered in the order in which they would preferentially be used.

As discussed in Section 7, it is worth taking care with the structure of the funding section in order to avoid any unnecessary circularities.

An example layout for a funding section is shown in Exhibit 15.1, but it is important to remember that the funding structure tends to be very deal-specific, and the details of layout will generally be unique to each transaction. The assumptions informing the example layout are:

(a) that equity is divided between pure equity and subordinated debt, with pure equity drawn up-front, as needed to meet expenditure;
(b) any funding requirement not met from drawings on pure equity is funded from senior debt, up to an amount equal to the senior debt facility size. The facility size can be an input value, or calculated from the percentage total funding to come from debt, and the total funding figure calculated via the recalc macro;
(c) any remaining funding requirement not met from pure equity and senior debt is met from subordinated debt; and
(d) all sub debt interest during construction is rolled up (i.e., funded from additional drawings on the subordinated loan).

This represents a fairly simple financing structure, but is adequate to illustrate the concept of the funding calculations 'cascading' through the funding sources.

The capital costs are picked up from the Capex sheet, broken down as required to support the funding calculations. This generally means that the figures for total capital expenditure, and any specific sub totals of costs eligible for ECA funding are required. The total legal, equity and finance fees in each period are added to the capital costs (in so far as the fees are not calculated with direct reference to drawings in the same period), and any net available revenues are deducted to give an initial funding requirement.

Pure equity drawings are calculated first, to match the net funding requirement in each period until the total pure equity amount has been drawn. A revised funding requirement is then calculated, deducting the equity drawings, and this is used to calculate senior loan principal drawings, until the full senior debt facility amount has been drawn.

The final net funding requirement is then calculated, deducting the senior debt principal and rolled up interest drawings and adding the senior debt interest to calculate a new net funding requirement. The subordinated loan then funds this final requirement, plus its own rolled-up interest.

Exhibit 15.1

Illustrative layout of funding calculations

	B		D	EF	G	H	I	J	K	L
1										
2	**Big Island Widget Plant Project**									
3	**Base Case**									
4					Pre	Jan-09	Jul-09	Jan-10	Jul-10	Jan-11	Jul-11
5					Yr	to	to	to	to	to	to
6	*All values in millions Zos*		Totals		One	Jun-09	Dec-09	Jun-10	Dec-10	Jun-11	Dec-1
8	**Total Capital Costs**		8,907.43			0.00	2,599.94	1,177.07	1,226.55	1,569.97	563.6
10	**Legal Fees paid at Financial Close**		8.00			0.00	8.00	0.00	0.00	0.00	0.0
11	**Total Loan Up-Front Fees**		127.93			0.00	127.93	0.00	0.00	0.00	0.0
12	**Total Loan Commitment Fees**		40.71			0.00	0.00	14.44	10.59	7.95	4.8
13	**Total Loan Agency Fees**		2.88			0.00	0.08	0.08	0.08	0.08	0.0
15	**Initial Funding of DSRA**		572.12			0.00	0.00	0.00	0.00	0.00	0.0
17	**Initial Funding Requirement**		9,659.07			0.00	2,735.95	1,191.59	1,237.23	1,578.00	568.5
18											
19	**Equity Calculation**										
21	**Equity Amount**		**120.00**								
23	**Equity as Drawn**		120.00			0.00	120.00	0.00	0.00	0.00	0.0
24											
25	**Net Funding Requirement after Equity**		9,539.07			0.00	2,615.95	1,191.59	1,237.23	1,578.00	568.5
26											
27	**Loan 1 Calculations**										
29	**Loan 1 Facility Size**		**8,528.5**								
31	**Loan 1 Interest Rate % p.a.**					6.75%	6.75%	6.75%	6.75%	6.75%	6.75
33	**Loan 1 Up-front Fees**		127.93			0.00	127.93	0.00	0.00	0.00	0.0
34	**Loan 1 Commitment Fees**		40.71			0.00	0.00	14.44	10.59	7.95	4.8
35	**Loan 1 Agency Fees**		2.88			0.00	0.08	0.08	0.08	0.08	0.0
37	**Loan 1 Principal Drawings**		7,801.76			0.00	2,615.95	1,191.59	1,237.23	1,578.00	568.5
38	**Repayments**		8,528.49			0.00	0.00	0.00	0.00	0.00	0.0
39	**Interest**		5,521.57			0.00	21.11	108.04	151.87	194.28	251.4
40	**Additional Drawings to Fund Interest**		726.73			0.00	21.11	108.04	151.87	194.28	251.4
41	**Loan 1 Balance Outstanding**		8,528.49			0.00	2,637.06	3,936.69	5,325.78	7,098.06	7,918.0
43	**Net Funding Requirement after Senior D**		6,532.14			0.00	0.00	0.00	0.00	0.00	0.0
44											
45	**Subordinated Loan**										
47	**Cash available for sub debt service**					0.00	0.00	0.00	0.00	0.00	0.0
49	**Sub Debt Interest Rate % p.a.**					9.00%	9.00%	9.00%	9.00%	9.00%	9.00
51	**Sub Debt Principal Drawings**		2,012.12			0.00	0.00	0.00	0.00	0.00	0.0
52	**Repayments**		2,207.49			0.00	0.00	0.00	0.00	0.00	0.0
53	**Interest**		2,040.65			0.00	0.00	0.00	0.00	0.00	0.0
54	**Additional Drawings to Fund Interest**		195.36			0.00	0.00	0.00	0.00	0.00	0.0
55	**Sub Debt Balance Outstanding**		2,045.68			0.00	0.00	0.00	0.00	0.00	0.0
57	**Sub Debt Target Balance Outstanding**					0.00	0.00	0.00	0.00	0.00	0.0
58											
59	**Sub Totals**										
61	**Total Up front fees**		127.93			0.00	127.93	0.00	0.00	0.00	0.0
62	**Total Commitment Fees**		40.71			0.00	0.00	14.44	10.59	7.95	4.8
63	**Total Agency Fees**		2.88			0.00	0.08	0.08	0.08	0.08	0.0
65	**Total Legal & Finance Fees**		179.52			0.00	136.01	14.52	10.67	8.03	4.
67	**Total Senior Loan Interest**		5,521.57			0.00	21.11	108.04	151.87	194.28	251.4
68	**Total Loan Interest**		7,562.21			0.00	21.11	108.04	151.87	194.28	251.4
70	**Total Senior Debt Interest and Fees**		5,701.08			0.00	157.11	122.56	162.54	202.31	256.2
71	**Total Interest & Fees**		7,741.73			0.00	157.11	122.56	162.54	202.31	256.2
73	**Total Loan 1 Drawings**		8,528.49			0.00	2,637.06	1,299.63	1,389.09	1,772.28	820.0
75	**Total Loan Drawings**		8,528.49			0.00	2,637.06	1,299.63	1,389.09	1,772.28	820.0
76	**Total Senior Loan Repayments**		8,528.49			0.00	0.00	0.00	0.00	0.00	0.0
78	**Total Senior Loan Interest and Repaym**		14,050.05			0.00	21.11	108.04	151.87	194.28	251.4
79											

|◄ ◄ ► ►|\ Fin /

Finance sub-totals are then calculated (see Section 2.2.2). These can feed into subsequent calculations, maintaining consistency, minimising the number of calculations in the model and simplifying the future incorporation of any additional loans into the model.

15.2 Equity calculations

Equity can be paid into the project in any number of ways, and in any combination of ways. The specific structure included in the model will depend upon the details of the deal, and the stage and structure of the deal will determine whether one equity structure will be sufficient or whether several structures need to be included, with a switch in the data to select between them.

Although it is impossible to anticipate all the available permutations of equity structure, certain common elements of the equity calculation can be considered.

Essentially, equity can be defined as a given value (for example, £20 million) or a calculated value (for example, 25% of total debt plus equity).

Timing of equity payments can be specified as given amounts in particular periods, drawings as needed up to a total figure, or drawings pro rata to debt.

15.2.1 Equity amount

15.2.1.1 Total equity as an input amount

If the value of some or all of the equity is to be specified as a given input amount, this can be accommodated easily by including a simple data item allowing the amount to be entered directly.

The considerations arising in relation to equity on this basis are essentially to do with timing rather than the calculation of the total amount. Some care must be taken, however, when equity is not denominated in the presentation currency. In this case, the equivalent value of the input equity amount will usually change over time in the presentation currency, and it is important to remember this and reflect it properly in the calculations.

15.2.1.2 Total equity as a percentage of funding

This calculation raises circularity issues because equity generally affects loan drawings and hence total debt. This figure should therefore be calculated using the recalc macro (see Section 7.4.2). The macro will probably include figures for total drawings for each loan, for use in the fee calculations, and adjustment should already have been made to these figures to reflect any currency issues (see Section 8.4). Add to the items iterated by the macro the amounts drawn for each type of equity in the appropriate presentation currency equivalent amount, and hence calculate a 'Total Funding' value via the recalc macro. Equity can then be calculated as a given percentage of this amount, and the macro will iterate to a solution for the values of debt and equity reflecting the required debt:equity ratio.

Calculation of a consistent debt:equity ratio in all periods, pro rata debt and equity drawdowns, is described in Section 15.2.2.3.

15.2.2 Equity timing

15.2.2.1 Equity spent first as needed

Under this structure, the input or calculated total equity figure is assumed to be paid into the project as needed to meet costs, until the total amount has been used. The costs to be met by equity would usually be calculated as the basic funding requirement less principal and rolled-up interest drawings on any loans to be drawn in preference to equity (export credit loans, grants, subsidies, etc.), plus interest on any such loans.

Care is needed with this calculation if the equity is denominated other than in the presentation currency. The presentation currency equivalent of remaining equity available for drawing must be adjusted from period to period to reflect any currency appreciation/depreciation. This generally requires calculation of the unused equity amount at the end of each period, which can then be carried forward and adjusted for currency movements to a point in time matching that of the costs which it is to fund (see Section 8.1).

15.2.2.2 Equity paid in at specified times

Some or all of the equity may be paid in up-front, or according to a specified schedule (perhaps representing a public share offer). In this case the funds paid into the project in a given period may exceed the funding requirement in that period. A deposit calculation must therefore be added to the funding section, which allows surplus funds to be carried forward to meet costs in later periods and calculates earned interest on such funds. The balance on such an account then comprises the first source of funds in the funding waterfall in subsequent periods. Where necessary, multiple rows can be included to calculate drawings on the balance to meet loan interest, etc., as required. If the equity is denominated in a currency other than the presentation currency, care must be taken when carrying funds forward to ensure that they are adjusted to reflect the appropriate presentation currency value.

15.2.2.3 Equity paid in pro rata to debt

This is usually the most intricate equity calculation because the equity drawings in each period influence the loan values on which they are based, apparently creating circularity. In practice however, applying the method of breaking down calculations into separate components, this calculation can be modelled with no circularity at all. The 'cascade' layout is very helpful in supporting this calculation, allowing an initial equity estimate to be calculated and adjusted through the funding cascade so that loan drawings will fund the correct percentage of the total funding requirement, leaving the correct amount unfunded, to be met from the equity drawings.

For example, to calculate a consistent debt:equity ratio of 20:80, which means 20% of total funding in each period comes from equity, and equity = 25% of debt:

1   calculate the total net funding requirement, excluding loan interest;
2   calculate 'first estimate equity' as 20% of (1), which will give equity drawings pro rata to the basic loan principal drawings;
3   calculate the remaining funding requirement after deducting the 1st equity estimate;
4   calculate principal drawings and interest for the next loan in the funding cascade. Calculate rolled up interest as 80% of the interest to be funded;
5   calculate an incremental equity estimate equal to 25% of the loan's drawings to fund rolled-up interest;
6   calculate the remaining funding requirement after taking account of interest and drawings on fixed loans and deducting the incremental equity estimate. Any negative values represent surplus funds;
7   repeat steps 4 to 6 for all but last loan in funding cascade, for which only step 4 is needed;
8   calculate the total of all loan drawings; and
9   calculate total equity as 25% of the total loan drawings in each period.

With reference to the net cash flow summary, check that the total loan drawings and equity correctly meet the project's funding requirement. Note that if the drawings on fixed loans in any period exceed 80% of the total funding requirement in the period, excess funds will be drawn in that period in order to maintain the specified debt:equity ratio. A deposit calculation should be included (see above) to carry forward such surplus for use in later periods, and to calculate interest earned on the surplus until it can be used. Such carried forward surplus should be deducted from 1 and should not be included in the 20% equity figure for that period.

The above procedure can be applied for any number of loans, simply revising the equity estimate and adjusting the remaining funding requirement after each loan.

15.3 Loan calculations

Each loan should be calculated as a complete item comprising fees, drawings, interest, repayments and balance.

For each loan, a number of basic masks (see Section 13.2 and below) should be created on the Worklines sheet, defining the permitted drawdown period ('availability'), the interest roll-up period, if different, and a repayment mask.

15.3.1 Data for loans

On the Data sheet, a table can be established giving all the loan data items, allowing a full set of inputs to be added easily for new loans (see Exhibit 15.2). This table can also include switches to determine which loans are to be included for a given model run.

Data items for inclusion in the table will vary according to the flexibility required in the finance structure and the details of individual loans, but will generally include a selection from the following list.

- Loan to be included (1 = Yes, 0 = No).
- Base interest rate % p.a.
- Margin pre-completion % p.a.
- Margin(s) post-completion % p.a.
- Last drawdown period (specified as a number of months from Financial Close, applied to the nearest half year or month, depending on timescale of drawdown calculations).
- Last period for roll-up (specified as number of months from Financial Close, applied to nearest half year or month, depending on timescale of drawdown calculations).
- Guide date for first repayment (specified as number of months from Financial Close, 1st repay at end of half year in which guide date falls).
- Repayment method (if choice available, for example, 0 = equal instalments, 1 = annuity basis).
- Number of repays.
- Percentage eligible foreign costs funded from loan (for example, for ECAs).
- Percentage interest rolled-up.
- Maximum permitted drawdown.
- Facility size used for fee calculation to be based on calculated loan drawings or input facility amount (for example, enter 0 or 1).
- Percentage increase in drawings when calculating facility size for fees.
- Calculated facility size rounding target (for example, to nearest £50 million).

Exhibit 15.2

Illustrative funding inputs

	Funding Data		ECA Loan Data	Foreign Commercial Loan Data	Local Commercial Loan Data
144	**Funding Data**				
145	Equity as needed (0) or pro-rata to debt(1)?	1			
146	Required equity as % of total funding	20.00%			
147	Loans 2&3 drawn pro-rata (0) or loan 2 1st (1)	1			
148	If pro rata, % from Loan 2	70.00%			
149					
150					
151					
152					
153	Loan used for this case? 1 = yes		1	1	1
154	% Foreign Costs Funded		85.00%	NA	NA
155	% Local Costs Funded (as % foreign costs)		15.00%	NA	NA
156	% Premium Funded		85.00%	NA	NA
157	Principal drawdown period/months from Fin.Close		27.00	27.00	27.00
158	Interest Rate pre-completion (% p.a.)		7.50%	7.00%	12.00%
159	Interest Rate post-completion (% p.a.)		6.75%	7.00%	11.75%
160	Up-front fees/premia as % facility amount		8.00%	1.50%	0.80%
161	Commitment Fees % p.a.		0.00%	0.25%	0.25%
162	Agency Fees millions Zgs p.a.		0.60	0.60	0.60
163	% Interest Rolled Up		85.00%	100.00%	100.00%
164	Months of Roll-up from Financial Close		24.00	24.00	24.00
165	1st Repayment (months from Financial Close)		36.00	36.00	36.00
166	Repayment Period/years		15.00	10.00	10.00
167	Facility Size Calculated(0) or Input(1)		0	0	0
168	Mark up on drawings for Calc. Facility Size		5.00%	5.00%	5.00%
169	Rounding Amount if Facility Calculated		10.00	10.00	10.00
170	Facility Size if Input/Maximum Facility Size			2,320.00	
172					

- Input facility size.
- Up-front fee as percentage of selected facility size.
- ECA premium as percentage of selected facility size.
- Percentage of ECA premium funded from loan.
- Commitment fees % p.a.
- Agency fees (for example, £ per annum).

15.3.2 Loan calculations

Each loan calculation should comprise the following rows (with the exception of 'Currency Devaluation' which only applies to loans denominated in a currency other than the presentation currency). Each item is discussed in detail below.

- Facility size.
- Fees.
  - Up-front fees.

    ○ Commitment fees.
    ○ Agency fees.
- Drawings.
- Repayments.
- Interest payable.
- Additional drawings to fund interest.
- Balance outstanding.
- Currency devaluation.

15.3.2.1 Facility size

A loan facility size must be specified or calculated for each loan. This provides a basis for the calculation of up-front and commitment fees, and for some loans fixes an upper limit on the drawings calculated by the model.

In the later stages of a deal, actual facility sizes will have been determined or be under negotiation and the appropriate figures can simply be included as data inputs. For some loans the facility size may be a fixed amount from the start and represent a constraint on drawdown, and again, the required figure can be entered directly in the data. In the early stages of the deal, however, a guide to the appropriate facility sizes will generally be one of the results required from the model, and a figure will be calculated for each loan based upon the calculated value for the total drawings made on that loan. It is useful to remember that in most cases the final facility size will not be equal to the base case drawings, but will be the product of negotiation, and part of a funding package sufficient to fund the deal under a number of downside assumptions. This is to satisfy lenders and investors that the project can be completed even if base case assumptions prove optimistic. It is therefore prudent, if setting facility sizes based on base case drawings, to include some increase on the total drawdown figure in order to give a realistic fee amount for the base case. Remember that this adjustment should be reduced or removed if sizing loans from a negotiated and agreed 'downside' case.

The model should have a facility size as part of each loan calculation. This value can select an input or calculated value, based on a switch set in the data, the calculated value being equal to total drawings plus the specified percentage mark-up. It might also be appropriate to round the calculated figure – rounding up to a multiple of a value specified in the data. This can be done by using:

$$\text{ROUNDUP}(\textit{total drawings} / \textit{multiple}, 0) * \textit{multiple}$$

This eliminates spurious accuracy from a value based on an estimated increment over base case drawings, and is closer to the likely format for actual agreed facility sizes, which may well be set in multiples of some suitable value.

Using total loan drawings as part of the fee calculation obviously creates a circular calculation and requires use of the recalc macro (see Section 7.4.2). This can be done simply by including in the macro a 'total drawings' figure for each loan. This should be the nominal total of principal drawings and rolled-up interest. If any loan is denominated in a currency other than the presentation currency, the value should be adjusted back to a given date by removing devaluation (see Sections 8.4 and 15.3.2.2).

The facility size in the loan calculation should be multiplied by the switch determining whether the loan is to be used for the given run.

15.3.2.2 Currency issues for facility size

For loans denominated in a currency other than the presentation currency, the facility size must be consistent with the currency assumptions in the model. The facility size can most usefully be represented as the equivalent presentation currency amount at a given date, ideally at financial close.

If the facility size is calculated based on total loan drawings (via the recalc macro), then the drawings must be converted to the underlying currency equivalents, totalled and converted to the presentation currency equivalent as at financial close. This can be calculated by dividing the calculated drawings in the presentation currency by the devaluation factors at the time of drawdown, and multiplying the total by devaluation at the time of Financial close. If a reciprocal of the devaluation factor is calculated in the worklines, then the total drawings converted to start-of-timeline presentation currency equivalent can be calculated in a single cell using the SUMPRODUCT(...) function.

15.3.2.3 Fees

There are, generally speaking, three types of fee to consider: (a) up-front fees, calculated as a percentage of the facility size (representing, for example, arrangement fees); (b) commitment fees, calculated as a percentage of the committed facility amount remaining undrawn in each period; and (c) agency fees, a given amount per annum paid during the life of the loan.

Up-front fees for each loan can be calculated simply, using the appropriate facility size for the loan (see above), multiplied by the percentage given in the data section, multiplied by the 'Financial Close mask' and any switch to determine whether the loan is to be included in the current run.

Agency fees should be calculated for each period of the loan life. This is also a simple calculation, taking the specified annual figure adjusted to reflect the model timescale – for example, divided by 2 for a semi-annual model, in all periods for which the previous period's loan balance plus 'Financial Close mask' is greater than zero, multiplied by any switch determining whether the loan is included in the current run. It is important not to refer to any other loan values in the current (rather than previous) period, because these will probably refer to the agency fees directly or indirectly, creating an unnecessary circularity in the model.

Commitment fees are calculated on the committed funds (i.e., the facility size) less the funds actually drawn, on which interest is payable. Unless loan agreements are determined in detail, and necessitate calculation of commitment fees as end-period values, taking account of drawings in the period, it is usually possible to make some simple assumptions when modelling commitment fees allowing avoidance of circularity. This can be done in a number of ways. An assumption can be made that the commitment fees are payable at the end of each period, based on the balance drawn at the start of the period (i.e., the balance at end of the previous period). Slightly more complex but probably more accurate is to assume that commitment fees for each period are based on the average undrawn balance over the period and are paid at the start of the next period. On this basis there should generally not be a problem with circularity.

If the commitment fees must be included in the model as end-period payments based on average drawings over the period, it may be simplest to exclude commitment fees from the initial funding requirement calculation, allowing them to be added separately as the calculation flows through the funding cascade. When doing this, it is helpful to remember that, because they are not paid until the end of the period, drawings to fund commitment fees, like those to fund interest, do not affect the average balance upon which they are based. Bear in mind that if values are denominated in a currency other than the presentation currency, they must be converted to end-period, rather than start or mid-period equivalent values, when using them to calculate end-period commitment fee values.

15.3.2.4 Interest rate

Even with a single input % p.a. interest rate, it is advisable to have a row across the timeline which gives the % p.a. interest rate applicable in each half-year period. This is consistent with maintaining flexibility in the model and anticipating future development.

For pre- and post-completion rates it is usually advisable to have separate rows for the two rates, since, in the period of completion, the pre-completion rate should be applied to the average balance, reflecting timing of drawings pre-completion, whilst the post completion rate should be applied to the full balance.

For changing margins within half years post-completion, generally a weighted average can apply since the balance is consistent throughout the half year.

15.3.2.5 Drawings

The principal drawings represent all drawings made on a given loan in each period, other than drawings to fund interest payable on that loan (rolled-up interest). The precise basis for loan drawings tends to be very specific to each project, and general guidelines only can be given here.

For all drawings, it is important to remember to multiply the formula by any data switch intended to specify whether the loan is to be included for the current run.

For each loan, a drawdown period should be specified in the data. This specifies the Availability Period for the loan, and is a simple and useful means of determining when costs cease to be funded from loan drawings. Obviously, for most loan calculations, drawdowns will in any case cease at or before this period, as the costs or funding requirement upon which drawings are based are fully spent. The drawdown period should be reflected in a simple mask calculated in the worklines section, with '1' in all periods in which drawdown is permitted, and '0' in all other periods, calculated on a semi annual basis, or reflecting more detailed timings if these have been modelled for capex. The formula calculating drawdown for each loan in any period should then be multiplied by the availability mask for that loan in that period.

Generally drawings are of three basic kinds – specified amounts on specified dates (for example, for bond issues), drawings tied to particular costs (for example, export credit loan drawings) and drawings made as needed to meet net costs.

Specified amounts on specified dates. If using a specified drawdown schedule it will need to be entered in the data. If the loan structure means that a single drawdown will be made, then the timing and amount can be entered as two data items. A drawdown mask can then be calculated in the worklines section and simply multiplied by the input amount to calculate the drawdown figures in the finance section.

If drawings are to be made in a number of periods, then the total drawings and a drawdown schedule from Financial Close, entered as percentages in the appropriate periods, can be included in the data. The drawdown schedule can be picked up into the appropriate periods on the model timeline in the same way as for capital expenditure, using 'SUMIF(...)' and the counter from Financial Close. The funding section then simply multiplies the total drawings by the percentage value in the drawdown schedule in each period, and makes any currency adjustments needed. This allows amount and timing of drawdowns to be varied independently, and allows the appropriate assumptions regarding currency

Exhibit 15.3

Calculation of availability mask (see Exhibit 14.1 for any calculation elements not displayed here)

	B	C	D	E
8	**Timing Inputs**			
9				
10	Scheduled Financial Close		01/07/2011	
28			Loan 1	
29	Availability period / months from Financial Close		33	

Inputs

=IF($D20=$D$53,1,0)*G$56+F63+MIN(1,F63)

	A	B	C	D	E	F	G	H	I	J	K	L	M	N	O
11															
12	Period start date						01/04/2011	01/10/2011	01/04/2012	01/10/2012	01/04/2013	01/10/2013	01/04/2014	01/10/2014	01/04
13	Period end date						30/09/2011	31/03/2012	30/09/2012	31/03/2013	30/09/2013	31/03/2014	30/09/2014	31/03/2015	30/09
14															
57							0								
58	Monthly counter from fin close in month 1 of half year period						0	4	10	16	22	28	34	40	46
59	" " month 2 of half year period						0	5	11	17	23	29	35	41	47
60	" " month 3 of half year period						0	6	12	18	24	30	36	42	48
61	" " month 4 of half year period						1	7	13	19	25	31	37	43	49
62	" " month 5 of half year period						2	8	14	20	26	32	38	44	50
63	" " month 6 of half year period						3	9	15	21	27	33	39	45	51
107	**Funding Worklines**														
108	Senior debt end of drawdown date			31 Mar 14											
109															
110	Senior Debt Availability mask month 1 of half year period						0	1	1	1	1	1	0	0	0
111	" " month 2 of half year period						0	1	1	1	1	1	0	0	0
112	" " month 3 of half year period						0	1	1	1	1	1	0	0	0
113	" " month 4 of half year period						1	1	1	1	1	1	0	0	0
114	" " month 5 of half year period						1	1	1	1	1	1	0	0	0
115	" " month 6 of half year period						1	1	1	1	1	1	0	0	0

Work

=IF(EDATE(G$12,$D19)<=$D$108,1,0)*MIN(1,G58)

=EOMONTH(Inputs!$D$10,Inputs!$D$38-1)

devaluation to be automatically reflected in the model. If currency issues do not arise and flexibility as to timing and amount is definitely not required, then the drawdowns can be entered directly as a row in the data section, and simply picked up in the appropriate periods in the funding section.

Drawings based on specific costs. Here, the drawdown can be specified in data as an input percentage(s) of the relevant costs. For example, an ECA loan might fund 85% of eligible foreign construction costs, local costs equal to 15% of eligible foreign costs and 100% of the loan's own up-front fee. Each of these figures can be entered as a separate data item, allowing them to be changed easily and independently, and also giving a clear indication of the loan drawdown assumptions in the data section.

The specific construction or other costs upon which drawings are to be based for a particular loan can be shown as a separate row(s) in the funding section.

Drawings to meet net costs. These can be calculated based upon the relevant net funding requirement in the funding cascade.

For all types of loans, provision may need to be made for a limit on drawings. Where required, this must be included in the principal drawdown calculation. This can be done simply by taking the lesser of the calculated drawdown amount and the input maximum drawdown amount less the closing balance at the end of the previous period. If the loan is denominated in a currency other than the presentation currency, then the remaining available loan amount must be adjusted in each period to give a presentation currency equivalent value at the same time point (probably mid-period) as that assumed for the drawings with which it is being compared.

In some cases, two or more loans will need to be drawn pro rata. Provided only principal drawings are to be made pro rata, then this can generally be done simply using a percentage split specified in the data. Alternatively, the split may be proportionate to input facility amounts specified for each loan. This can again be modelled without difficulty by converting the facility size ratio into a percentage value.

If the pro rata split is to include rolled-up interest then the calculation becomes a little more complicated, but can be adjusted through the rolled-up interest calculation (see below) without affecting the principal drawdown calculations. It is worth noting that if the first repayment period is the same for both tranches, and they are to be drawn fully pro rata throughout the availability period, then the drawdowns can be calculated as though for a single loan.

15.3.2.6 Currency adjustments for drawings

Drawings should be calculated as the presentation currency equivalent of amounts in the underlying currency, converted at the time the drawings are made. Given that drawings will generally be made to meet costs, and such costs will already be calculated in the model in the presentation currency or presentation currency equivalent at the time of expenditure, no currency adjustment should be required between the funding requirement and the drawings made to meet it.

Careful treatment is, however, needed when a maximum facility size is specified, to ensure that the value used to restrict drawings is the correct value (in presentation currency terms) in each period. Drawings will generally be assumed to occur at mid-period, or averaged over the period. The remaining facility amount must therefore be calculated at the same time-point for proper comparison with the drawings.

The total permitted facility size as at the middle of each period can be calculated by dividing the Facility Size in the presentation currency at Financial Close by devaluation at Financial Close, and multiplying by devaluation to the point of drawdown (see Section 8.4), usually at the mid-point of each period. From this amount, the total drawings to date must be deducted, calculated as the previous period's closing balance, divided by the previous period's end-period devaluation factor, multiplied by the current period's mid-point devaluation factor. The remaining facility amount defines the maximum permissible drawdown at the period mid-point. An end period value must be similarly calculated to restrict drawings to fund rolled up interest, which occur at the end of the period.

15.3.2.7 Principal repayments

Loan repayments most often follow one of a number of standard formats, and can be fully specified from the data.

Repayments can be:

- by means of a specified number of equal instalments;
- on an annuity basis over a specified number of periods (i.e., repayment plus interest is a constant amount in each period);
- sculpted to meet cover factor constraints, according to an input profile, or using a specified percentage of net revenues (the most complex to model); or
- a single 'bullet' repayment, on its own, or combined with another repayment method for part of the loan.

In addition, a scheduled repayment profile may be constrained by available cash once other debt service commitments have been met – usually the case for some types of subordinated debt.

Repayment masks. For equal or annuity repayments, a special repayment mask should be calculated in the worklines section. Prior to the first repayment period specified in the data, the mask should take a value of zero. In the first repayment period, the mask should take a value equal to the number of repayments specified in the data (or calculated from the total loan maturity and first repayment period specified in the data), and should reduce by 1 in each subsequent period until the last scheduled repayment period, in and from which, it should take a value of 1. This mask indicates in each period the remaining number of periods over which any outstanding debt should be repaid and allows repayments to be adjusted for any drawings that overlap with repayments, or for any shortfall in achieved versus scheduled repayments, while maintaining the scheduled loan life. If the scheduled loan life is exceeded, then the mask will attempt to repay all outstandings as quickly as possible. It also allows each repayment to be calculated with reference to the closing balance at the end of the previous period, and eliminates the need to extract a total drawings value upon which the repayments can be based, very useful if currency adjustments are required. This flexibility would not be available if a simple '1' and '0' mask was to be used.

Note that the formula in Exhibit 15.2 requires an input zero in the pre-timeline column. This is to avoid problems with the MIN(…) function, which ignores an empty cell, rather than treating it as zero. This means that the MIN(…) function gives, for example, '1', not zero, as the lesser of '1' and an empty cell.

Exhibit 15.4

Loan repayment mask calculation

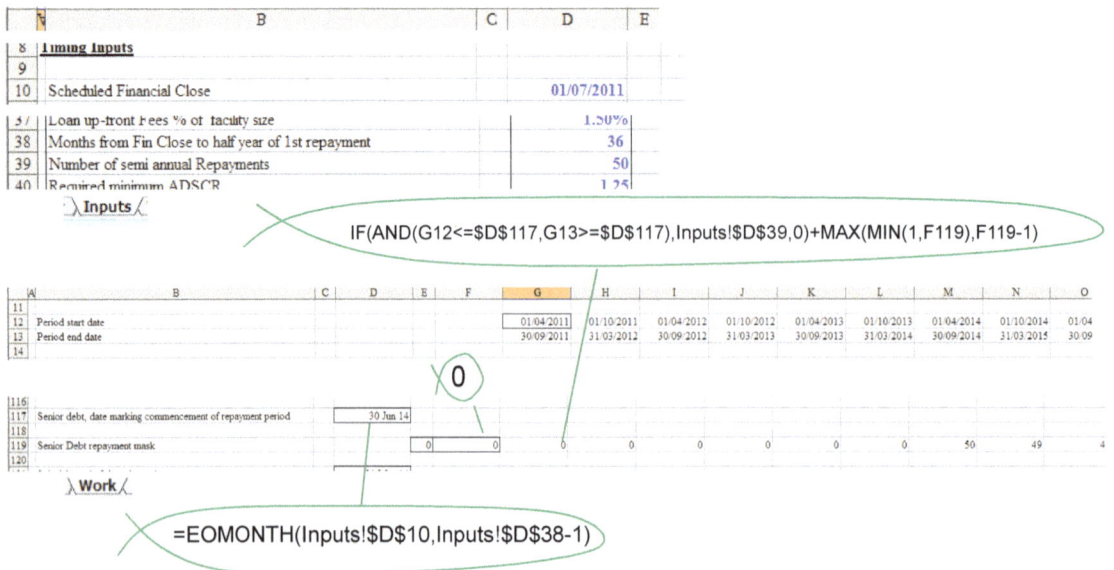

	B	C	D	E
8	Timing Inputs			
9				
10	Scheduled Financial Close		01/07/2011	
37	Loan up-front Fees % of facility size		1.50%	
38	Months from Fin Close to half year of 1st repayment		36	
39	Number of semi annual Repayments		50	
40	Required minimum ADSCR		1.25	

Inputs

IF(AND(G12<=$D$117,G13>=$D$117),Inputs!$D$39,0)+MAX(MIN(1,F119),F119-1)

	B	C	D	E	F	G	H	I	J	K	L	M	N	O
11														
12	Period start date					01/04/2011	01/10/2011	01/04/2012	01/10/2012	01/04/2013	01/10/2013	01/04/2014	01/10/2014	01/04
13	Period end date					30/09/2011	31/03/2012	30/09/2012	31/03/2013	30/09/2013	31/03/2014	30/09/2014	31/03/2015	30/09
14														

0

	B	C	D	E	F	G	H	I	J	K	L	M	N	O
116														
117	Senior debt, date marking commencement of repayment period			30 Jun 14										
118														
119	Senior Debt repayment mask			0		0	0	0	0	0	0	0	50	49	4
120														

Work

=EOMONTH(Inputs!$D$10,Inputs!$D$38-1)

The following guidelines all assume that repayments are to be made at a rate of one in each model period, and will fall at the end of the period.

Calculation of **equal repayments**. In each period for which the repayment mask for the loan is greater than zero, simply take the previous period's closing balance, plus any drawings in the current period, divided by the repayment mask (calculated as described above).

Annuity repayment calculations. Use the PMT or PPMT function to calculate the repayment amount. The principal value in each period is given using these functions by taking the previous period's closing balance plus any drawings in the current period as the loan amount to be repaid, the value in the repayment mask as the required number of payments, and the per annum interest rate converted to a per period rate (for example, divide by two for semi-annual interest) as the interest rate. If the loan is denominated in a currency other than the presentation currency, then the balance and drawdown figures should be adjusted to give presentation currency equivalent values as at the end of the period. If using PMT(...) which calculates the total debt service amount, the repayment in each period is calculated by deducting the interest payable in the period from the calculated total payment amount. The calculation can be checked by totalling the repayment and interest amounts in each period (removing any currency adjustments, if applied). The total should have the same value in all repayment periods, and should exactly repay the outstanding balance of the loan in the last repayment period.

Calculating a sculpted repayment profile. Constraining a repayment profile, generally in order to meet ADSCR targets (see Section 10.2.1), requires a non-circular calculation of appropriate available cash flows and a means of avoiding early final repayment of the loan.

Early repayment can be avoided by establishing a base repayment method, such as equal or annuity instalments, and using this to calculate a target balance outstanding at the end of each period. Repayments can then be calculated in each half year following the first repayment date as the lesser of the maximum payment which complies with ADSCR constraints and the difference between the opening balance and the target closing balance for the period.

The ideal source of available cash values for this calculation would be the CFADS calculated on the cover factor sheet. However, sometimes this will create circularity, and it is preferable to calculate equivalent values in a way which avoids circular issues. For example, the CFADS may be net of transfers to/from the MRA, which are themselves affected by the debt service. For the sculpting calculation therefore it may be appropriate to handle such items by simply deducting the full difference between the target MRA balance and the opening MRA balance. The DSRA is very tightly linked to debt service, and creates a greater issue regarding circularity. A simple way to deal with this is to define the DSRA as equal to debt service using the base repayment method, rather than the sculpted payments.

The cash available for repayments within ADSCR constraints is equal to the total cash available for debt service divided by the target ADSCR, less interest in the period.

Using an input sculpted repayment profile. To simplify the handling of variable total drawings, currency adjustments, and any constraints which cause repayments to fall below the scheduled value in some periods, it is convenient to specify sculpted profiles as the percentage of total debt still outstanding at the end of each period. This profile should be input on a timeline from financial close, or 1st repayment, to ensure that the model flexibility is not compromised. The input values can then be positioned on the timeline using SUMIF(...) or INDEX(...) functions. In each period the repayment due can be calculated as:

$$\frac{\textit{Opening balance on the loan} \times}{\textit{(Previous period's scheduled \% closing balance} - \textit{Current period's scheduled \% closing balance)}}}{\textit{Previous period's scheduled \% closing balance}}$$

For loans in a currency other than the presentation currency, the percentage repayment should be applied to the loan balance adjusted to the presentation currency equivalent at the end of the period.

Repayments constrained by available revenues, for example subordinated debt repayments. Assuming that repayments fall at the end of each period and do not therefore influence interest (and hence, generally, tax) until the following period, use of post-tax net revenues less any senior debt service should not generally generate any intrinsic circularity. As for sculpted repayments (see above), ideally, a 'target' balance outstanding should be calculated, based on the preferred repayment method, for example, equal instalments over twenty years, then used to constrain repayments where sufficient cash is available to exceed the specified repayment rate.

Calculation of **bullet repayment**. The calculations associated with bullet repayments depend upon whether they are assumed to be made using accumulated cash, or to reflect an assumption that the loan will be wholly or partially refinanced, with the repayment funded from a single drawdown on a new loan, which is in its turn repaid over a specified period. The purpose of this is usually to extend the loan life or to provide an early cash payment to investors. In either case the bullet repayment can easily be controlled from data, with a repayment date and the percentage of the loan or an input monetary amount to be repaid on a bullet basis being specified as data items. If refinancing is to be modelled, then an additional loan must be specified in the data and added to the funding section.

15.3.2.8 Currency adjustments for loan repayments

Assuming that repayments occur at the end of the period, they should be based on the previous period's closing balance, plus any drawings in the repayment period, plus the currency devaluation adjustment in the repayment period.

15.3.2.9 Interest payable

The details of the interest calculation depend on the assumptions made regarding timing of drawdowns, currency adjustments, etc. It is assumed here, however, that interest is paid once in each half-year model period, at the end of the period, and this has proved a generally applicable assumption.

Interest should generally be calculated on an average balance basis – i.e., taking account of the timing of drawings in the period to calculate the average balance outstanding during the period. If costs, and hence the associated loan drawings, are assumed to be made evenly throughout the period, or at the mid-point of the period, then the average balance can be calculated as the previous period's balance outstanding, plus half the principal drawings in the period for semi annual calculations. Applying the same principals to monthly drawings gives an average balance during the half year equal to the opening balance plus 11/12 of the first months drawdown, plus 9/12 of the second months drawdown, and so on to 1/12 of the final, sixth month's drawing. It is simplest to model this using a set of factors in the worklines and a SUMPRODUCT(...) function in the interest calculation (see Exhibit 15.5). The average balance is then multiplied by the annual interest rate divided by two (assuming semi-annual interest payments).

For significant specific amounts that are known not to be drawn evenly throughout the period, or at mid-period, special adjustments can be made. For example, up-front fees are known to fall at the

Exhibit 15.5

Average balance calculation for monthly loan drawings

	B	C	D	E	F	G	H	I	J
40									
41	Monthly (single column) calculations		Month Numbers			Month of financial close within half year	Monthly Completion Mask	Proportions for interest average balance	
42			0			01-Jul-09	01-Jan-12		
43	Month 1 of half year		1			0	0	92%	
44	Month 2 of half year		2			0	0	75%	
45	Month 3 of half year		3			0	0	58%	
46	Month 4 of half year		4			0	1	42%	
47	Month 5 of half year		5			1	0	25%	
48	Month 6 of half year		6			0	0	8%	
49									

Work =(F77+SUMPRODUCT(G67:G72,Work!$I$43:$I$48))*G60/2

	B	C	D	E	F	G	H	I	J	K	L
52											
53	**Loan 1 Calculations**										
54											
55	**Loan 1 Facility Size**		8,528.49								
56											
57	Cash flows available for senior debt service		40,281.55			0.00	157.11	122.56	137.51	177.28	216
58	Cash flow available for repayments		25,667			0.00	99.75	0.00	0.00	0.00	0
59											
60	**Loan 1 Interest Rate % p.a.**					6.75%	6.75%	6.75%	6.75%	6.75%	6.7
61											
62	**Loan 1 Up-front Fees**		127.93			0.00	127.93	0.00	0.00	0.00	0
63	**Loan 1 Commitment Fees**		40.71			0.00	0.00	14.44	10.59	7.95	4
64	**Loan 1 Agency Fees**		2.88			0.00	0.08	0.08	0.08	0.08	0
65											
67	Loan 1 Principal Drawings in month 1 of 1/2 year					0.00	0.00	182.33	124.58	124.97	156
68	Loan 1 Principal Drawings in month 2 of 1/2 year					0.00	0.00	139.47	84.59	117.02	151
69	Loan 1 Principal Drawings in month 3 of 1/2 year					0.00	0.00	196.30	84.59	117.02	88
70	Loan 1 Principal Drawings in month 4 of 1/2 year					0.00	0.00	139.47	715.42	117.02	57
71	Loan 1 Principal Drawings in month 5 of 1/2 year					0.00	2,444.19	451.39	114.07	117.10	57
72	Loan 1 Principal Drawings in month 6 of 1/2 year					0.00	171.76	82.63	113.99	984.87	57
73	**Loan 1 Principal Drawings**		7,801.76			0.00	2,615.95	1,191.59	1,237.23	1,578.00	568
74	**Repayments**		8,528.49			0.00	0.00	0.00	0.00	0.00	0
75	**Interest**		5,521.57			0.00	21.11	108.04	151.87	194.28	251
76	**Additional Drawings to Fund Interest**		726.73			0.00	21.11	108.04	151.87	194.28	251
77	**Loan 1 Balance Outstanding**		8,528.49			0.00	2,637.06	3,936.69	5,325.78	7,098.06	7,918
78											
79	**Target balance for Loan 1**					0.00	2,637.06	3,936.69	5,325.78	7,098.06	7,918
80											
81	Loan balance as % profile					0%	31%	46%	62%	83%	9

Fin

start of the period. The average balance calculation for a loan that funds specific up-front fees can therefore be adjusted to reflect this. Items occurring at the end of the period should have no effect on that period's interest payable. If the principal drawings include drawings to fund end of period payments, therefore, these could be excluded from the principal drawings when calculating the average balance (ensuring that they are not omitted from the end period balance).

The annual interest rate should be divided by the number of interest payments per year when calculating interest payments. This reflects the fact that, unlike inflation rates, interest rates are quoted assuming a particular payment frequency. Thus 12% per annum payable annually means 12% of the average balance during the year, paid at the end of each year; 12% per annum payable semi annually means 6% of the average balance over the half year paid at the end of each half year; 12% per annum payable quarterly means 3% of the average balance over the quarter paid every three months and 12% per annum payable monthly means 1% of the average balance during each month, paid at the end of the month. Clearly these alternatives have quite different costs, when considering the time cost of money, and care should be taken to be consistent in the treatment of such interest timings in the model and avoid inappropriate compounding or decompounding of interest.

15.3.2.10 Currency adjustments for interest calculations

Currency adjustments for the interest calculations must take account of the different timing of drawings, etc. Assuming that interest is payable at the end of the period, the calculation should be based on an end-period presentation currency value equal to the average balance during the half year. This can be calculated by dividing values such as previous period's balance outstanding, and mid-period drawings or monthly drawings, by the devaluation factors applicable to the timings for these amounts, and multiplying the result by the end-period devaluation factor for the period. The interest calculation is then performed as normal, using these adjusted values.

15.3.2.11 Additional drawings to fund interest

Interest roll-up is the funding of interest payments on a loan from additional drawings on that loan. It is also often referred to as 'capitalised interest', but this description can cause confusion between this calculation and the capitalisation of interest for tax and accounting purposes.

Although the division of total loan drawings between principal and rolled-up interest may not be of great interest in the reports sections, particularly as principal drawings on one loan may include funding for interest on other loans, the distinction is extremely useful for funding calculation purposes.

For project finance deals, all interest during the construction period must generally be funded from loan drawings or equity. It is common, therefore, for each loan to fund all its own interest during the applicable drawdown period. Some loans, however, will not explicitly fund any interest (for example, bond issues), some will only fund a given percentage of their own interest (for example, some export credit loans), and some will fund interest for a shorter or longer period than that for which principal drawings are permitted. Data items for these parameters need to be included as required.

If the period for interest roll-up is to be specified in the data, then a mask for the period of roll-up should be included in the worklines.

In addition to multiplying by the drawdown mask, or a specific interest roll-up mask, and any specified percentage for interest roll-up for a given loan, the roll-up calculation must also take account, in the same way as the principal drawings, of any restriction on total drawings. For loans that are based on the net funding requirement, the rolled-up interest calculation needs to take account of any surplus funds available in the period, and assume that these will be used to pay interest if all other funding needs have been met. If equity is being calculated pro rata to debt (see above), then the rolled-up interest for loans calculated net of equity (i.e., not loans based on a specific percentage of construction costs or similar) needs to take account of this by limiting the rolled-up interest to the percentage of funding required from debt (i.e., interest payable, less any surplus funds to be used to pay interest, multiplied by 1 less the equity percentage of total funding).

Note that for subordinated debt, one of the differences in calculation versus senior debt is often that interest can be rolled up throughout the loan life to the extent that insufficient cash is available to make interest payments in full in any period.

15.3.2.12 Balance outstanding

The balance outstanding in each period represents the total outstanding loan at the end of the period.

The balance outstanding is thus calculated in each period as the previous period's balance outstanding, plus the current period's principal drawings, interest roll-up and currency devaluation (see below), less repayments.

15.3.2.13 Currency adjustments for loan balance outstanding

The loan balance outstanding for a non-presentation currency denominated loan will be represented by changing amounts of presentation currency as the exchange rate between the loan's actual currency and the presentation currency changes over time. An adjustment is therefore needed to reflect the effect of currency movements over time on the balance and drawings. This adjustment is calculated in any period as the difference between the presentation currency values for opening balance and the loan drawings, and the same values adjusted for currency movements to the end of the half year. The adjustment is calculated by dividing the opening balance by the start period (end of previous period) devaluation factor, and the drawings by the devaluation factor(s) at the time of drawdown, then multiplying the results by the devaluation factor at the end of the period and deducting the unadjusted values. It is useful to show this adjustment as a separate row, simplifying checking of the loan calculation and allowing equivalents at the time of payment or receipt of loan amounts to be clearly calculated and shown.

If it is preferred not to show this as a separate item, then the adjustment can be calculated directly as part of the balance calculation.

16 Operations

The operations section covers values associated with operations, giving the operating costs and revenues which feed into the cash flow and other calculations. This section will vary most according to the industry being modelled.

16.1 Operating levels

For most projects some sort of operating level is determined, either an output or a throughput, from which some or all of the revenue and variable operating cost values can be calculated. This operating data will usually be one of the factors varied for the purposes of sensitivity analysis, and is a useful information item in its own right. The operating section should therefore generally calculate such information as a separate item, rather than simply including it as part of the revenue formula, etc. For example, for power projects, items that could be calculated and shown clearly as separate items would include capacity in MW, availability % and production in MWh.

For some projects a number of throughputs and outputs are needed to calculate costs and revenues, and again, all these can probably usefully be calculated and shown as separate items. For example, water treatment plants have a number of revenue sources, and infiltration of ground water into pipes can mean that the volume of water passing through the works is different to the assumed waste water volume to be treated. Operating items for such a plant might therefore include waste water volumes /M^3, treated volumes /M^3, potable water sales /M^3 and treated solids /tonne.

16.2 Input of operations values

Input of operating values via the data can take a number of forms. For some items, single values can be entered, combined with some timing information: for example, for power plant capacity, the capacity figure for each unit can be given, together with data about the start of operations. The timing information can be used to create one or more operating masks for each unit: one mask, for example, simply taking a value of 1 for all periods in which operation occurs, and one giving the number of operating months in each period.

Operating period masks can be used to control the analysis period of the model, for example, to reflect an input concession period by returning to zero at the end of the period under consideration (see Exhibit 16.1). Such masks are often extremely useful throughout the operations and other calculation sections.

Operating values based on input timing data can easily be adjusted for delay case sensitivities.

For operating data requiring time-based inputs, such as a production profile or traffic forecast, inputs should be entered on a suitable timeline, such as periods from start of operation, and should then be positioned using appropriate counters with the SUMIF(...) or INDEX(...) functions, as for capital expenditure profiles (see Section 3.1.3 and Exhibit 14.1).

It is often useful to be able to run sensitivities whereby operating values are increased or reduced by a simple factor. The data should therefore include an input for 'operating costs sensitivity factor', which will initially take a value of 1.00. The formulae for the basic operating values calculated or picked up in the operating section can then include multiplication by this factor. When including this

Exhibit 16.1

Calculation of operations masks

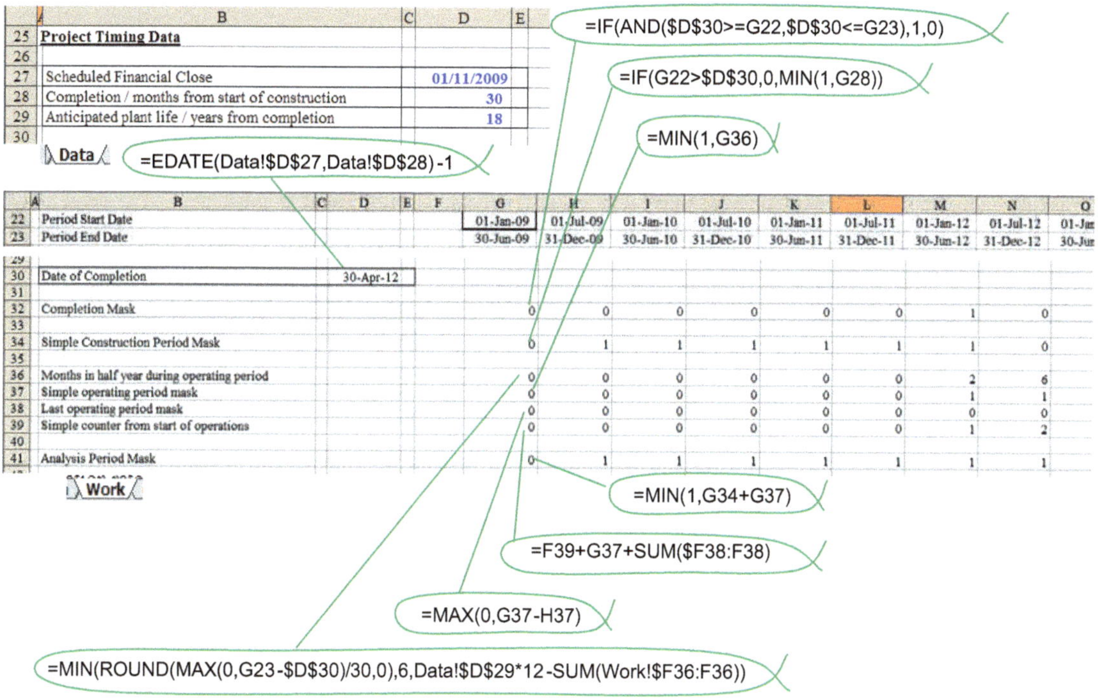

option it is important to ensure that the values forming the bases for all calculations are adjusted, but that the adjustment is not double counted by applying the factor to items calculated using values already adjusted. Such errors will not be apparent when checking base case figures with the factor set to a value of 1.00.

16.3 Operating revenues

Once the underlying values have been calculated as regards operating levels, then the operating revenues can be calculated. This basically involves the calculation of appropriate nominal values for any tariffs, sale prices, annual capacity payments, etc., all shown as separate items in the operations section, and their multiplication by the appropriate operating values – for example, availability, production or capacity.

Revenues should be calculated in nominal values in the presentation currency. Any tariffs, etc., that are denominated in a currency other than the presentation currency should be calculated in presentation currency equivalents and will therefore automatically give correct presentation currency values when used to calculate revenues.

Revenues are calculated in each period in relation to the operations that generate them, without adjustment for any delay between production or processing and the receipt of payment. This adjustment is calculated and applied explicitly through the receivables element of the working capital adjustment (see below).

When several revenue streams, based on different price or operating values, are to be calculated, they should be shown separately and a total operating revenue figure calculated that totals all operating revenue sources. However, when multiple bands of revenue are assumed to arise from a single operating stream – for example, if sales of a total production stream are to be made to various categories of purchaser who will pay different charges – it may sometimes be appropriate for the purposes of the financial model to apply an average tariff that will give a correct revenue figure while maintaining simplicity in the model. This would be most appropriate where the ratio of different purchasers will remain constant throughout the analysis, allowing a single average tariff to be input, or where revenues are being calculated to meet certain criteria. Simple operation of the model is maintained, and a detailed breakdown between categories of purchaser can be included in the model, if necessary, in the later stages of the deal.

16.4 Operating costs

For modelling purposes operating costs are divided into two types – fixed costs and variable costs. Fixed costs are costs which do not vary with operating levels such as throughput or production and will generally be specified in data as a cost per annum. Variable operating costs, on the other hand, are costs which vary directly with operating levels and will be quoted in data as a value per unit of operation – for example, £/kWh, $/tonne.

Costs may be quoted in relation to a unit of fuel, feedstock, employees and so on, which in turn must be calculated based upon the operating period or operating levels also calculated in the operations sheet.

Costs per unit should be input as real-terms values at a stated value date then converted on the operations sheet to nominal values in the presentation currency, reflecting any devaluation adjustments necessary if the costs are denominated in a currency other than the presentation currency. They can then be multiplied by the operating period mask or calculated production/throughput values to give actual operating cost values. Each category of cost should be shown as a separate item, with subtotals for fixed and variable costs and a total operating cost figure.

16.5 Stocks

Many projects will require stocks of fuel, feedstock or equivalent to be maintained. Once purchased, it can generally be assumed that any stocks used will be replaced by purchases already included in the operating cost calculation. It is changes in the levels of stocks that therefore impact the cash flows, and it is the cost of these that need to be calculated. If stock levels reduce, then a negative cost (i.e., positive cash flow) arises.

It is important to establish whether initial stock purchases are included in the capital cost data, and if so, what level of stocks they represent so that subsequent stock calculations can correctly reflect this.

16.6 Payables/receivables

Payables and receivables are calculated based on a specified delay for payment of revenues and operating costs. If detailed data is available, then separate delays can be specified for different categories of cost and revenue.

When modelling payables/receivables delays of less than six months, it is simplest to calculate the amount to be carried forward from each half year. This gives the payables/receivables balance for the balance sheet, and the figures required to calculate the cash adjustment in each period.

The data inputs can specify the number of months delay for the relevant categories. Since delays in excess of six months require an alternative modelling approach, to ensure consistency inputs can be restricted using the Data Validation tool (see Section 12.5.2) to ensure that values cannot be entered which are incompatible with the model calculations. Values should, for example, be limited to whole numbers between 0 and 6, if specifying delays as months. The restriction need only activate if inappropriate data is entered, i.e., there is no need to display a message whenever the input cell is selected.

To calculate the delayed values, first one month's worth of the cost or revenue value needs to be calculated. Assuming that a mask has been produced giving the number of months of operation in each half year, then the cost or revenue in the period can be divided by this mask. To avoid generating errors by zero division, the division can be by MAX(1, number of months operation), since if operating months are less than 1, the costs or revenues will be zero, so there is no problem dividing by 1. For all operating periods except the final period, at the end of the analysis period, the amount delayed will be the lesser of the total cost or revenue value in the period, or one month's worth of the cost or revenue multiplied by the number of months delay. In the final period, only costs or revenues generated in the last n months of the half year, where n = number of months delay, should be delayed to the next period. So the delayed amount is one month's worth of costs or revenues multiplied by the lesser of the number of months delay and the number of months of operation in the final period less (6-number of months delay).

Exhibit 16.2

Calculation of payables/receivables delay

	B	C	D	E	F
180	Fixed Operating Costs Payables Delay / months		1		
181	Recievables Delay / months		1		

↘ Data ↙

	B	C	D	E	F	G	H	I	J	K	L	M	N	O
36	Months in half year during operating period					0	0	0	0	0	0	2	6	
37	Simple operating period mask					0	0	0	0	0	0	1	1	
38	Last operating period mask					0	0	0	0	0	0	0	0	
39	Simple counter from start of operations					0	0	0	0	0	0	1	2	

↘ Work ↙

	B	C	D	E	F	G	H	I	J	K	L	M	N	O
17	Widget Sale Revenues		37,749			0.00	0.00	0.00	0.00	0.00	0.00	193.61	600.80	621
18														
30														
31	Fixed Operating Costs		155			0.00	0.00	0.00	0.00	0.00	0.00	0.79	2.46	2
32														
37	Payables					0.00	0.00	0.00	0.00	0.00	0.00	1.09	1.12	1
38	Receivables					0.00	0.00	0.00	0.00	0.00	0.00	96.80	100.13	103
39	Net Payables/Receivables Adjustment		0			0.00	0.00	0.00	0.00	0.00	0.00	(95.72)	(3.30)	(3.

↘ Ops ↙ F

=G37-G38-F37+F38

=G31/MAX(1,Work!G$36)*(MIN(Data!$D$180,Work!G$36)*(1-Work!G$38)+MAX(0,Work!G$36-(6-Data!$D$180))*Work!G$38)

111

The net payables/receivables cash adjustment can then be calculated in each period as the payables value less the receivables value, less previous period's payables value plus previous period's receivables value. This will give positive values when the net payables/receivables figure gives an increase to cash flows, and a negative value where a net reduction in cash flow results.

Working capital loans. Rather than assuming that the full effects of payables/receivables delay will feed into the cash flows, a working capital loan may be assumed. The precise amount and terms of such a loan can vary enormously, however, and it can be difficult to establish a meaningful basis for calculating the costs of such a loan. If included in the model, the drawings should be added to cash flows, and interest and repayments deducted, together with the normal payables/receivables adjustment.

17 Tax

Tax calculations will vary considerably from country to country, and even from project to project. Details of the calculations, particularly with regard to depreciation, will have to be provided from expert sources and reflected in the model as they become available. Careful consideration is required in order to distinguish between essential data and inappropriate detail when trying to incorporate such information into the model. It is, for example, not usually appropriate to break out the costs of one or two staff vehicles in order to calculate capital allowances for them on a different basis to the other costs. When selecting the level of detail to be reflected in the model, consideration should be given to the likely effect of any simplifying assumptions on the tax calculations, and the extent to which the tax values critically affect the project.

Given the above, a general layout can usually be assumed for tax calculations, and can certainly be used in a feasibility model if no useful tax information is initially available. The basic data for which assumptions are required are as follows.

- The tax rate as a percentage.
- The basis for depreciation/capital allowances:
  - straight line or declining balance;
  - periods of depreciation or percentage per annum; and
  - assignment of capital costs between different depreciation bases.
- The basis for timing of payment of calculated tax.

A tax sheet (as illustrated in Exhibit 17.1) will include components as described below.

Net Operating Revenues, as calculated on the Ops sheet, with no payables/receivables adjustments applied.

Interest earned on deposited funds.

Loan Interest and Fees are the interest payable on all loans or overdrafts, together with the financing fees, to the extent these costs are not capitalised and included in the capital allowances.

Immediately Expensed Costs, any costs other than operating costs and loan interest which are deducted for tax purposes as they arise, rather than via capital allowances or depreciation.

Capital Allowances/Tax Depreciation are calculated based upon the construction costs and financing costs during construction. They can generally be calculated either on a straight line basis or on a declining balance basis (see Section 17.1).

Taxable Profits, the net figure calculated by deducting Loan Interest and Fees, immediately expensed costs and Capital Allowances from the Net Operating Revenues plus Earned Interest.

Annual Taxable Profits are calculated based upon the Net Taxable Profits, grouped into annual totals in the second half of the tax year. This can be done using a simple annual mask, as shown in Exhibit 17.1. Grouping figures annually at this point avoids any problems with second half year losses being offset against profits in the first half of the tax year.

Losses Carried Forward can be calculated in each period as any negative total for the previous period's Losses Carried Forward, plus the current period's Annual Taxable Profits.

The Tax Basis is then calculated as any positive total for the previous period's Losses Carried Forward, plus the current period's Annual Taxable Profits.

Tax Payable is then calculated as the Tax Basis multiplied by the applicable tax rate in each period.

Tax Paid is based on Tax Payable, but reflects the actual timing of tax payments, which usually incorporates some delay, or some system of estimated payments followed by a 'catch-up' payment. The calculation in Exhibit 17.1 assumes payment in equal semi-annual instalments in the following tax year.

Exhibit 17.1

Illustrative tax calculation sheet

	B	C	D	E F	G	H	I	J	K	L	M	N	O
11	Annual Mask (1=2nd half year)				0	1	0	1	0	1	0	1	
	i) **Work**												

	B	C	D	E F	G	H	I	J	K	L	M	N	O
8													
9	Net Operating Revenues		37,329		0.00	0.00	0.00	0.00	0.00	0.00	191.43	594.11	614
10													
11	less	Interest and Fees Costs	4,678.17		0.00	0.00	0.00	0.00	0.00	0.00	0.00	273.60	264
12	plus	Interest Earned	1,021.16		0.00	0.00	0.00	0.00	0.00	0.00	0.00	10.61	12
13													
14	less	Costs immediately expensed	425.63		0.00	0.00	0.00	0.00	0.00	0.00	35.50	0.00	0
15	less	Capital Allowances	7,845.76		0.00	0.00	0.00	0.00	0.00	0.00	419.98	419.98	398
16													
17		**Taxable Profits**	25,400.86		0.00	0.00	0.00	0.00	0.00	0.00	(264.05)	(88.86)	(36.
18		Annual Taxable Profits	25,400.86		0.00	0.00	0.00	0.00	0.00	0.00	0.00	(352.91)	0
19													
20		Losses Carried Forward			0.00	0.00	0.00	0.00	0.00	0.00	0.00	(352.91)	(352.
21													
22		Tax Basis	25,466.42		0.00	0.00	0.00	0.00	0.00	0.00	0.00	0.00	0
23													
24		Tax Payable	7,639.93		0.00	0.00	0.00	0.00	0.00	0.00	0.00	0.00	0
25													
26		Tax Paid	7,639.93		0.00	0.00	0.00	0.00	0.00	0.00	0.00	0.00	0
27													
28	_) **Tax** (_												

=F24/2+E24/2

=MIN(0,F20+G18)

=SUM(F17+G17)*Work!G11

=G22*Data!$D$197

=G9-G11+G12-G14-G15

=MAX(0,F20+G18)

If the tax rate varies over time, or tax holidays apply, then a row in the worklines, masks, factors and counters section, or in the tax section itself, can be used to pick up the applicable rate in each period. Remember that, where several types of tax are payable, they are often calculated as percentages of the same tax basis, with the same payment assumptions, and can therefore be calculated as a single tax value using a total of the rates for the separate tax types. It is generally not significant for the model that the tax bill is paid to several parties rather than one – just the total amount that is paid, and the timing of the payments.

17.1 Tax depreciation or capital allowances

These can often prove the most complex part of the tax calculation. Information must be obtained giving appropriate estimates of the division of capital costs between different depreciation categories, and what categories are to be included in the model. Depreciation is generally calculated on one of two bases – straight line or declining balance. Straight line depreciation is the depreciation of a value in equal annual amounts over a specified period. Declining balance depreciation is calculated as an annual value equal to a given percentage of the remaining undepreciated costs, for a specified or an unlimited period. There are other methods specific to certain fiscal systems and deal types, such as the 'Finance debtor' method. It is beyond the scope of this book to address these individually, but they can be addressed, like any other calculation by intelligent application of the methods and ideas described throughout this text.

When first setting up the depreciation calculations, if the actual depreciation basis is unknown, then include options for both methods with several assumptions for period or percentage per annum. A table can then be included in the data that lists all elements of construction costs, plus ongoing maintenance and capitalised interest and fees, and specifies the percentage of each item included in each depreciation category. Each category should allow input of the period over which straight line depreciation will apply or the percentage to be used for declining balance depreciation (see Exhibit 17.2).

Exhibit 17.2

Flexible specification of depreciation, and calculation of costs for each depreciation category

	B	C	D	E	F	G	H	I	J	K
195	**Tax & Accounting Data**									
196										
197	Corporation Tax Rate		30%							
198										
199	**Capital Allowance/Depreciation Data**					For Tax			For P&L		
200			% expensed immediately		% for wdb @	% for wdb @	% SL over	% SL over	% SL over	% SL over
201					25%	5%	8	5	15	20
202					per annum	per annum	years	years	years	years
204	Site Purchase		0%		0%	0%	0%	0%	0%	0%
205	Civil Works					100%				100%
206	Start-up Costs		10%		70%		20%		100%	
207	Plant and Machinery						100%	10%	80%	10%
208	Engineers and Consultants					100%			100%	
209	Major Maintenance Costs		30%		70%			100%		
210	Capitalised Interest and Fees				30%	70%		10%	60%	30%
211										
212										

Data

Callout: =Data!F201

Callout: =Fin!G91*Work!G34

Callout: =Fin!G91-Work!G136

Callout: =SUMPRODUCT(G$130:G$136,Data!$D$204:$D$210)

	B	C	D	E	F	G	H	I	J	K	L	M	N	
34	Simple Construction Period Mask					0		1	1	1	1	1	0	
121	**Tax and Accounting Worklines**													
123	Tax and Capallow specifications													
124	Tax capallow type 1, % p.a. wdb		25%			P&L Depreciation type 1, years SL		5						
125	Tax capallow type 2, % p.a. wdb		5%			P&L Depreciation type 2, years SL		15						
126	Tax capallow type 3, years SL		8			P&L Depreciation type 3, years SL		20						
128														
129	Costs for Depreciation & Capallow													
130	Site Purchase		884.52		0.00	884.52	0.00	0.00	0.00	0.00	0.00	0.00	0.
131	Civil Works		2,926.47		0.00	686.80	653.60	499.72	547.32	408.89	130.14	0.00	0.
132	Start-up Costs		355.00		0.00	0.00	0.00	0.00	0.00	0.00	355.00	0.00	0.
133	Plant and Machinery		3,881.45		0.00	891.02	368.67	572.04	867.85	0.00	1,181.86	0.00	0.
134	Engineers and Consultants		860.00		0.00	137.60	154.80	154.80	154.80	154.80	103.20	0.00	0.
135	Major Maintenance Costs		1,300.42		0.00	0.00	0.00	0.00	0.00	0.00	0.00	0.00	0.
136	Capitalised Interest and Fees		858.75		0.00	141.54	59.28	99.13	136.89	188.85	233.05	0.00	0.
137														
138	Interest and Fees expensed		4,678.17		0.00	0.00	0.00	0.00	0.00	0.00	0.00	273.60	264.
139														
140	Costs for Immediate Expense for tax		425.63		0.00	0.00	0.00	0.00	0.00	0.00	35.50	0.00	0.
141														
142	Costs for 25% p.a. wdb for tax		1,416.42		0.00	42.46	17.78	29.74	41.07	56.65	318.41	0.00	0.
143	Costs for 5% p.a. wdb for tax		4,387.59		0.00	923.48	849.90	723.91	797.94	695.88	396.47	0.00	0.
144	Costs for 8 years straight line capallow for tax		3,952.45		0.00	891.02	368.67	572.04	867.85	0.00	1,252.86	0.00	0.
145														
146	Costs for 5 years SL depreciation		1,774.44		0.00	103.26	42.80	67.12	100.47	18.88	141.49	0.00	0.
147	Costs for 15 years SL depreciation		4,835.40		0.00	935.34	485.31	671.91	931.22	268.11	1,543.52	0.00	0.
148	Costs for 20 years SL depreciation		3,572.23		0.00	818.37	708.25	586.66	675.17	465.54	318.24	0.00	0.

Callout: ="Costs for "&TEXT($D124,"#0%")&" p.a. wdb for tax"

Callout: =SUMPRODUCT(G$130:G$136,Data!$F$204:$F$210)

Creating a block of rows in the worklines picking up the depreciable costs in the same order as the cost items in the depreciation allows isolation of the costs for each depreciation category using a simple SUMPRODUCT(...) function, as shown in Exhibit 17.2.

Allowing flexible input of the period over which straight line depreciation is to be applied requires some care in the calculations if costs can arise post-completion (for example, on-going major maintenance) or if some are depreciated from an earlier start date than others (for example, for a phased-completion project). Because these costs will be depreciated over a different, but probably overlapping, period to the main capital costs, the simplest approach, taking the cumulative depreciable costs to date, divided by the number of periods for depreciation, up to a total value equal to the depreciable costs, does not work. A possible methodology is shown in Exhibit 17.3, using the INDEX(...) function. This requires costs to be allocated to the time period from which they will be depreciated. The depreciation figure is then carried forward from period to period, adding an amount for new costs, and deducting an amount for fully depreciated costs. The fully depreciated costs are found by looking back for the relevant number of periods.

Exhibit 17.3

Declining balance depreciation can be calculated using the difference between the total of the relevant costs up to and including the calculation period, less the depreciation in all previous periods. For the first period of each tax year, this value multiplied by the percentage depreciation per annum gives the amount to depreciate in the year, and half this amount gives a value per half year. The second period in each tax year can then repeat the value in the first period (see Exhibit 17.4).

Exhibit 17.4

Calculation of written-down balance depreciation

If annual depreciation is required, this can be calculated by grouping the semi-annual data into totals in the second half of the year. If depreciation is required to fall annually in fiscal years, and to reflect an initial partial year, this can be achieved by adjusting the calculations using percentage values in the Mask From Final Completion, rather than simply 1s and 0s.

Capitalised Interest and Fees will be calculated as the total loan interest and fees over a specified period. This period may not be identical for the purposes of tax and accounting calculations, in which case the data should allow it to be separately specified for each. If a project involves some kind of phased completion and start of operations, then the capitalisation of interest may be determined as percentages of the total costs applicable to the various completion dates of each phase. It is important to ensure that the interest and fees expensed directly as costs are calculated on a compatible basis with the capitalised interest and fees – i.e., that all interest and fee costs are either capitalised or expensed, unless a particular tax system specifically requires otherwise.

18 Profit and loss summary

The profit and loss section in a project finance model is generally important only for its contribution, if any, to the distributable dividend calculation. If profit and loss constraints on dividends do not apply or are not being considered as part of an early analysis, the profit and loss calculations should not be considered a priority.

It is important to allow for the fact that accounting profit and loss is not inevitably the same as taxable profits, and provision should therefore be clearly made in the data and the code allowing them to be specified and calculated separately, unless definite information is available to indicate that they are the same. This particularly applies to depreciation or capital allowances for tax purposes and accounting depreciation.

As for tax, details of the profit calculation (such as any reserve requirements) will depend upon the location and nature of the project, and expert advice will be needed to establish the correct treatment for use in the final version of the model. In the early stages of the project, however, a simple profit calculation can be included, if needed, to give an indication of returns taking account of profit constraints. It is important that the assumptions used for profit calculations are documented along with other model assumptions, as they may make a significant difference to projected equity returns.

An example profit and loss calculation layout is shown in Exhibit 18.1. This sets out the calculation of cumulative retained earnings as the cumulative total of net profit/loss less distributed

Exhibit 18.1

Illustrative profit and loss sheet

	B	C	D	E	F	G	H	I	J
214	Reserve requirement		10%		% of revenues up to		20%	% of equity	

Data

	B	C	D	E	F	G	H	I	J	K	L	M	N	O
38	Net Cash Available for Dividends		16,835.23			0.00	(0.00)	0.00	0.00	0.00	0.00	(159.37)	150.97	15

Cascade

	B	C	D	E	F	G	H	I	J	K	L	M	N	O
7														
8	Net Operating Revenues		37,329			0.00	0.00	0.00	0.00	0.00	0.00	191.43	594.11	614
9														
10	less Interest and Fees Costs		4,678			0.00	0.00	0.00	0.00	0.00	0.00	0.00	273.60	264
11	plus Interest Earned		1,027			0.00	0.00	0.00	0.00	0.00	0.00	0.00	10.61	12
12														
13	less Depreciation		9,964			0.00	0.00	0.00	0.00	0.00	0.00	297.89	297.89	297
14														
15	Net Pre-tax profits		23,714			0.00	0.00	0.00	0.00	0.00	0.00	(106.45)	33.24	64
16														
17	less Tax Payable		7,642			0.00	0.00	0.00	0.00	0.00	0.00	0.00	0.00	(
18														
19	Net Profits		16,073			0.00	0.00	0.00	0.00	0.00	0.00	(106.45)	33.24	64
20														
21	Required Reserves		408			0.00	0.00	0.00	0.00	0.00	0.00	19.14	59.41	61
23	Dividends		16,583			0.00	0.00	0.00	0.00	0.00	0.00	0.00	0.00	(
25	Retained Earnings		(511)			0.00	0.00	0.00	0.00	0.00	0.00	(106.45)	33.24	64
27	Cumulative Retained Earnings					0.00	0.00	0.00	0.00	0.00	0.00	(106.45)	(73.22)	(8.

P&L

=MAX(0,MIN(G19+F27-G21,Cascade!G38+CBals!F38))

=F27+G25

=G19-G23

=MIN(SUM(Fin!$F$42:G42) * Data!$H$214,SUM(Ops!$F35:F35) * Data!$D$214)

dividends. If simple P&L constraints apply then distributable dividends in each period will be the lesser of the cash available for distribution (including previously undistributed cash sitting in the surplus cash account), and any positive value for the total of P&L in the period plus cumulative retained earnings from the previous period less any required balance on reserves. Although reserves can significantly affect returns via their effect on dividend distribution, it is useful to remember that accounting reserve requirements usually relate to levels of retained earnings in the P&L calculation, rather than any direct requirement for cash deposits. Confusion over this point can have a dramatic effect on returns and related values.

Modelling issues for depreciation are generally the same as those for capital allowances/depreciation for tax, discussed in Section 17.1.

19 Cash cascade

This sheet produces the cash flow sub totals required for various calculations in the model. Details of layout will be specific to each project, but an illustrative layout is shown in Exhibit 19.1.

Exhibit 19.1

Illustrative content of cascade sheet

	A	B	C	D	E	F	G	H	I	J	K	L	M	N	O
8															
9		Net Operating Cash Flow		37,329.25			0.00	0.00	0.00	0.00	0.00	0.00	95.72	590.81	611
10															
11	less	construction costs		8,907.43			0.00	2,599.94	1,177.07	1,226.55	1,569.97	563.69	1,770.20	0.00	(
12	less	tax paid		7,575.23			0.00	0.00	0.00	0.00	0.00	0.00	0.00	0.00	(
13	less	major maintenance costs		1,300.42			0.00	0.00	0.00	0.00	0.00	0.00	0.00	0.00	(
14															
15	plus	loan drawings		8,162.38			0.00	700.89	1,236.35	1,325.69	1,706.86	752.53	2,440.05	0.00	(
16	plus	equity drawings		2,040.59			0.00	2,040.59	0.00	0.00	0.00	0.00	0.00	0.00	(
17															
18		Net Cash Available to Fund MRA		29,749.14			0.00	141.54	59.28	99.13	136.89	188.85	765.56	590.81	611
19															
20	less	transfers to MRA		1,193.72			0.00	0.00	0.00	0.00	0.00	0.00	93.61	10.01	3:
21	plus	transfers from MRA		1,018.89			0.00	0.00	0.00	0.00	0.00	0.00	0.00	0.00	(
22															
23		CFADS for Cover Factor Calcs		29,574.30			0.00	141.54	59.28	99.13	136.89	188.85	671.95	580.80	579
24															
25	plus	transfers from DSRA		553.45			0.00	0.00	0.00	0.00	0.00	0.00	0.00	0.00	(
26															
27		Net Cash Available for senior debt service		30,127.75			0.00	141.54	59.28	99.13	136.89	188.85	671.95	580.80	579
28															
29	less	Senior Debt Interest and Fees		5,812.47			0.00	141.54	59.28	99.13	136.89	188.85	233.05	279.04	27(
30	less	Senior Debt Repayments		8,162.38			0.00	0.00	0.00	0.00	0.00	0.00	0.00	161.40	166
31															
32	plus	Interest earned on deposits		1,081.06			0.00	0.00	0.00	0.00	0.00	0.00	0.00	10.63	1:
33															
34		Net Cash Available to fund DSRA		17,233.97			0.00	(0.00)	0.00	0.00	0.00	0.00	438.90	150.99	154
35															
36	less	transfers to DSRA		553.45			0.00	0.00	0.00	0.00	0.00	0.00	436.88	0.00	(
37															
38		Net Cash Available for Dividends		16,680.52			0.00	(0.00)	0.00	0.00	0.00	0.00	2.02	150.99	154
39															
40	less	Dividends		16,428.04			0.00	0.00	0.00	0.00	0.00	0.00	0.00	0.00	(
41															
42		Net Cash after dividends		252.48			0.00	(0.00)	0.00	0.00	0.00	0.00	2.02	150.99	154
43															
44		Transfers (to)/from surplus cash account					0.00	0.00	0.00	0.00	0.00	0.00	(2.02)	(150.99)	(154.

╲ Cascade ╱

20 Cash deposits

In most models, one or more cash deposits will be required, either to meet some specified cash requirement, such as for a DSRA, or a maintenance reserve, or to simply 'mop-up' surplus funds. While all such deposits might reasonably be included in some specific model section (the DSRA in the finance section, for example), there are benefits to grouping them together in a separate section of their own. The benefits include:

- easy location of all cash deposit calculation;
- reduced risk of accidental omission of any cash balance values from other calculations; and
- easy location of all earned interest values for collection and use in other calculation sections.

Each deposit calculation will have its own peculiarities, but some general principles can be applied to particular types of deposit. In all cases, deposits should be reflected in the cash flow by deducting transfers to deposits and adding transfers from deposits and earned interest in all periods.

20.1 DSRA

Most projects have a requirement for a debt service reserve account – a deposit to hold a balance equal to a given number of months projected debt service, usually six months, which includes one period's interest and repayment amount. The deposit may be funded from debt or from surplus revenues.

Care must be taken with this calculation to avoid circularity, particularly if funding from debt, if more than six months worth of debt service is required, or if loan repayments are based on available cash.

Although it is generally desirable to specify model assumptions in the data so far as possible, the nature of the debt reserve calculation means that, unless the period of debt service to be included in the target balance is specifically subject to uncertainty, it is better to make the period covered by the DSRA balance an implicit assumption of the model. If it is really necessary to consider more than one option for the period of debt service to be covered by the deposit, then it is recommended that an input be included in the data section which specifies how many periods of debt service are to be taken into account, rather than offering an input as, for example, a number of months.

If the account is initially funded from debt, the re-calc macro can be used to avoid circularity. The SUMPRODUCT(...) function can be used with the DSRA target balance and the completion period mask to calculate an initial funding amount which can be iterated through the re-calc macro. This amount, assumed drawn at completion, can then be included as part of the funding requirement in the funding calculations. The DSRA calculation must then ensure that the full amount is transferred into the account.

Exhibit 20.1 shows the basic elements and layout of an illustrative DSRA calculation, assuming initial funding of the account from debt.

20.2 MRA

This can take various forms, but it is important to remember that there are costs to be covered from the funds placed on deposit, and the cash flow movements associated with actually paying the costs, not just funding the account, must be properly taken into account.

Exhibit 20.1

Illustrative DSRA calculation

	B	C	D	E	F	G	H	I	J	K	L	M	N	O
8	Interest rate for Deposit Accounts %p.a.					0.00%	4.00%	4.00%	4.00%	4.00%	4.00%	4.00%	4.00%	4.
9														
10	Debt Service Reserve Account													
11														
12	Cash Available to fund DSRA		17,389			0.00	(0.00)	0.00	0.00	0.00	0.00	277.50	150.97	15
13	Initial Drawdown to Fund DSRA		437			0.00	0.00	0.00	0.00	0.00	0.00	436.88	0.00	
15	Target Balance on DSRA		13,498			4.91	42.76	84.51	124.79	179.73	387.74	436.88	436.88	43
17	Transfers to DSRA		553			0.00	0.00	0.00	0.00	0.00	0.00	436.88	0.00	
18	Transfers from DSRA		553			0.00	0.00	0.00	0.00	0.00	0.00	0.00	0.00	
19	Interest Earned on DSRA		251			0.00	0.00	0.00	0.00	0.00	0.00	0.00	8.74	
20	Balance on DSRA		437			0.00	0.00	0.00	0.00	0.00	0.00	436.88	436.88	43

Callouts:
=Fin!G22
=MAX(0, Cascade!G42)
=Fin!H89+Fin!H96
=MAX(0,MIN(G15-F20,G12),G13)
=MAX(0,F20-G15)
=F20+G17-G18
=F20*G8/2

It is common to see funding of an MRA as a lender's requirement, with the required balance in each period defined as the sum of various percentages of the costs in subsequent periods. This requirement can most easily and flexibly be accommodated in the model using a percentage profile to represent the required level of future costs to be funded, and multiplying this profile against future maintenance costs using the SUMPRODUCT(...) function, see Exhibit 20.2.

Transfers to and from the MRA, unlike transfers to and from the DSRA, are commonly included in the calculation of CFADS for ADSCRs (see Section 10).

20.3 Cash balance/overdraft

If no profit constraints are assumed to apply to dividends, then it is the general assumption that all post-tax and finance cash, net of transfers to/from deposits, will be distributed. In this case there will be no cash balance and (hopefully) no overdraft.

If there is cash that cannot be distributed, then funds should be assumed to be placed on a cash deposit until they can be distributed. The cash balance calculation is simple: the balance is increased by any positive value for net cash flow after transfers to and from compulsory deposits, less dividends, and reduced by any negative value for the same calculation.

It is worth noting that for financing structures that may involve drawing of excess funds in some periods to be used in later periods, a separate 'surplus funds' balance should be calculated in the funding sheet. This reduces the likelihood of creating unnecessary circularity in the code.

The cash balance interest can reasonably be based upon an average balance calculation. If this is done, it is probably advisable to assume interest payments are received at the start of the following period, which avoids multiple potential problems with circularity.

Exhibit 20.2

Illustrative MRA calculation

	B	C	D	E	F	G	H	I	J	K	I
191					half years from calculation period>>>>>						
192					1	2	3	4	5	6	
193	Profile for target MRA balance % future maint costs				100%	100%	80%	80%	50%	50%	

⟍ Data ⟋

	B	C	D	E	F	G	H	I	J	K	L	M	N	O
43	Major Maintenance Costs		1,300			0.00	0.00	0.00	0.00	0.00	0.00	0.00	0.00	

⟍ Ops ⟋

=SUMPRODUCT(Data!$F$193:$BC$193,Ops!H43:BE43)

=MAX(0,MIN(G26-F31,G24))

	B	C	D	E	F	G	H	I	J	K	L	M	N	O
8	Interest rate for Deposit Accounts %p.a.					0.00%	4.00%	4.00%	4.00%	4.00%	4.00%	4.00%	4.00%	4.0
22	Maintenance Reserve Account													
23														
24	Cash Available to fund MRA(less int & fees)		24,146			0.00	0.00	0.00	0.00	0.00	0.00	532.51	317.21	346.
26	Target Balance on MRA		5,982			0.00	0.00	0.00	25.03	25.03	40.05	93.61	103.63	135.
28	Transfers to MRA		1,194			0.00	0.00	0.00	0.00	0.00	0.00	93.61	10.01	32.
29	Transfers from MRA		1,019			0.00	0.00	0.00	0.00	0.00	0.00	0.00	0.00	0.
30	Interest Earned on MRA		106			0.00	0.00	0.00	0.00	0.00	0.00	0.00	1.87	2.
31	Balance on MRA		711			0.00	0.00	0.00	0.00	0.00	0.00	93.61	103.63	135.

⟍ CBals ⟋

=MAX(0,F31-G26)

=F31*G8/2

=(F31+G28-G29)*Work!G41

21 Investor returns

The calculation of equity returns is often one of the key functions of the model. For project finance purposes, equity returns are usually calculated as an IRR expressed as a percentage per annum over a given period, rather than as an annual return on equity (ROE). There has been some discussion about the appropriateness of IRR as a measure of project quality, with alternative measures, such as modified IRR (MIRR) being proposed.

The key issue here is to understand what the IRR tells us, and then decide whether that information answers the investor's questions about the value of the project. The IRR is effectively the 'interest rate' earned on equity whilst it remains invested in the project. If the project is thought of as a savings account, then the IRR equates to the effective per annum interest rate earned on the account, considering all transfers to and from the account, and leaving the account empty at the end of the analysis period.

The IRR does not, therefore, indicate the annual return earned on the whole investment over the whole project life, just the return on invested funds *while they remain in the project*.

There is an argument that, when comparing projects, the IRR does not capture the period of time for which the given return is actually available. The MIRR attempts to fudge this by including an assumed reinvestment rate for funds released from the project, and calculates an overall IRR on the basis that all funds remain invested either in the project or elsewhere at the reinvestment rate, until the end of the project life. I think this actually raises more questions than it answers, and produces a figure more difficult to interpret than a simple IRR.

21.1 Calculating IRR

Mathematically an IRR is the discount rate at which an NPV of the input equity is equal to an NPV of the cash flows to equity, both being discounted to the same point in time. This calculation can only be resolved by trial and error, and this is the method employed by the 'IRR' and 'XIRR' functions in Excel.

The IRR(...) function therefore allows the input of a 'guess' from which the process of seeking the correct discount rate can commence. This is necessary because the calculation can have multiple solutions, and failure to find a solution, or production of a ridiculously high or low result may need to be corrected by starting the calculation from a lower or higher initial 'guess'. If the cash flow to investors has initial negative values and an overall positive total, then an IRR should be calculable.

If there are issues with finding sensible solutions for the IRR, then a 'guess' table can be used (see Exhibit 21.1). This is particularly important if calculated IRRs are being used (via the re-calc macro) in other model calculations.

If using the IRR(...) function remember that the result will be the percentage return per period, and will need to be converted to a per annum value. For a semi-annual model, therefore, the annual IRR will be calculated as:

$$(1+IRR\text{ (}\textit{semi annual investor cash flow}\text{))}^2-1$$

Exhibit 21.1

IRR 'guess table'

=IF(ISERR(IRR($G$12:$CR$12)),0,IRR($G$12:$CR$12))

	B	C	D	E	F	G	H	I	J	K	L	M	N
6	Pure Equity Investor Returns												
8	Pure Equity Drawn		1,015			0	1,015	0	0	0	0	0	0
10	Dividends (less witholding tax)		58,505			0	0	0	0	0	0	0	0
12	Net Cash Flow to Pure Equity Investors		57,490			0	(1,015)	0	0	0	0	0	0
14						*Trial and Error Guess Testing Table for IRR*							
15	Pure equity Returns for $a Investors					no guess	13%	2%	1%				
16	IRR for Pure Equity Investment (nominal $a) % p.a.		31.46%			14.66%	0.00%	0.00%	0.00%				
17	IRR for Pure Equity Investment (real $a) % p.a.		26.27%			12.37%	0.00%	0.00%	0.00%				

Ret

=(1+SUM(G16:J16))^2-1

0.1

=IF(OR(SUM($G$16:G16)>0,ISERR(IRR($G$12:$CR$12,H$15))),0,IRR($G$12:$CR$12,H$15))

For models with monthly funding calculations, or to capture more detailed timing assumptions in semi-annual calculations, the XIRR(...) function allows dates to be allocated to each cash flow item. Dates can be in any order, but the first cash flow item in the range used by the XIRR function must be a negative value, or the function will return 0%. Since Financial Close may be in any period, this condition is not inevitably met by the equity cash flows. However, the problem can be simply resolved by including one of the spare columns to the left of the timeline in the range used by the function and entering −1 and 1 in the first two periods, and using the same date (timeline start date −1) for both. This provides the required initial negative value in a way which has no impact on the calculated IRR, see Exhibit 21.2.

The overall return to investors, taking account of all relevant cash movements and distribution constraints, is generally one of the final outputs of the model, based on the 'bottom line' of the cash flow. In some circumstances, however, a target return provides the basis for the revenue or funding calculations (see Section 11.4.3).

It is generally necessary to provide both nominal and real equity return values – i.e., values including and excluding the effects of inflation, respectively. The figures calculated in the model are nominal figures, and will therefore provide the basis for a nominal return calculation. The real return figure can be calculated by discounting the nominal investor cash flow using the general inflation factor applicable to the currency in which the results are presented and appropriate to the assumed timing of the cash flows. A quick alternative method would be to adjust the nominal rate by dividing by (1 + inflation rate). This, however, implies that values in each period are inflated to the same point within the periods, and is also of course, not appropriate with inflation rates that are assumed to vary over time.

If a model includes subordinated debt then equity returns are usually calculated for pure and blended equity.

21.2 Calculation of specific investor returns

When a project receives equity funding from different sources on different terms, then, in addition to calculating an overall return to investors, separate returns may be required for each category of

Exhibit 21.2

Using the XIRR function to calculate the IRR

	B	C	D	E	F	G	H	I	J	K	L	M	N	
22	Period Start Date					01-Jan-09	01-Jul-09	01-Jan-10	01-Jul-10	01-Jan-11	01-Jul-11	01-Jan-12	01-Jul-12	01-
23	Period End Date					30-Jun-09	31-Dec-09	30-Jun-10	31-Dec-10	30-Jun-11	31-Dec-11	30-Jun-12	31-Dec-12	30-

	B	C	D	E	F	G	H	I	J	K	L	M	N
			Month			Mo fina close hal	=G60-1						
41	Monthly (single column) calculations		Numbers			01-							
42			0										
43	Month 1 of half year		1				=F60						
44	Month 2 of half year		2										
45	Month 3 of half year		3										
46	Month 4 of half year		4					=EDATE(G$22,$D42)+14					
47	Month 5 of half year		5										
48	Month 6 of half year		6										

	B	C	D	E	F	G	H	I	J	K	L	M	N	
58	Detailed dates for XIRR calculations													
59														
60	mid point month 1 of half year					14 01	15-Jan-09	15-Jul-09	15-Jan-10	15-Jul-10	15-Jan-11	15-Jul-11	15-Jan-12	15-Jul-12	15-.
61	mid point month 2 of half year					14 01	15-Feb-09	15-Aug-09	15-Feb-10	15-Aug-10	15-Feb-11	15-Aug-11	15-Feb-12	15-Aug-12	15-F
62	mid point month 3 of half year						15-Mar-09	15-Sep-09	15-Mar-10	15-Sep-10	15-Mar-11	15-Sep-11	15-Mar-12	15-Sep-12	15-M
63	mid point month 4 of half year						15-Apr-09	15-Oct-09	15-Apr-10	15-Oct-10	15-Apr-11	15-Oct-11	15-Apr-12	15-Oct-12	15-/
64	mid point month 5 of half year						15-May-09	15-Nov-09	15-May-10	15-Nov-10	15-May-11	15-Nov-11	15-May-12	15-Nov-12	15-M
65	mid point month 6 of half year						15-Jun-09	15-Dec-09	15-Jun-10	15-Dec-10	15-Jun-11	15-Dec-11	15-Jun-12	15-Dec-12	15-:
66	end date for half year						30-Jun-09	31-Dec-09	30-Jun-10	31-Dec-10	30-Jun-11	31-Dec-11	30-Jun-12	31-Dec-12	30-:
67								=G23						

Work

	B	C	D	E	F	G	H	I	J	K	L	M	N	O
7														
8	Equity Drawings		120.00			0.00	120.00	0.00	0.00	0.00	0.00	0.00	0.00	
10	Dividends		22,496.34			0.00	0.00	0.00	0.00	0.00	0.00	0.00	0.00	
11														
12	Pure Equity Cash Flow		22,376.34			0.00	(120.00)	0.00	0.00	0.00	0.00	0.00	0.00	
13				-1										
14	Cash flows to/(from) pure equity investors													
15	assumed mid month 1 of half year			(1)		0.00	0.00	0.00	0.00	0.00	0.00	0.00	0.00	
16	assumed mid month 2 of half year			1		0.00	0.00	0.00	0.00	0.00	0.00	0.00	0.00	
17	assumed mid month 3 of half year			+1		0.00	0.00	0.00	0.00	0.00	0.00	0.00	0.00	
18	assumed mid month 4 of half year					0.00	0.00	0.00	0.00	0.00	0.00	0.00	0.00	
19	assumed mid month 5 of half year					0.00	(120.00)	0.00	0.00	0.00	0.00	0.00	0.00	
20	assumed mid month 6 of half year					0.00	0.00	0.00	0.00	0.00	0.00	0.00	0.00	
21	assumed at end of half year					0.00	0.00	0.00	0.00	0.00	0.00	0.00	0.00	
22														
23														
24	Nominal Pure Equity IRR % p.a.		47.65%											

Ret

=XIRR($F15:$BD21,Work!$F$60:$BD$66)

investor. This requires division of both equity payments and returns between the various categories of investor, together with inclusion of any costs or benefits specifically relating to particular investors.

The division of input equity amounts should be fairly straightforward. Complications may arise if some investors are assumed to have invested beyond the direct equity paid into the project – for example, expenditure of development costs. These can be entered in the 'pre-year one' column (and special adjustments made as required using XIRR to reflect timing issues, as described in Section 21.1). If such expenditure is subsequently recovered as a charge to the project, then the payments to investors, included as a cost for the project cash flows, should appear as a positive payment in the investor(s) cash flows.

The division of returns between investors will, of course, depend upon the detail of the finance structure. Once the total distributed dividends have been calculated, they can be divided between the investors according to the hierarchy and proportions specified in the data for the proposed financing structure.

Exhibit 21.3

Illustrative returns calculation layout

A	B	C	D	E	F	G	H	I	J	K	L	M	N
7													
8 Pure Equity Drawings		436.78			0.00	436.78	0.00	0.00	0.00	0.00	0.00	0.00	0.00
9													
10 Dividends		14,589.33			0.00	65.41	35.81	167.17	83.75	137.78	132.18	153.39	143.82
11 Cash Shortfalls/Final Cash Balances		(209.90)			0.00	(0.00)	0.00	0.00	0.00	0.00	0.00	0.00	0.00
12													
13 Cash Flow to pure equity investors		13,942.65			0.00	(371.37)	35.81	167.17	83.75	137.78	132.18	153.39	143.82
14													
15 Nominal Pure Equity Return % p.a.		73.78%											
16													
17													
18 Sub Debt Drawings		1,310.35			0.00	1,310.35	0.00	0.00	0.00	0.00	0.00	0.00	0.00
19													
20 Sub Debt Interest and Repayments		2,420.86			0.00	19.66	95.36	93.73	92.09	90.45	88.81	87.17	85.54
21													
22 Cash Flow to sub debt		1,110.52			0.00	(1,290.69)	95.36	93.73	92.09	90.45	88.81	87.17	85.54
23													
24 Total Cash Flow to Investors		15,053.17			0.00	(1,662.06)	131.17	260.90	175.84	228.23	220.99	240.57	229.35
25													
26													
27 Nominal Blended Equity Return % p.a.		30.89%											
28													
29													
30 Real Terms Cash Flow to pure equity investors		9,427.75			0.00	(365.56)	35.07	162.93	81.22	132.30	125.06	143.00	132.11
31 Real Terms Cash Flow to Investors		10,029.81			0.00	(1,631.99)	128.16	253.64	170.10	217.54	207.55	222.62	209.13
32													
33 Real Pure Equity Return % p.a.		70.53%											
34 Real Blended Equity Return % p.a.		27.79%											

Once the cash flows for a given investor have been calculated, then real and nominal returns can be calculated as required. When analysing returns for an investor whose cash flows are denominated in a currency other than the presentation currency, returns should be calculated for the underlying currency. If purchasing power parity has been assumed between the underlying currency and the presentation currency (i.e., no real appreciation/depreciation), then the real returns should be the same on either basis, while nominal returns will reflect any different inflation rate assumptions for the two currencies.

In order to adjust for currency effects, the cash flows can simply be converted into presentation currency values at a constant exchange rate. This is done by adjusting the investor cash flow using the devaluation factor including real appreciation/depreciation. This will take account of any assumed real appreciation/depreciation between the currencies (see Section 8).

21.3 Calculating an IRR waterfall

The calculation of an IRR waterfall, where cash flows to investors are allocated based on specified IRR allocations to particular investors, is actually fairly straightforward. What is required is to keep in mind the mathematical definition of an IRR as the rate at which the NPV of cash flows to/from investors equals zero. The calculation therefore simply needs to keep track of the NPV of cash flows to each specific investor so far. This allows the appropriate additional transfers to be calculated at each stage in the waterfall.

Exhibit 21.4

Illustrative IRR waterfall calculation. Assumes two investors, A and B, investor A receives 80% of cash flows to investors until they achieve a 15% IRR, then 60% until they achieve a 25% IRR, then 30% of cash flows thereafter.

	A	B	C	D	E	F	G	H
			% share of dividends		IRR Limit			
7	Returns to investor A							
8	Target One		80%		15%			
9	Target Two		60%		25%			
10	Target Three		30%		n/a			

=NPV((1+Data!$E$8)^0.5-1,$F$18:$BC$18)

=MIN(F20*Data!$C$8,-MIN(0,E26*(1+Data!$E$8)^0.5))

=-C22

=E26*(1+Data!$E$8)^0.5+F24

	A	B	C	D	E	F	G	H	I	J	K	L	M	N	
13	Equity as Paid in					0.00	1,294.01	568.20	110.98	0.00	0.00	0.00	0.00	0.00	
14	Dividends					0.00	0.00	0.00	0.00	405.27	481.82	535.67	592.25	651.69	71
16	Investor Net Cash Flow (nominal)		5,071.89			0.00	-1,294.01	568.20	-110.98	405.27	481.82	535.67	592.25	651.69	71
18	Investor A Equity paid in		1,254.61			0.00	970.51	284.10	0.00	0.00	0.00	0.00	0.00	0.00	
20	Cash flow for allocation between investors		7,045.09			0.00	0.00	0.00	0.00	405.27	481.82	535.67	592.25	651.69	71
22	NPV of Investor A Equity at 1st target IRR		1,074												
24	Initial Cash to Investor A		1,721.91			0.00	0.00	0.00	0.00	324.22	385.46	428.54	473.80	109.89	
26	Cumulative NPV to Investor A 1st IRR				-1,074.29	-1,152.05	-1,235.44	-1,324.86	-1,420.75	-1,199.37	-900.72	-537.38	-102.48	0.00	
28	Initial Cash to Investor B		430.48			0.00	0.00	0.00	0.00	81.05	96.36	107.13	118.45	27.47	
30	Investor A 1st IRR cross-check		15.00%			0.00	-970.51	-284.10	0.00	324.22	385.46	428.54	473.80	109.89	
32	Remaining Cash					0.00	0.00	0.00	0.00	0.00	0.00	0.00	0.00	514.32	71
34	NPV of Investor A Equity at 2nd target IRR		980												
36	Stage Two Cash to Investor A		470.69			0.00	0.00	0.00	0.00	0.00	0.00	0.00	0.00	308.59	16
38	Cumulative NPV to Investor A 2nd IRR				-979.70	-1,095.33	-1,224.62	-1,369.17	-1,530.77	-1,387.24	-1,165.52	-874.56	-503.98	-144.99	
40	Stage Two Cash to Investor B		313.79			0.00	0.00	0.00	0.00	0.00	0.00	0.00	0.00	205.73	10
42	Investor A 2nd IRR cross-check		25.00%			0.00	-970.51	-284.10	0.00	324.22	385.46	428.54	473.80	418.49	16
44	Remaining Cash		4,108.22			0.00	0.00	0.00	0.00	0.00	0.00	0.00	0.00	0.00	44
46	Stage Three Cash to Investor A		1,232.47			0.00	0.00	0.00	0.00	0.00	0.00	0.00	0.00	0.00	13
47	Stage Three Cash to Investor B		2,875.76			0.00	0.00	0.00	0.00	0.00	0.00	0.00	0.00	0.00	31
49	Net Cash Flow to Investor A		2,170.45			0.00	-970.51	-284.10	0.00	324.22	385.46	428.54	473.80	418.49	29
50	Net Cash Flow to Investor B		2,901.44			0.00	-323.50	-284.10	-110.98	81.05	96.36	107.13	118.45	233.20	41
52	Investor A IRR		36.72%												
53	Investor B IRR		46.04%												

=F24/Data!$C$8*(1-Data!$C$8)

=E38*(1+Data!$E$9)^0.5+F36+F24

22 Cover factor calculations

A key part of the role of a financial model is to establish the amount of debt supportable by the project and the robustness of the project in terms of its ability to service and repay debt under a range of downside assumptions. The debt cover factors provide a simple way of reviewing this information and are discussed in detail in Section 10.

22.1 Calculating the debt service cover ratios

These are the simplest of the cover factors, and are basically a measure of the extent to which available cash flow in each period covers the scheduled loan repayments plus interest in the period. A minimum value of 1.00 or above shows that the scheduled interest and repayment can be met directly from the projected cash flows. It is possible, however, that intermittent costs, for example irregular maintenance costs, may give rise to a shortfall in some periods, even though cash from previous periods is more than adequate to cover the shortfall. To allow this to be reflected in the cover factors, the values can be presented on two bases – one based upon available cash flows as they arise, and the other based upon available cash flows net of transfers to and from specific cash deposits, particularly the MRA.

The formula calculating the cover factor in each period should include a check to ensure that scheduled debt service is greater than zero; if not, the formula should give a blank string as the result. Because the MIN(...) function ignores empty cells, this makes it straightforward to find the lowest cover factor value. Also with regard to avoiding misleading values for the minimum cover factor figure, it is probably worth eliminating the drawdown period from the calculation because, if funding is matched to costs, the DSCRs should inevitably equal 1.00 during the construction period.

22.2 NPV loan and project life cover factors

These cover factors compare the outstanding debt at a point in time with all projected cash flows available to service that debt.

In order to properly take account of the timing of available revenues over the specified period, the future revenues are discounted back using the loan interest rate. If more than one loan is being included in the calculation, then a weighted average interest rate must be calculated.

There are a number of defensible methods for calculating the weighted average interest rate. For example, the rate in each period can be calculated in proportion to the loan balances outstanding in that period. The calculated rate can then be used as the discount rate in each period when calculating the NPV of projected CFADs.

When calculating the NPV cover factors, it is important to decide whether the figure is to be calculated for the beginning or the end of the period in which it is to appear, and ensure that the loan balance and NPVs are consistent with this.

For the loan life cover factors, the NPV should be calculated using CFADS during the scheduled loan life. The scheduled end of the loan life can be established with reference to the loan repayment mask. If the previous period's repayment mask = 1.00, then the current period is after the end of the scheduled loan life.

As for DSCRs, the formula calculating the cover factors should check in each period to ensure that the loan balance has a value greater than zero to avoid DIV errors.

22.2.1 Including deposits in NPV cover factors

This can be accomplished in one of several ways:

- the funds on deposit may be added to the NPV of available revenues;
- funds on deposit may somehow be allocated between funds added to the NPV of available cash, and funds deducted from the loan balance outstanding; or
- the total funds on deposit may be deducted from the loan balance outstanding.

These will have an increasingly positive effect on the resultant cover factor value.

Exhibit 22.1

Illustrative cover factor calculation sheet

`=IF(F15*MIN(1,Work!E23)>0.001,(F13*MIN(1,Work!E23)+E13*MIN(1,Work!D23))/(F15*MIN(1,Work!E23)+E15*MIN(1,Work!D23)),"")`

`=IF(F15*MIN(1,Work!E23)>0.001, F13/F15,"")`   `=F9+F11`   `=F9`   `=IF(Work!E51=1,0, F21)`

	A	B	C	D	E	F	G	H	I	J	K	L	M	N	O
9	Available cash for Cover Factor Calculations		26,893			0.00	0.00	480.20	609.92	525.19	577.82	569.42	589.02	577.92	6(
11	Transfers (to) & from MRA		3			0.00	0.89	(0.53)	(0.53)	(0.88)	(1.13)	1.09	2.42	(0.06)	(
13	Cash for ADSCR Calculation		26,896			0.00	0.89	479.67	609.39	524.31	576.69	570.51	591.45	577.86	5
15	Senior Debt Service		10,766			0.00	69.19	356.55	356.55	356.55	356.55	356.55	356.55	356.55	3
17			Min												
18	Semi Annual Debt Service Cover Factor		1.35					1.35	1.71	1.47	1.62	1.60	1.66	1.62	
19	Annual Debt Service Cover Factor		1.35					1.35	1.53	1.59	1.54	1.61	1.63	1.64	
21	Cash for NPV cover factor calculations		26,893			0.00	0.00	480.20	609.92	525.19	577.82	569.42	589.02	577.92	6(
22	Cash for NPV cover factor calculations over loan life					0.00	0.00	480.20	609.92	525.19	577.82	569.42	589.02	577.92	6(
24	FNPV of available cash		427,672			14,492	14,492	14,926	14,894	14,731	14,648	14,509	14,375	14,217	1<
25	FNPV of available cash over loan life		253,361			11,831	11,831	12,185	12,071	11,823	11,653	11,424	11,198	10,944	1(
27	Senior Debt Balance Outstanding at start of half year		0			0	0	6,989	6,842	6,690	6,534	6,374	6,209	6,038	
29			Min												
30	Project Life NPV Cover Factor		2.14					2.14	2.18	2.20	2.24	2.28	2.32	2.35	
31	Project Life NPV CF with balances on MRA and DSRA		2.19					2.19	2.23	2.26	2.30	2.33	2.37	2.41	
33	Loan Life NPV Cover Factors		1.74					1.74	1.76	1.77	1.78	1.79	1.80	1.81	
34	Loan Life NPV CF with balances on MRA and DSRA		1.79					1.79	1.82	1.82	1.84	1.85	1.86	1.87	

CFactor

`=(G24+F21)/(1+Fin!F$52/2)`   `=MIN(F30:BC30)`

`=IF(F$27>0.001,(F25+CBals!E$19+CBals!E$31)/F$27,"")`

`=IF(F$27>0.001,F24/F27,"")`

`=IF(F$27>0.001,F25/F$27,"")`

`=IF(F$27>0.001,(F24+CBals!E$19+CBals!E$31)/F$27,"")`

22.3 Currency issues when modelling cover factors

For debt denominated in a currency other than the presentation currency, future cash flows in the presentation currency do not have a consistent value with respect to given loan balances. This must be resolved for LLCR and PLCR calculations. One approach is to calculate the NPVs using cash flows with devaluation adjustments removed to give values based on a consistent exchange rate. This can be achieved by dividing the CFADs by the total devaluation factors in each period. The NPVs can then be adjusted to reflect devaluation to the appropriate calculation date by multiplying by the devaluation factor at the time point of the NPV Figure.

23 Net cash flow (NCF) summary

The NCF is a key report for project finance purposes, and can give a very full picture of the project and the particular case being presented. The details of rows included in the cash flow summary will vary from deal to deal, reflecting the nature of the project – the industry type and the figures of particular concern for the project at a given point in the project development path.

In addition, the content of the cash flow summary will depend upon who is preparing the model and who will ultimately see the printed results. Detailed equity returns, for example, may well be considered confidential if the model is being prepared by the investors for presentation to banks or as part of a bid. Similarly, banking advisers may not wish to provide details of assumed fee amounts when presenting model output to potential lenders, with whom fees will be a matter of negotiation. The following comprise the general categories of information to be expected on an NCF sheet.

- **Production.** It is worth including some indicative figures for operating levels, whether it be production (in tonnes, MWh, Bbls, etc.), availability (as a percentage), throughput (passenger miles, traffic units) or some combination of these or other appropriate values. This gives an indication as to the basic assumptions used for the case being run, and gives quick identification of operating sensitivities.

- **Sales Price/Unit.** The sales price per unit is often an important figure in its own right, either as a key input or calculated result. For some projects several values, relating to different categories of production, can helpfully be shown.

- **Gross Operating Revenues.** This represents the total revenue generated in relation to operations. If there are several categories of revenue, each should probably be shown along with the total figure.

- **Fixed/Variable Operating Costs.** Operating costs should be shown, broken down between any appropriate categories – for example, fixed, variable, fuel, other.

- **Total Operating Costs.** A sub-total of all the categories of operating cost shown.

- **Net Operating Revenues.** A sub-total comprising Gross Operating Revenues less Total Operating Costs.

- **Working Capital Adjustment.** As calculated in the operations section of the calculations, this row shows the adjustment needed to reflect payables/receivables timing delays, and purchase of stocks. It can helpfully be shown as a single row comprising a mix of positive and negative values, reflecting the effect of the adjustment on cash flow in each period.

- **Net Operating Cash Flows.** A sub-total comprising Net Operating Revenues plus the Working Capital Adjustment.

- **Capital Costs.** Comprising construction costs, development fees, etc., but not including any finance costs. A number of separate items can be shown here, if appropriate, and sub-totalled into the total Capital Costs figures.

- **Pre-Tax Project Cash Flow.** This sub-total comprises the Net Operating Cash Flows less the Capital Costs. If required, a pre-tax and finance Project IRR can be calculated based on the values in this row.

- **Tax Paid.** Tax payments as made – i.e., as they affect the cash flow, rather than when the tax liability is calculated or incurred.

- **Post-Tax Project Cash Flow.** This sub-total gives the basic project economics, and comprises the Pre-Tax Project Cash Flow less the Tax Paid. The Post-tax Project IRR can be calculated based on the values in this row. It is worth noting that the project cash flows are intended to represent the 'pure' cash flows of the project, without taking account of funding choices, but the tax figure will reflect the finance assumptions through deducted interest costs. While this is normally acceptable, it should be a clearly documented assumption.

- **Loan Drawings.** Rows showing the loan drawings, broken down, as appropriate for the project and the finance structure, between loans, types of loans, etc. Total Loan Drawings can be shown as a sub-total of these categories, or as a single value if no breakdown is required.

- **Debt Service.** Rows showing the finance costs, including loan interest and fees, legal costs associated with the financing, ECA premia, debt and equity arrangement fees, advisory fees, etc. As for drawings, these costs can be shown in categories appropriate to the deal and the finance structure. An additional issue when showing the finance costs is consideration of the extent to which an explicit breakdown of fees should be provided to likely recipients of the cash flow summary printout. It may be desirable, for example, to group legal, equity and finance fees together into one row, rather than showing each explicitly.

  Total Debt Service should give a total of all the loan fees, interest and repayments, including interest during construction.

- **Post-Tax and Finance Cash Flow.** Calculated as Post-Tax project Cash Flow, plus Loan Drawings, less Total Debt Service. This reflects the net input and output for the project, with finance in place, before taking account of placement of funds in accounts, etc.

- **Transfers (To)/From Accounts.** In this section transfers to and from accounts can be shown, either separately or as a single row for each account, showing transfers to accounts as negative values and transfers from accounts as positive values. This can comprise all accounts, including debt service reserve, sinking funds, and the surplus cash account. Interest earned on the accounts can also be added at this point in the net cash flow. This gives a logical layout, and separates actual cost and revenue values from these figures that represent movement of funds, and the interest consequent upon those movements. If required, however, some or all of these values can be sited elsewhere in the cash flow. It could be argued, for instance, that transfers to/from the debt service reserve should be taken into account when calculating the Post-Tax and Finance Cash Flow, and likewise some or all of the earned interest.

- **Net Cash Flow to Investors.** Calculated as the Post-Tax and Finance Cash Flow, less transfers to, plus transfers from accounts, plus interest earned on deposits.

  This row represents the total cash flow to investors, excluding taxes other than those paid directly by the project and should show negative values equal to the calculated pure equity payments into the project, and positive values equal to calculated distributable dividends. This provides a key checking point for the model, highlighting any periods where there are cash flow shortfalls, or cash flows which are not allocated to any costs, deposits or dividends.

- **Equity as Paid In and Calculated Dividends.** These information lines allow easy checking that the investor net cash flow balances.

- **Cash Balances.** Showing the closing balances on all cash accounts helps give a complete picture of the cash position in each period.

If withholding taxes are payable on dividends to all investors, it might be appropriate to show such tax charges just above the net cash flows to investors row, and deduct them from the total. Otherwise they can be shown as an information line below the net cash flow, with the distributed dividends.

Clearly the detailed contents of the Net Cash Flow Summary will vary according to the specific industry and deal being summarised, but the example layout in Exhibit 23.1 gives a general guide as to the recommended contents and appearance of an NCF. Note that only the various subtotals are actually calculated on this sheet, all other values are calculated elsewhere in the model and simply re-presented here in the simplest possible way, using, for example, '=Ops!F18', '=Capex!F32', etc.

Exhibit 23.1

Illustrative NCF layout and contents

	Totals	Pre Yr One	Jan-09 to Jun-09	Jul-09 to Dec-09	Jan-10 to Jun-10	Jul-10 to Dec-10	Jan-11 to Jun-11	Jul-11 to Dec-11	Jan-12 to Jun-12	Jul-12 to Dec-12
Big Island Widget Plant Project										
Base Case										
Net Cash Flow Summary										
All values in millions Zgs										
Plant Capacity / tonnes per hour			0.00	0.00	0.00	0.00	0.00	0.00	1.20	1
Plant Operating Hours	40,000		0.00	0.00	0.00	0.00	0.00	0.00	333.33	1,000
Plant Production / tonnes widgets	48,000		0.00	0.00	0.00	0.00	0.00	0.00	400.00	1,200
Widget Sale Price / Zgs per tonne			452,698.18	468,274.64	484,387.06	501,053.87	518,294.15	536,127.64	554,574.74	573,656
Widget Sale Revenues	51,485		0.00	0.00	0.00	0.00	0.00	0.00	221.83	688
Power Costs	143		0.00	0.00	0.00	0.00	0.00	0.00	0.62	1
Feedstock Costs	183		0.00	0.00	0.00	0.00	0.00	0.00	0.79	2
Other Variable Operating Costs	57		0.00	0.00	0.00	0.00	0.00	0.00	0.25	0
Total Variable Operating Costs	383		0.00	0.00	0.00	0.00	0.00	0.00	1.65	5
Fixed Operating Costs	184		0.00	0.00	0.00	0.00	0.00	0.00	0.79	2
Total Operating Costs	567		0.00	0.00	0.00	0.00	0.00	0.00	2.44	7
Net Operating Revenues	50,918		0.00	0.00	0.00	0.00	0.00	0.00	219.39	680
Net Payables/Receivables Adjustment	0		0.00	0.00	0.00	0.00	0.00	0.00	(110.52)	(3.
Net Operating Cash Flow	50,918		0.00	0.00	0.00	0.00	0.00	0.00	108.87	677
Major Maintenance Costs	1,300		0.00	0.00	0.00	0.00	0.00	0.00	0.00	0
Construction Costs	8,907		0.00	2,599.94	1,177.07	1,226.55	1,569.97	563.69	1,770.20	0
Pre-tax project Cash Flow	40,710		0.00	(2,599.94)	(1,177.07)	(1,226.55)	(1,569.97)	(563.69)	(1,661.33)	677
Tax	10,997		0.00	0.00	0.00	0.00	0.00	0.00	0.00	0
Post-tax Project Cash Flow	29,713		0.00	(2,599.94)	(1,177.07)	(1,226.55)	(1,569.97)	(563.69)	(1,661.33)	677
Loan 1 Principal Drawings	7,802		0.00	2,615.95	1,191.59	1,237.23	1,578.00	568.59	610.40	0
Loan 1 Additional Drawings to fund interest	727		0.00	21.11	108.04	151.87	194.28	251.43	0.00	0
Sub Debt Principal Drawings	2,012		0.00	0.00	0.00	0.00	0.00	0.00	2,012.12	0
Sub Debt Additional Drawings to fund interest	195		0.00	0.00	0.00	0.00	0.00	0.00	33.56	0
Total Loan Funding	10,736		0.00	2,637.06	1,299.63	1,389.09	1,772.28	820.03	2,656.08	0
Loan 1 Principal repayments	8,528		0.00	0.00	0.00	0.00	0.00	0.00	0.00	225
Loan 1 Interest	5,522		0.00	21.11	108.04	151.87	194.28	251.43	277.83	287
Legal and Finance fees	180		0.00	136.01	14.52	10.67	8.03	4.91	2.37	0
Sub Debt Principal Repayments	2,207		0.00	0.00	0.00	0.00	0.00	0.00	0.00	26
Sub Debt Interest Payments	2,041		0.00	0.00	0.00	0.00	0.00	0.00	33.56	92
Total Debt Service	18,478		0.00	157.11	122.56	162.54	202.31	256.34	313.76	632
Net Cash Flow	21,971		0.00	(120.00)	0.00	0.00	0.00	0.00	680.99	44
Transfers (to)/from DSRA			0.00	0.00	0.00	(0.00)	0.00	0.00	(572.12)	71
Transfers (to)/from MRA			0.00	0.00	0.00	0.00	0.00	0.00	(93.61)	(9.
Transfers (to)/from Cash at Bank			0.00	0.00	0.00	0.00	0.00	0.00	(15.26)	(120.
Interest Earned on Deposits			0.00	0.00	0.00	0.00	0.00	0.00	0.00	13
Net Cash Flow to Investors	22,376		0.00	(120.00)	0.00	(0.00)	0.00	0.00	0.00	0
Equity as Paid in to Project	120		0.00	120.00	0.00	0.00	0.00	0.00	0.00	0
Calculated Dividends	22,496		0.00	0.00	0.00	0.00	0.00	0.00	0.00	0
Balance on DSRA			0.00	0.00	0.00	0.00	0.00	0.00	572.12	500
Balance on MRA			0.00	0.00	0.00	0.00	0.00	0.00	93.61	102
Balance on Surplus Cash Account			0.00	0.00	0.00	0.00	0.00	0.00	15.26	136

NCF

24 Single page summary

It is often useful to provide a one-page printout giving a summary of the key data values for a given run, together with the important results. This is often a difficult page to set up when first creating the model, because it may be far from clear which results and which data items will be significant as runs are produced. It can therefore be a good idea to begin with the sources and uses summary, returns, etc., together with a descriptive title for the case being run, and add or remove values as appropriate, as the deal progresses.

Data items should be shown by means of a formula picking up values from the data section, rather than by moving the cells from the data section that are actually picked up and used by the code. This means that the summary sheet can be changed without any risk of affecting the operation of the model.

This sheet can often usefully display text controlled by or incorporating particular data inputs. See Section 9.3 for helpful techniques.

25 Investment period sources and uses

Either as a report on its own, or as part of a key inputs and results summary, it is generally useful to produce a Sources and Uses summary showing totals for the elements of funding and expenditure during construction. This can be very simple, with two columns giving values and sub-totals for the total Sources and Uses respectively. Alternatively, this can be expanded into a sophisticated report showing values for various currencies and giving percentage breakdowns between different funding sources.

In principle, this summary is easily calculated, either using totals for values that are inherently limited to the construction period, or taking totals of values multiplied by a construction period mask. The mask can be applied either by creating a row in the worklines and multiplying the relevant items by the mask or using a single cell using the SUMPRODUCT(...) function.

Difficulties can, though, arise from the details of costs, revenues and funding in the periods around the end of the construction period.

Through retentions or for other reasons, some construction costs may overlap with final completion. In some deals, production builds up as construction is completed. In both cases, operating revenues may be used to fund some part of the construction costs. This could reasonably be reflected in the Sources and Uses by including the total figure for construction costs in the construction period uses, with the appropriate operating revenues added to the construction period sources. The operating revenue figure can be calculated fairly simply as the total of: the lesser in each period of revenues; *or* construction costs less other funding. The confusion arises with regard to loan interest and fees, where revenues overlap with the construction period, possibly paying all interest in some of the later periods. It then becomes a matter of judgement as to which interest costs are included as construction period costs, and hence the amount of revenue to be included in the sources figures to cover these costs. The period selected may well not coincide with the whole period of expenditure of construction costs, particularly where, as mentioned above, this period overlaps with final completion. More than one mask may therefore be needed to establish the costs included in the summary. A simple mask will not necessarily give the required result if applied to the revenue figures, because revenues in a given period might well exceed the selected construction costs for that period, and only those actually used to meet such costs should be included in the sources figures. The calculation therefore requires calculation in each period of the costs to be treated as construction period costs, less funding from all non-revenue sources, and the amount of net revenues available from operations.

The Sources and Uses summary can be a very helpful check on the funding calculations, in that a failure of total Sources to balance with total Uses can highlight a funding mismatch, or indicate that a cost or funding item has been omitted from other calculations. It is therefore preferable, subject to ultimate time constraints, to independently calculate all items included in this summary, rather than replacing detailed calculations with a 'balancing item' calculated as the difference between the required total and the total of other elements in the Sources or Uses category.

26 Balance sheet

For project finance purposes, the balance sheet is essentially useless. Its ubiquity is presumably a function of the predominance of financiers with accounting or corporate finance backgrounds who just cannot get comfortable without seeing things presented in a P&L and balance sheet format.

If time is short when the model is being developed, the balance sheet can usually be left until last because it does not feed into any other calculation and does not provide any information likely to be critical for evaluation of a project finance deal. Eventually, however, this sheet will generally have to be included, and the process is often viewed with fear and loathing by the modeller involved. Although the balance sheet can include a number of accounting 'twiddly bits', the basic report can usually be put together (and made to balance) quite painlessly if the underlying principles are understood and borne in mind.

Exhibit 26.1

Items tracked in the balance sheet

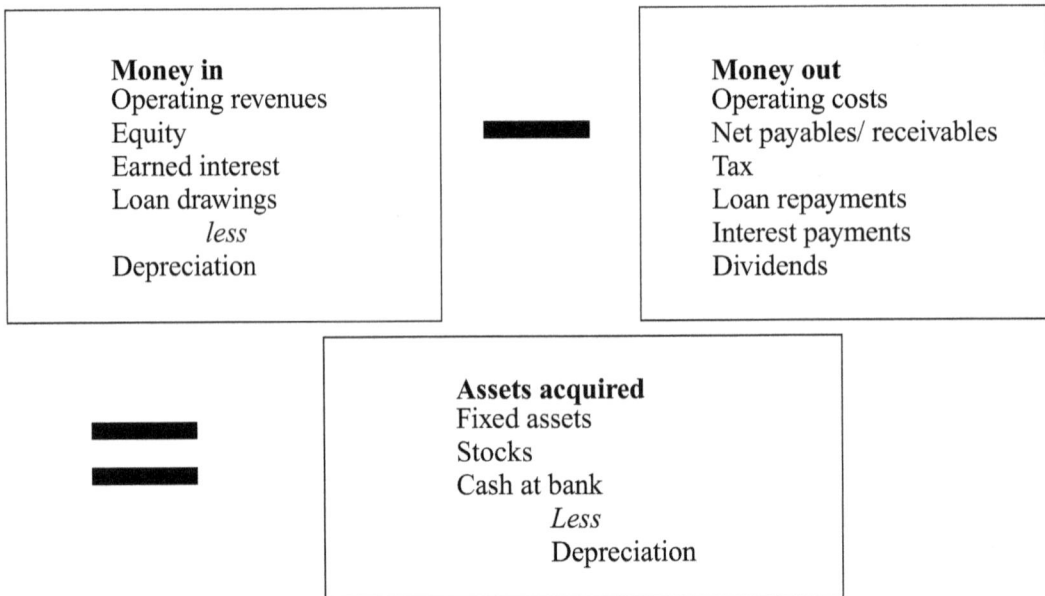

Money in
Operating revenues
Equity
Earned interest
Loan drawings
less
Depreciation

Money out
Operating costs
Net payables/ receivables
Tax
Loan repayments
Interest payments
Dividends

Assets acquired
Fixed assets
Stocks
Cash at bank
Less
Depreciation

The balance sheet can be thought of simply as a means of keeping track of the money paid into a project, ensuring that the net funds paid in are matched by assets acquired, whether using a UK 'net assets versus shareholders' funds', or a 'total assets versus total liabilities' format. The balance sheet thus lists the source and ultimate destination of all funds retained within the project. The picture is slightly complicated by the inclusion of depreciation, but, based upon the cash flow and profit and loss figures, the balance sheet should balance automatically if other calculations are correct.

The key items in allowing the balance sheet to balance are the retained profits and cash at bank, through which many items flow into the balance sheet. This can be illustrated by considering specific items and checking their application in the balance sheet.

Exhibit 26.2

Illustrative balance sheet layout

Base Case Balance Sheet All values in millions Zgs	1st half 2009	2nd half 2009	1st half 2010	2nd half 2010	1st half 2011	2nd half 2011	1st half 2012	2nd half 2012	1st half 2013	2nd half 2013
Assets										
Fixed Assets	0	1,889	2,783	4,210	6,608	10,434	10,434	10,434	10,434	10,43
less depreciation	0	0	0	0	0	0	260	573	885	1,19
Cash	0	0	0	0	0	0	334	704	732	73
Receivables	0	0	0	0	0	0	177	182	191	20
Stocks										
Total Assets	0	1,889	2,783	4,210	6,608	10,434	10,685	10,748	10,472	10,17
Liabilities										
Overdraft	0	0	0	0	0	0	0	0	0	
Loans	0	867	1,222	2,587	5,090	9,091	9,297	9,155	9,000	8,83
Payables	0	0	0	0	0	0	0	0	0	
less Forex Losses	0	273	301	351	455	630	836	1,012	1,179	1,33
Tax Provision	0	0	0	0	0	0	0	0	0	
Total Net Assets	0	1,294	1,862	1,973	1,973	1,973	2,224	2,604	2,650	2,67
Shareholder Funds										
Shareholder Equity	0	1,294	1,862	1,973	1,973	1,973	1,973	1,973	1,973	1,97
Retained Earnings	0	0	0	-0	-0	-0	-0	251	631	67
This Year's P&L	0	0	-0	-0	-0	-0	251	381	46	2
Total Shareholder's Funds	0	1,294	1,862	1,973	1,973	1,973	2,224	2,604	2,650	2,67
Check	0	0	0	0	0	0	0	0	0	
Difference	0	0	0	0	0	0	0	0	0	
half difference							0	0	0	

It is useful to include a row below the balance sheet that simply takes the absolute value of total net assets less shareholders' funds. A total of the values for this row will show at a glance whether or not the balance sheet is balancing. The timing and amount of any differences, visible across the row, may also help to identify the source of any problems.

27 Model development

27.1 How to start

When confronted with a blank screen and the prospect of creating a new model from scratch, it can be hard to decide what to do first. Here are some suggestions regarding the initial stages leading to the first draft.

When entering a new model, or making significant changes to an existing model, it is advisable to save the model regularly, perhaps as each new calculation is entered and checked. For maximum safety, save the model alternately under two slightly different names (for example, modelwithbellsV1a, modelwithbellsV1b). This gives a fallback position if the model is saved with an unresolvable error, or if there is a system failure during save, because the previous saved version of the model is preserved.

Select a suitable set of icons for the toolbar or quick access menu. Suggested sets of icons are shown in Exhibit 27.1.

Exhibit 27.1

Toolbar icons

Excel 2003

Excel 2007

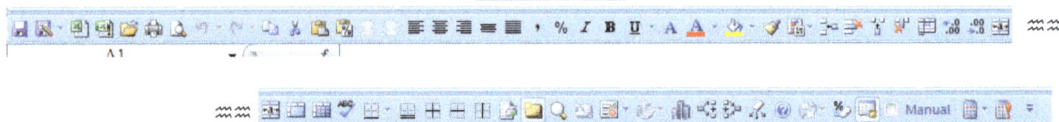

Use the 'Tools', 'Options' (2003) or 'Office' button, 'Excel Options' (2007) menus to select suitable settings for the Excel enviroment.

Set calculation to manual, no iteration, and no recalculation before save (see Section 2.1.8 for reasons!). In addition, deselect the option which moves the cursor on entry. For a process of entering and copying specific formulae, rather than primarily typing in endless rows or columns of data, having the cursor move to another cell every time the cell content is entered generates completely unecessary work moving the cursor repeatedly back to the required cell, and also has the potential to cause error.

Ensure that the Analysis Toolpak Add-in is activated to provide access to useful date functions. In 2003 this is done via 'Tools', 'Add-ins'. In 2007, use the 'Office' button, then 'Excel Options', 'Add-ins' and 'Go' next to 'Manage' and 'Excel Add-ins'. In both cases ensure that 'Analysis Toolpak' is ticked in the drop-down list.

Although it is not really necessary to plan a spreadsheet model in detail on paper, it is worth spending a little time clarifying your thoughts in advance. Consider what the model is primarily intended to calculate (revenue, equity return, supportable debt:equity ratio, etc.), and the implications of this for the structure of the model and the details of the calculations. Similarly, plan ahead regarding possible circularities and ways of dealing with them in the model (see Section 7).

1   Decide which sections will be needed in the model, the length and start date for the timeline, and the timing of the model half-year periods (for example, April to September and October to March).

2   Open a blank file.

3   Set up column widths and print header/footer on one page and make a copy of the page using 'Edit', 'Move or Copy Sheet', 'Create copy'.

4   Label one sheet 'work'. Leaving around ten blank rows at the top of the sheet, add two rows containing the start and end dates for each column of the timeline, and use the values in these rows to create the timeline heading at, say rows five and six of the sheet.

5   Copy formatting for the timeline heading onto the second page with column widths set up, and pick up values for this heading from the timeline in the 'Work' sheet. Set up basic print header and footer for this sheet and create as many copies of this sheet as needed for all the model sections, plus one to spare.

6   Label the sheets (Data, Work, Capex, Fin, etc.), remembering to keep sheet names short but meaningful.

7   Create inputs for all the data items you know you will need, laid out in the data sheet by category (for example, timing data, capex data, funding data, operating data, etc.). Where no values are yet available, use some arbitrary value as test data, but ensure that such inputs are very clearly identified. Colour the background of the relevant cells, not just the font, then the figures will still be highlighted if printed in monotone.

8   When the basic data is in place, begin to fill in the calculation sections. Start with the capital costs. Add items to the 'Masks, worklines ...' section as you find you need them. When inputting formulae that need to refer to values you have not yet calculated, simply enter a row heading ready for the missing figures on the appropriate sheet. Formulae can then be written including references to that row, even though the cells are initially empty. The correct formula or data can then be entered in the blank row as you work your way through the model. It is important to remember to treat any row with a row header as a whole row when moving things around in the model, even if the cells are still empty, so that formulae picking up cells from the row will continue to reference the correct cells. As each row or set of rows is entered, check the results produced.

9   As the calculations are entered, it will often become clear that additional data items are required. Add new items to the data sheet as needed, using test data where necessary until valid inputs are available.

10 Enter row headings for the 'Net cash flow summary', and pick up values as they become available during the model-building process. This will help to provide an overview of the results at each stage of model development, giving a quick check on the magnitude of various values, and on the calculated funding amounts.

11 If needed, set up a re-calc macro. Once in place, it is easy to incorporate new values into the iterative process simply by adding them to the 'Macrosupport' sheet.

12 When the first draft is complete, print and check all figures, from the data sheet(s) through to the report sheets.

13 Once a full printout has been checked, with one or more ticks against the values in each row, you have a basic model, provisionally checked and ready for use.

> Remember that the complexity of the first draft should be appropriate to the level of detail in the available data.

When deciding what level of detail to include in the first draft of the model, it is also worth considering which detail is easy to add subsequently. For example, it is easy to expand semi-annual construction cost calculations into monthly figures, but difficult to retro-fit currency treatments. Based on this, simplify where appropriate with the aim of producing a model which works, in that it can process inputs appropriately through to key output figures. Then add detail where needed. This approach has a number of benefits vs. attempting to create an all-singing all-dancing version from scratch.

- It produces something which can give useful, if not final, results in a manageable timeframe.
- It allows complex calculations to be tested and adjusted individually, in a framework which is known to function properly.
- It eliminates the risk of investing a lot of time in producing something which may prove ultimately unworkable.

27.2 Further development of the model

Whether building from a simplified first draft, or enhancing a 'finished' model as a deal progresses, there are a number of ways in which expansions can be made, utilising the benefits of the recommended model structure, and maintaining the principles of flexibility, clarity and robustness which will support later changes, and easy model use.

27.2.1 Adding new data choices

Wherever possible, preserve simple links between data and calculations. If adding multiple options for an existing single input, have the chosen value picked up into the original input cell, so no change is required in the model calculations.

27.2.2 Adding additional funding options

To add a new loan:

1 create a new column in the loan input data table and enter appropriate inputs for the new loan;
2 establish where in the funding cascade the new loan should be included, and make room for it by inserting rows *above* the net funding requirement used by the next source of funds;
3 create a new net-funding requirement to be used by the new loan, and copy into it the calculation for the funding requirement you have just displaced;
4 copy and paste row headings and first few columns of formulae from an existing loan calculation into the rows for the new loan;
5 add availability and repayment masks for the new loan on the 'Work' sheet;

6   edit or replace the headings and formulae for the new loan to correctly calculate the required drawings, repays and interest, etc., adding values to the 'Macrosupport' sheet as required;

7   change the net funding requirement following the new loan to use the previous funding requirement adjusted for drawings and interest on the new loan; and

8   update funding sub totals, NCF, sources and uses, etc., to include the new loan.

27.2.3 Adding timing breakdowns

The accuracy of available data will often be limited during the early stages of model development. Incorporation of greater timing accuracy by including additional rows to represent, for example, months within the half year (see Section 3.2) has the additional advantage that it can easily be added to an existing semi-annual model when better data becomes available.

Adding monthly data essentially requires replacing single row inputs with the six rows giving the monthly breakdown within the half year. On calculation sheets, six new rows should be inserted above each semi annual item for which monthly figures are being added. The monthly calculations are then entered in the new rows, and the original semi-annual row overwritten with a total of the new monthly figures. This ensures that the new monthly values automatically feed into all the existing semi annual calculations in the model.

28 Checking and debugging

28.1 Introduction

In the very early days of computing, people believed that producing a computer program involved careful design, followed by coding and then using the program. But what quickly became apparent was that there is another stage in the process – 'debugging' – i.e., finding the typos and errors of logic inevitable in new computer programs, spreadsheets being no exception. The process of modelling therefore needs to include, as a matter of course, checking and debugging procedures.

Time constraints will often limit the extent to which any model can be double-checked and fully documented at all stages but, overall, it is not possible to short-cut the basic checking procedure as it is essential to ensure that valid figures and results are being produced by the model. If a time-table does not allow time for reasonable checking, then it is not possible to produce figures to that timetable.

It is worth bearing in mind how figures can come to 'haunt' a deal. There is a worrying tendency for any released figures to become firmly fixed in some mind or document, and to reappear repeatedly over the subsequent life of the deal. This is particularly true of the first figures released, even though these are usually based on incomplete data and are issued covered in health warnings. Once circulated, they will generally form a key part of someone's understanding of the deal, and later figures, based on complete data and justifiable assumptions, will have to be reconciled back to the original 'back of the envelope' figure. It is therefore worth making certain that, at all stages, everything possible has been done to ensure that the results produced by the model do correctly reflect the data and assumptions upon which they are supposed to be based.

In order to make the process of checking as quick, reliable and efficient as possible, and so help to produce reasonable results as soon as possible, a number of standard methods and techniques can be applied, as described in this text. While it is best to assume that the perfect model does not exist, and that for some or all of its life every model will include at least one error, taking a systematic approach to checking, and using all the cross-checks possible within the model, can contribute to minimising any errors in the final figures.

In addition to built-in errors in structure or code, results can be compromised by 'run-time errors' – i.e., errors arising from data entries made while running the model, which give rise to inherently incorrect figures or figures that do not reflect the assumptions and data apparently used. These can be limited to some extent by habitual checking of output and comparison of the results for each case against the base case or previous sensitivities, and can ultimately be minimised by the consistent use of a case control table (see Section 9.4).

28.2 Debugging while developing the model

It is important to check the model as a whole once the first draft is complete. Checking each section as it is completed, and sometimes each formula as it is entered, can make this process a simple one of verifying a basically correct model, rather than a complex one of trying to resolve multiple errors.

28.2.1 Debugging tips

Whilst entering the model, either initially or when adding new sections to a developed model, it is possible to check new code at three levels.

1   A single row can be checked when it is entered.
2   A section of the model can be checked as completed.
3   The overall calculation can be monitored and checked by reviewing reports, etc., that bring together the results from various sections, allowing them to be compared and reviewed.

At these three levels, the debugging process should become an intrinsic part of the model development process. To assist with this, it can be helpful to recalculate the model as each calculation, or set of calculations is input. This has various advantages, including:

- any figures feeding from the calculation into the key summaries can be reviewed and checked;
- it gives immediate warning if any circularity has been introduced (see below); and
- ensures that all figures reflect the same stage of model development, ready for input of the next stage.

28.2.2 Complex formulae

If, when verifying a single formula, it is too complex to allow quick checking without interrupting the flow of work, try using data items to allow different elements of the formula to be checked separately. For example, inflation rates for different currencies could be set to the same level to allow calculations to be checked without the complications of currency adjustments obscuring the underlying calculation. Consider whether such calculations can usefully be broken down into meaningful intermediate calculations that might be included in the 'Work' sheet. There is always a trade-off between clarity of the model and clarity of individual formulae. Complex formulae are not inconsistent with good modelling, unnecessarily complex formulae are.

28.2.3 The 'totals' column

Nominal totals can form part of the checking process, so use the totals column as code is entered. For example, if no currency adjustments are involved, then the total of principal drawings plus total rolled-up interest for a loan should equal the total repayments figure for that loan. Rows representing totals or sub-totals of other rows can quickly be checked using the totals column. In order to have this check available, it is important that all row totals are calculated as the total of values in the row to the right, not simply as totals of other values in the totals column.

28.2.4 Percentage values

Where input profiles are entered as a series of percentage values, then a total can be calculated (on a temporary or permanent basis) to quickly check that the values add to a total of 100%. If not, then the schedule can be checked in detail, item-by-item. Remember that simply selecting a range of cells will usually cause the total value of the cell contents to be displayed by Excel.

28.2.5 Masks and counters

These should be checkable by simple observation of their calculated values. Once a mask has been prepared correctly, then correct reflection of the timing assumptions involved should be reliably transferred to all subsequent calculations prepared using the mask.

28.2.6 Inflation

When checking inflation factors, for a semi-annual model assuming inflation from the start of the first period, end-period values should show whole multiples of the annual rates in the second, fourth, sixth, etc., periods.

The capital costs section can be checked with zero inflation to ensure that the nominal total for each category of capital costs is equal to the value input in data for the costs. If inflation assumptions are then restored, a quick comparison can be made between nominal totals and input values to ensure that the appropriate values have increased or remained unchanged. The application of currency assumptions can also be checked by manipulating inflation assumptions and any real appreciation/depreciation assumptions in this way.

28.2.7 Loan calculations

The 'cascade' basis for the funding section allows loan drawings to be checked easily against the preceding 'funding requirement' row. It also makes any underfunding or overfunding fairly easy to observe. Within any loan calculation, once the principal drawings have been checked, the rolled-up interest can be checked by comparison with the interest payable, the loan balance can be checked by looking at the drawings, roll-up and repayment, and the repayments (if no currency adjustments apply) should have a nominal total equal to the principal drawings plus the rolled-up interest. The repayments and balance outstanding can be checked in combination by looking at the scheduled last repayment period: there should be a repayment of an appropriate amount, which should exactly reduce the balance outstanding to zero. This check will apply even when currency adjustments are required.

If a loan calculation requires 'annuity' style repayments, then the repayment calculation can be checked by adding a temporary row which adds together the interest payable and repayment figures in each period. This total figure should be the same for all periods, including the last repayment period, subject only to changes reflecting currency issues, and should exactly pay the loan to zero on the final repayment period.

28.2.8 Pro rata equity

If payment of equity into the project is to be calculated pro rata to loan drawings, then the equity drawings used in the model should be calculated as the appropriate percentage of total loan drawings, rather than as a total of the equity values calculated in order to produce the appropriate loan drawings. This allows the pro rata calculation to be instantly checked, because it will result in inappropriate underfunding or overfunding if the pro rata calculation is not being correctly applied.

28.2.9 Funding calculation

The best overall check for the funding calculation is provided by the cash flow summary. If laid out on the basis indicated in the 'Cash flow summary' (see Section 23), the cash flow will clearly indicate the costs and funds drawn in each period, and will show any unintentional mismatch between funding and costs during the construction period. This can also be reviewed with the construction period sources and uses summary. If either fail to balance, then there is an error to be tracked down (although, of course it may not be in the funding section, but may rather indicate an omission or error of some sort in one of the summaries).

28.2.10 Operations

In the operations section, timing of operations should be largely checkable by simple observation. For complex formulae, quick checks can be performed by checking that figures give the expected result when various data items are changed. This can be accomplished by deleting portions of the formula in one column, and restoring the original formula (when checks are complete) by copying across from other columns.

There is generally no simple overall check for operations calculations, although common sense suggests that revenues should exceed operating costs by a reasonable margin. Correct application of the project life input can be checked by scanning down the columns at the end of the project life to ensure that values do not stop too soon, nor continue past the specified last period.

28.1.11 Optimised revenues

If a calculated revenue is being used, then equity returns or cover factor values may provide a straightforward check that the tariff and revenue calculations are working.

28.2.12 Tax

For the tax section, all the standard checking techniques apply, together with simple visual checks on the timing of net taxable profits, tax payable and tax paid. The nominal totals for tax payable and tax paid can be compared. These would be expected to be equal or nearly equal, with any difference being due to tax 'falling off the end of the analysis period'. This can be checked by reviewing the last period(s) of the model.

28.2.13 Cover factors

These should make sense, and values should appear over the proper period – for example, loan life or project life.

For NPV cover factors, ensure that values used are all calculated at the same point in time and include all the appropriate amounts. For example, for start of period cover factors, use the previous period's closing balance on loan, with NPV of available revenues to the beginning of the period, including the revenues in that period.

28.2.14 Profit and loss

In the P&L, check sub-totals and cross-check values with equivalent values in cash flow. Check totals to ensure that loan interest and fees are equal to the values used in the cash flow, less the amounts capitalised for depreciation.

28.2.15 Returns

For returns, check that figures correspond to equity values and calculated net cash flow or dividend amounts. Ensure that IRRs correspond to the indicated period – for example, ensure that a calculated IRR in a semi-annual model is properly adjusted if it is presented as an IRR per annum.

28.2.16 The net cash flow summary

This summary, if presented in accordance with the layout suggested in Section 23, provides a self-check and a check on many other items in the model. The bottom line should take negative values during the construction period, equal to equity amounts as paid into the project. Thereafter, if profit constraints are assumed to apply to dividend distribution, the net cash flow should equal distributed dividends.

28.2.17 Balance sheet

The basic check on the balance sheet is so obvious, and the reason for a very visible failure to balance can be so obscure, that hours of frustration can go into the production of this relatively unimportant report.

The first key step to achieving a balanced balance sheet is to believe that it should balance and understand why! See Section 26. As suggested in that section, the first thing to do when beginning to debug a balance sheet is to set up a row that identifies and locates in time any failure to balance – a row that gives the absolute value of any difference between total net assets and shareholders' funds, or total assets and total liabilities. A single cell in the totals column can show at a glance whether or not the balance sheet balances over the whole model life.

If the balancing check shows that there is an imbalance in the balance sheet, begin by checking the simplest possible sources of error -sub-totals and totals within the balance sheet itself. Next, check that the net cash flow itself balances (see Section 28.2.16). Assuming that this does not lead to a resolution of the problem, return to the checking row, looking across the row to see where the imbalance starts, and what value it takes. Try additional rows with half or double the values in the error row, and one with the change in the error period by period. Review of the balance sheet, cash flow and P&L may then show an item equal to the imbalance, hopefully allowing the problem to be quickly corrected. If nothing is found with a value equal to the difference, look at the period in which the problem begins. Items that first take a non-zero value in the period in which the problem arises can then be checked, and items that have a zero value beyond the period in which the problem arises can probably be ignored.

Checking through the balance sheet provides a cross-check on the relationship between cash flow and profit and loss – one of the useful results of including a balance sheet in the model. For each of the simple items that initial checks show might be contributing to the problem, verify that the figures in the balance sheet are equal to, or properly reflect, the figures elsewhere in the model, remembering that the balance sheet gives the cumulative position at the end of each period. If none of the simple values gives the solution, then begin checking back to the values that feed into the more complex figures, such as retained earnings and cash balance. In so far as these should be based on identical figures, check that the same figures are in fact being used. Where different items feed into these calculated figures, ensure that the differences are properly balanced through other items in the balance sheet. If this still fails to solve the problem, then check through the cash flow and P&L line-by-line, confirming the reflection of each value in the balance sheet. If this still does not work, check your 'check' row, then go back to the start and do it all again!

28.3 Removing unintentional circularities

Given the undesirability of including circular code in the model (see Section 7), this section assumes that no circularities will intentionally be included in the code. The problem, therefore, concerns the identification and elimination of any circularities unintentionally introduced whilst creating the model.

As code is entered and the model periodically recalculated, then circularity should be indicated automatically by the spreadsheet. If the model has been recalculated after entry of each new calculation, then it should be apparent that the circularity has arisen within a small area of recently added code. Although Excel will often give some sort of indicator to assist with the location of circularity, the rows involved in the circular code can be widely dispersed through the model, and it is very helpful to be able to locate the immediate source of the circularity in a few rows of code. It is prudent to save the model as each calculation is satisfactorily entered, and most prudent to do this under two names used alternately. If this has been done, then a version of the model prior to inclusion of the new calculation should be safely saved. Before starting work to remove a circularity, save the model (including the new code) under an alternate file name. This ensures that if ERRs are propagated through the model while trying to remove the circularity, the model can be restored to the start position, and another attempt can be made.

If the spreadsheet gives guidance as to the location of a circular calculation, then start by considering the indicated row. If the row is within the new or revised code, then start checking with that row. If the indicated row is outside the new code, it may still give a clue as to the likely source of the problem.

In the absence of a clear automatic indication from the spreadsheet as to which row is originating the problem, and given that several rows have been entered prior to discovering the circularity, the source of the problem can be identified by a process of elimination. Assuming that all rows contain a formula that is consistent across the row, each row in turn can be removed from the calculation by converting the formula in the first period to text and storing it in an unused cell, and entering '1's across the row. To convert a formula to text, simply insert an apostrophe in front of the formula. Having effectively removed one row, recalculate the model and see whether the circularity has disappeared. If it has not, then restore the formula in the first period and copy it back over the row. Repeat the process with each of the rows in question. Once the row(s) involved in the circularity has/have been identified, check the formulae to see whether any obvious typos or errors are causing the circularity. If not, then investigate the source of the circularity by entering an error message into the selected row, recalculating the model, and checking: (a) rows above the selected row; (b) periods before the column in which the error message was entered; or (c) rows referenced by the formula in the selected row, to see if any are now displaying an error message.

If the circularity remains throughout this process then check the formulae in the nominal totals column. Assuming all is well with the totals, then either more than one of the introduced or amended rows is involved in a circularity, or the circularity has actually arisen elsewhere and been overlooked. In order to discover which is the case, neutralise all the rows under consideration using the method described above, and see if the circularity disappears. If it does not, then the problem lies outside the area being considered and must be traced through the model using the circularity tracker in the formula auditing tool.

28.3.1 Tracing circularity through the model

Start by considering key calculations where logical circularities might be expected. Try temporarily removing key rows from such calculations using the method described above, and see if the circularity message disappears. If you suspect that more than one circularity may be present, then, keeping a careful note of the rows adjusted, do not restore each row after checking but continue temporarily removing rows until the spreadsheet indicates that no circularities remain. The removed rows can then be restored one at a time and the model recalculated for each row in order to see which rows cause the circularity indicator to return.

Sadly, this process will not work if the model contains a small circularity – say within one cell or row. However, in this case, the formula audit circularity tracking tool should straightforwardly identify the problem formula.

28.3.2 Checks after identifying rows involving circularity

Once a given row is identified as part of a circular calculation, then the cause of the circularity must be identified and resolved. First retrieve the version of the model saved before introduction of any error messages. The first possibility is to see whether a typo has led to one of the formulae referencing itself, or unintentionally picking up a value from a later column into which the formula itself feeds a value. If this does not appear to be the case, enter an error message into the identified row by adding it to the existing formula in one or two columns, some periods from the start of the analysis. Recalculate the model several times, then check whether any of the values feeding into the row now show an error message. Follow the calculation back in this way until the whole circle is identified.

If the circularity appears to arise from an error, or from a methodology that can easily be amended to give a linear calculation, then implement the changes necessary to make the code linear. If not, then select the best point at which to break the calculation and remove the circularity by using the recalc macro (see Section 7). Once this has been done, recalculate the model, remove the input error messages from the originally identified row, recalculate the model again, and check that all error messages have disappeared. This check can easily be done by looking at the ultimate output from the model, equity returns, nominal totals in the cash flow summary, etc. Once the identified circularity is removed, save the model, and repeat (if necessary) the process of identifying a row forming part of the next circularity. Continue repeating the process until all circularities have been removed or diverted via the recalc macro.

The process of identifying elements of the circular code can be made quicker by reviewing the nominal totals from the start of the model through the calculation sections, and finding the first appearance of an introduced error message. This can often show the row in which values are picked up and fed back into the calculation from which they arise. It can also be helpful to look for the first error messages appearing when reviewing values in relation to time – i.e., the first occurrence in a given row. This may indicate a point at which values are picked up from later periods, or may at least isolate a few rows showing the error message in an early column, before the message propagates through many calculations in later columns.

28.4 Common errors

A number of errors are so easy to make that they will appear repeatedly at the development stage of the model. Looking out for these during development means they can be eliminated at an early stage, before the model is used to provide any results.

28.4.1 Units

Check the units in which data is input and calculations are presented, and ensure that the treatment of values in the calculation sections is appropriate to their units. This includes consideration of orders of magnitude to ensure consistency – for example, power plant capacity input in MW feeding into a calculation of power output presented in GWh, then being used to calculate revenues in millions of pounds, using a tariff defined in pounds per kWh.

28.4.2 Timing

Ensure that input values are properly adjusted to reflect the timing of model periods. For example, annual interest rates used in a semi-annual model, fixed costs per annum used to calculate fixed costs in each half year, or calculated IRRs presented as annual values.

28.4.3 Wrong sign

Values should be presented in absolute terms throughout the model, with sub-totals etc., reflecting the role of a value when adding or subtracting it (see Section 2.1.6). If this recommendation is not followed, it is easy to include a value in a formula using the wrong sign. This can be checked for when values seem suspiciously large or small.

28.4.4 Periods

Ensure that formulae refer to the correct columns. In most cases this should be the same column as that in which the formula is placed. Where this is not the case (for example, picking up a closing balance from the previous period), ensure that this is properly reflected. It is easy to forget and use same-period values.

28.5 Checking the 'completed' model

The checking and correcting procedures outlined above will contribute to the production of a basically sound and correct model. No model can safely be depended upon, however, until a full check of the output has been carried out. Once this has been done, the base case, with the existing data, might be considered probably reliable. The model itself, for general use, should be further checked by documenting the formulae, as described below. In addition to providing a useful reference with regard to the model's underlying assumptions and structure, this audits each formula in the model and helps to check the functionality of the model if used with alternative data. Finally, the running of sensitivities and careful cross-checking of results against the base case and other sensitivities may throw up some further issues missed in the rest of the checking process.

28.6 The importance of checking

As explained in several sections elsewhere, it is not safe to assume that input code will automatically work as expected and required. Because the output of the model may form the basis for key decisions at all stages of the project's life, it is essential that all possible steps are taken to ensure that results produced by the model correctly reflect the assumptions upon which they claim to be based, and that such assumptions are reasonable and the best available. In order to do this, it is important to check the 'finished' version of the model before providing results, even if a process of care and checking (such as that described above) has been applied during the development of the model.

It is usually the case that tight deadlines apply to the production of results from the model at all stages of the project's development. The checking procedures must therefore be flexible enough to adapt to the availability of time. Checking cannot, however, simply be omitted as a non-essential element of the process when trying to save time. Incorrect results are not merely useless, they are dangerous, and, just as a certain minimum period of time will inevitably be required to create a model or to input changes to a model and to produce some figures, so a certain period of time is required to carry out some checking of those figures before they can be considered valid results; if this cannot be fitted within the deadline, then the required figures simply cannot be produced within the specified deadline.

Having said this, obviously the checking process must incorporate some flexibility. Once the model has been fully checked and documented then amendments can be separately checked, rather than rechecking the whole model every time a change is made. For urgently required figures, great care should be taken while inputting data or making code changes, and the figures directly output from the revised items should be carefully checked, together with a review of the main summaries to ensure that results still make sense, and that changes to the results, compared with previous values, are consistent with the amendments made. Results might then be issued with a caveat that final confirmation will be given subsequently, following more thorough and detailed checking.

28.7 Checking output

The minimum requirement for verifying that the model code is working as anticipated with a given set of data values, is to check the output results of the model's calculations. The only really thorough way to do this is to produce printout of the model and confirm all input against its source, and check each calculation with a calculator.

If checking a new model, start by producing a full printout of the data section. Check each item against its source, working with the screen to use any documentation included in the spreadsheet, and to create temporary totals of input values where this will help to check them quickly against source material. As each data item is confirmed, insert a tick against it on the printout. This ensures a thorough check is carried out, and the printout can be kept to document the checking process.

Once the data is confirmed, then a print of the worklines, masks, factors and counters section can be taken, together with the capital costs section. The worklines, etc., section need not be checked on its own account. The printout provides figures needed to check other calculation sections, and allows rows in the worklines to be verified when they are first used as part of another calculation. Once the calculation of a given row in the worklines section has been checked (and ticked on the printout), it is only necessary to confirm that it is the appropriate row for use in any other calculations in which it appears.

Each section can then be printed and checked in turn, with any errors being corrected as they are discovered. If a section is changed as the result of an error correction, then the printout should be amended either by hand, if only a few values have changed, or by reprinting the section and transferring any ticks as appropriate. The checked printout thus builds a reference source of checked values for use in the auditing of subsequent sections.

Ensure that the model has been recalculated using the recalc macro, if available, before starting the checking process and following any changes made during the checking process. This eliminates apparent errors and mismatching of funding arising because the numeric values in the recalc macro have not been updated.

Every row in the calculation section should be checked – even simple sub-totals, etc. – because the uncomplicated formulae can often be the ones that slip through the checks during development. When checking each row, verify at least two values from different stages of the project (for example, pre and post-completion, and during and after the loan repayment period). It is also often worth reviewing the nominal totals and following up any apparent anomalies that they indicate.

Check, at least briefly, through the values in the last period of the model, or the last period being analysed for the current run. Ensure that all values stop in the correct period. Consider the best treatment for items that are carried forward a period, such as receivables or tax payable, and for any outstanding balances on deposits, etc.

Once this process has been completed for all sections and for the reports, it is reasonable to say that the figures (though not necessarily the output of the model with any other data) have been checked.

As sensitivities are run, ideally the above process should be repeated for the sections that will be changed in comparison with the base case, together with a quick review on screen of other sections to ensure that they have, as expected, remained unchanged. Any apparent anomalies in relation to the base case values should be carefully checked and an explanation established or a correction made before the results are used. This is also helpful when dealing with questions from parties provided with the results, because they will probably query these same items and it is helpful to have a confident explanation prepared.

The checking of output, carried out thoroughly, can be sufficient to validate the checked results. In order to validate the model, however, so that sensitivities and changes to base case data can confidently be performed without necessarily requiring a complete check of the output for each run, the code should be further checked, as described below, but even the most careful checking of code should not be regarded as sufficient to validate results without checking output values.

28.8 Using sensitivities to check the model

Running sensitivities provides a further checking mechanism for the model. As sensitivities are produced, compare the key output with the base case and other sensitivity values, and check that the changes seem reasonable. Surprising results should be checked, and either a satisfactory explanation found or any necessary corrections made to the model.

28.9 Checking the code

As explained earlier, while results can be checked based upon the figures produced by the model, and no figures can be relied upon until such checks have been completed, the operation of the model can be depended upon with confidence only following a careful check of the code.

The code is more difficult to check than the model output, requiring careful consideration of the logic in each formula, and assessment of its operation under all the circumstances that the model might reasonably be required to address.

Adherence to the principle of using a single consistent formula across each row means that there is only one formula to check per row. Even so, this is a time-consuming process. Kept to a minimum, and used in association with output checks, such checking can be restricted to the more complex formulae and those that incorporate switches or operate differently under different assumptions. If time permits, however, a complete review of the code in the model can be carried out, and this is most usefully and efficiently done as part of a process of documenting the model, as described in the next section.

When checking a particularly complex formula, it may be useful to make temporary changes to data in order to confirm the operation of the code. Alternatively, to verify different elements of a formula – perhaps options comprising part of an 'IF' function – the formula in one period can be changed by, for example, erasing part of the formula to cause one element to operate on its own. When the check has been completed, the original formula can be restored by copying from other periods in the row.

28.10 Documenting the code

Whenever time permits, the preparation of full documentation for the model, giving a detailed item-by-item account of the assumptions and calculations included, both provides a useful supporting document for the model and gives structure to a complete check of the model code.

If at all possible, full documentation should be prepared at least for the early model and for the 'final' version of the model upon which the raising of funding or preparation of the final bid will be based. The ideal in the absence of time constraints would be that documentation should be prepared and should be updated following any changes to the code, prior to the issue of results based upon the revised model incorporating such changes.

Time may not, however, always be available for preparation of full documentation at any stage. It is essential though, that a basic list of the data and assumptions used in the model be prepared and supplied to those making decisions based upon the model's results. Much of this can be provided from a full printout of a properly constructed data section. This should be supplemented by a list of the main calculation assumptions not specified in the data but reflected directly in the code.

To prepare full documentation, row-by-row consideration of the model is the most appropriate approach. For some worklines it may be best to actually document the formulae when working through the formulae that make use of them. This is because the purpose of a particular workline may be obscure until it is reviewed in the context of the calculation to which it contributes. Otherwise, the safest approach is to start at row one of the first page and work methodically through to the last row of the model.

In order to allow calculations to be described and explained with reasonable succinctness, it is useful to include row headers as definitive titles in the documentation, which can then be used in the descriptions of later calculations. For each data item or formula, a brief explanation can be given of the source, basis, nature or purpose of the item if this is not apparent from a straightforward description of the value or calculation. For each formula, a full description of the calculation should be given, referencing other rows by their row headings, allowing the detailed calculations to be reviewed and checked via the documentation.

28.11 Shadow models

A relatively recent development in model auditing is the use of a 'shadow model'. This comprises construction of a simple model reproducing the functionality of the model being audited, and allowing validation of various cases by comparison of the outputs from the two models. Shadow modelling is particularly appropriate for checking complex PFI models, where a large part of the model code is devoted to generating values which are then fixed as part of the bid. The shadow model can omit all the calculations required to generate the relevant debt, revenue, or subsidy figures, and can instead simply process the bid figures to ensure that consistent results are generated for net cash flows, cover factors, IRRs, etc.I believe this technique, and versions of it, has much to offer the model checking and auditing process.

29 Presentation

The purpose of the model is to produce results that can be used to make or confirm decisions about the financing of a given project. The clear presentation of results, and the correct identification of the assumptions upon which they are based, is thus a key part of the function of any model.

It is useful to have a single page summary which captures key information for each case, it is also necessary, however, to be able to produce a full printout of data and calculation sections for detailed checking and auditing, and a full set of reports sheets to present the model results in detail.

To produce printed figures readable without a microscope, calculations and reports across the timeline will need to be printed across more than one page. To make multi-page printouts readable without intrusive and inflexible repetition of the timeline or row headings within the sheet, the title plus timeline and the row headings can be fixed as print titles via the 'Page' 'Set-up' 'Sheet' menu. This will ensure that row headings and timeline information will appear in relation to the appropriate figures for all pages of a given printout.

Exhibit 29.1

Using the 'Page Setup, Sheet' options in Excel

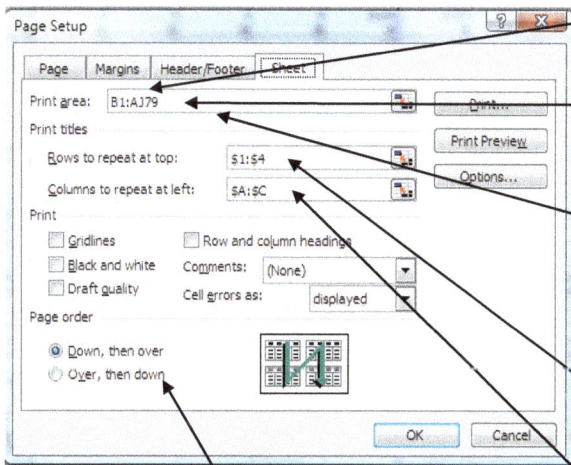

Default print area includes all rows and columns on the sheet with non-empty cells

The total print area and the position of page breaks can be adjusted via the 'Page break preview' view

Complex print areas can be defined by specifying a series of ranges, separated by commas, eg.

A1:V60,A63:P85,A86:V194

Rows repeated as a header at the top of every printed page

Columns repeated on the left of every printed page

For print ranges spanning multiple pages, determines whether to print first rows across the timeline, then next set of rows ie. 'Over then down' or to print first part of timeline for all rows, then next part of timeline and so on, ie. 'Down then over'

The compression used for printing can be set as a specific percentage, or using the 'Fit to...' option, which can specify a given number of pages wide or high. To set just one of these parameters and have the other automatically adjusted, simply leave one of the input boxes empty.

Exhibit 29.2

Using the 'Page Setup, Page' options in Excel

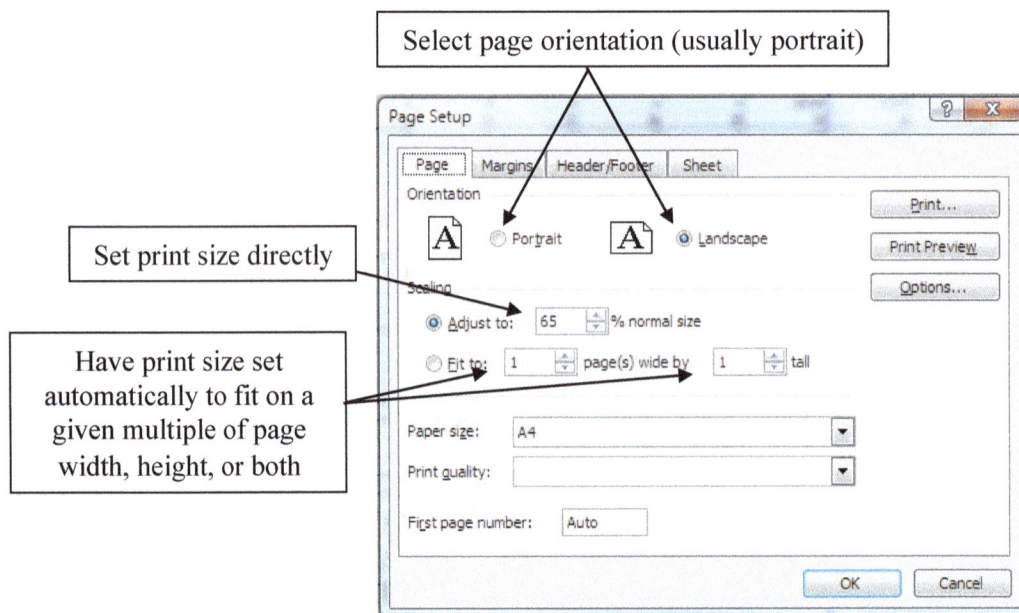

It is usually a good idea to incorporate headers and footers to set a title printed at the top and/or bottom of each page. These can include page numbers, the name of the sheet or file being printed, the date of printing, and other optional text (see Exhibit 29.3).

To save time when producing printout, it may be appropriate to set up some automation of the print process using macros. This can be done most simply by ensuring that each model sheet has appropriate print settings specified, then recording a macro (see Section 6.5.1) which simply selects 'File', 'Print'.

An 'index' page can be included in the model which lists the sheets in the model, perhaps with a brief explanatory note, and offers two buttons for each sheet, one to go to the sheet, and one to print it. The print macros can then include the 'goto' macro and a final instruction which returns the user to the 'Index' page after printing (see Exhibit 29.4). Printing multiple sheets, for example, all 'report' sheets or all 'calculation' sheets can be provided via a simple second stage macro, which records activation of the relevant individual macros in a suitable order.

Remember to recalculate the model before printing. It is disappointing to produce volumes of printout, only to discover that the numbers printed are not those of the run required, and if such an error is not noticed the printed figures may mislead those making critical decisions about the deal.

Exhibit 29.3

Using the 'Page Setup, Header/footer' options in Excel

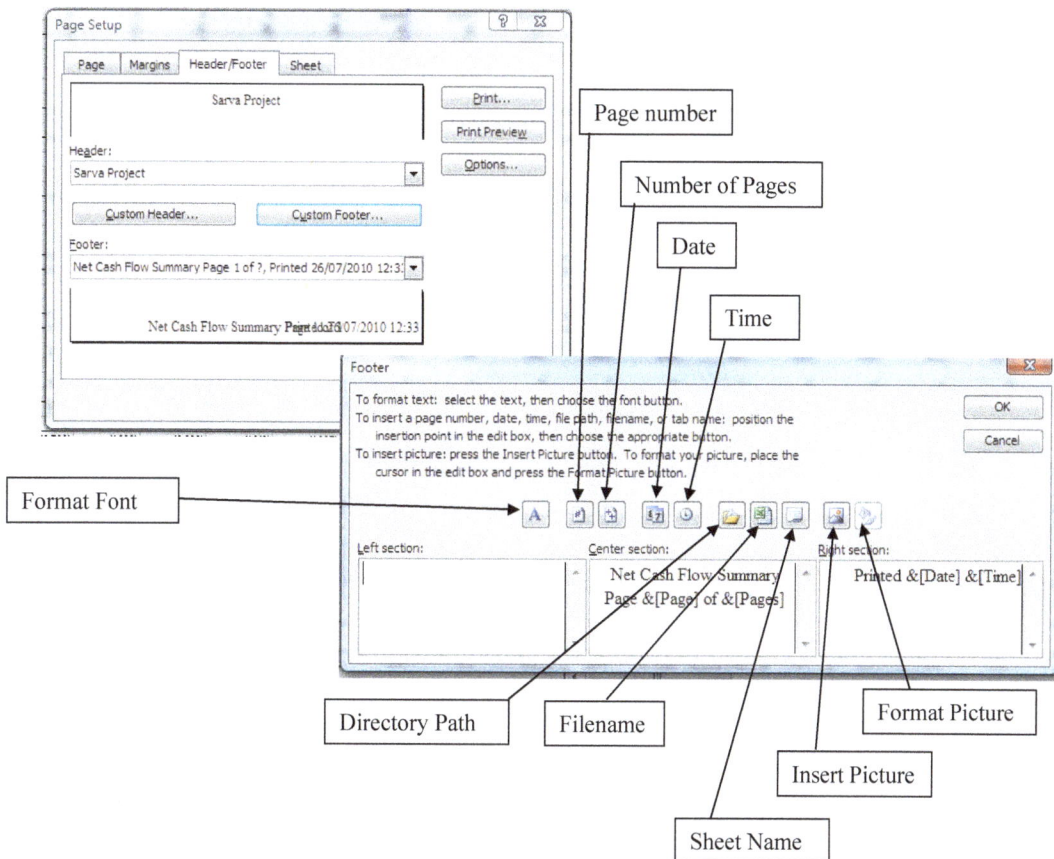

29.1 The use of graphics

Graphs have instant impact, and can sometimes impress those with limited understanding of the model to a disproportionate degree! Ideally, graphs should be used when information can be conveyed more clearly using a visual image than if presented in numeric form. Sadly, graphs are often included for the sake of appearances rather than clarity, leaving the modeller with the task of finding something that can be attractively, if not usefully, converted into a graphic format.

A number of graphs can, however, be usefully incorporated into the key input and results summary, including graphs of cover factors and cash flow breakdown.

The basic rules applying to graphs in spreadsheets are mainly those applicable to graphs in general. A graph without titles is useless. It must be clear what is being graphed, in what units and over what period.

It is often the case that figures for use in graphs require some manipulation (for example, changing semi-annual to annual values). It is also useful to group together on the spreadsheet the values to be used in a given graph, because this can simplify the setting of ranges for the graph. The lines used to

Exhibit 29.4

Illustrative 'Index' sheet and macros

	A	B	C	D	E
1	**Super-duper Project**				
2					
3	See notes on running model	See Notes			
4					
5	Sheet	Go to this sheet	Print this Sheet	Notes on model sheets	
6					
7	**Data**				
8	Inputs			Contains all input values for the model	
9					
10	**Results**				
11	Summary			One page summary of key results	
12	NCF			Net Cash Flow Summary	
13					
14	**Calculations**				
15	Capex			Capital cost calculation sheet	
16	Fin			Funding Calculations - Equity and debt	
17	Ops			Operating costs and revenue calculations	
18	Tax			Tax calculations	
19	P&L			Profit and loss calculations	
20	Deposit			Cash deposit calculations - DSRA, MRA and cash at bank	
21	Cover			Cover Factor Calculations	
22	IRR			Equity Return Calculations	
23					
24	**Support sheets**				
25	Cascade			Calculates cash available for debt service, deposits, dividends etc.	
26	Work			Various background calculations, inflation factors, etc.	
27	MacroSupport			Values in circular calculations converted to numbers by re-calc macro	
28					
29					
30					
31					
32					
33	Notes on use of the model.				
34					
35	Excel Settings required to run the model				
36	Calculation should be set to 'manual'.				
37	The add-in 'Analysis ToolPak' should be activated				
38	Macros should be enabled.				
39					
40	Re-calculation after changes				
	In order to avoid circular code, the model uses a simple copy and paste macro to solve for				
	some figures. This macro should therefore be used instead of 'F9' to recalculate the model				

▶| \ Index /

continued

prepare the graph numbers can be included in the worklines, masks, factors and counters section, but if the graph figures are not matched to the model timeline this must be made very clear, ideally with a border around the aberrant rows, and a distinctive font. Ideally, such values should also be placed at the bottom of the sheet.

The basic process for adding a graph to a model starts with the Chart wizard or the 'Insert' 'Chart' menu. Next select a chart type, for example, line, bar, pie, etc., then a specific sub-type from that general category.

The next option is whether to enter the graph data as a 'data range', or as data series. Specifying data as a data range simplifies the allocation of multiple data series to the graph, provided the relevant data has been gathered in a contiguous block in the model, with the series titles in the cells next to the first cell of the range to be graphed. The data range includes the titles as well as the figures. Specifying data series allows easy inclusion of items physically separated in the model. For Excel 2003, the selection is made by choosing between two dialog boxes, one for specifying a data range, one for inputting data series. In Excel 2007 both methods are accessed from a single panel.

For individual data series the values to be graphed and the title for them are entered separately. In Excel 2007 the labelling for the option allowing input of a new data series is rather obscure. Using the 'Add' button under the text 'Legend Entries (series)' produces a suitable input format for specification of a new series.

Once the basic chart has been created, changes can be made by selecting the chart and then using the options displayed under the 'Chart' menu item (2003), or 'design' 'Layout' and 'Format' ribbon items (2007), which will appear whenever a chart is selected. 'Change chart type' can be used to change the type of the whole chart, or can be selected after clicking on a particular data series on the chart to change the type for just that data series, for example, to display one item as a line on a bar chart (see Exhibit 29.5).

Selecting a data series on the chart, then right-clicking, will access menu options for formatting and chart type options which will be applied only to that data series. Having selected a data series, clicking on a single point in the series to select it, then right clicking on the same point, will offer similar menu options, but will allow formatting of the individual point rather than the whole series. Although rather inflexible, this does allow quite tight customisation of the appearance of a graph around a given set of results, which may be appropriate for generating final graphics for inclusion in documentation.

The horizontal scale

The horizontal 'x' scale can be defined using values in a row of the spreadsheet. Labels can be set to appear only at yearly intervals for semi-annual figures. This is only appropriate for values such as flow

Exhibit 29.5

Illustrative bar chart with one data series graphed as a line

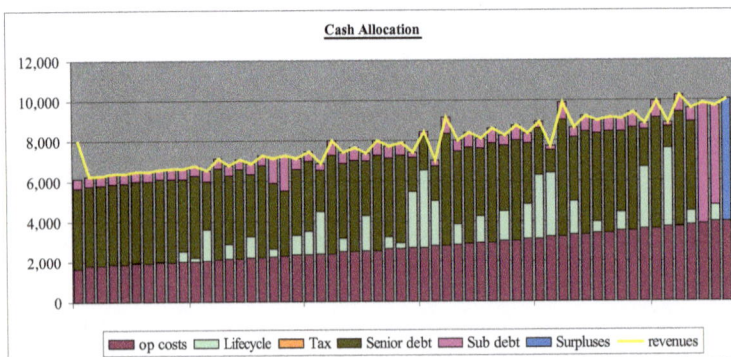

rates or prices per unit of production, not for simple monetary values, such as revenues or costs, which must be totalled to give proper annual values. If trying to include labels intermittently, effort can be saved by using a formula that takes a value equal to an empty string in the unlabelled periods, rather than entering separate values in each cell where a label is required.

The vertical scale

The vertical scale will usually be calculated automatically. It is important to remember, however, that if several graphs are to be used to allow comparison of several sets of values, it is helpful for a consistent 'y' scale to be used. This can be achieved by manually fixing the maximum and/or minimum values for the 'y' scale (see Exhibit 29.6).

The options for formatting either axis are accessed by double clicking the relevant axis on the graph.

Titles, labels and notes

Provision is made for various titles to be included in a graph. If these do not meet requirements, various techniques can be used to add information in other formats and positions in the graph.

The font formatting for the built-in graph titles can be amended by double-clicking the titles on the graph. Text for titles can also be changed directly in this way, although changes can sometimes be lost in subsequent updates if not made via the Chart Options menu.

Although graphs can be presented very stylishly on the screen using coloured lines and bars, it is important to remember that the model may need to be printed in black and white, and may need to be photocopied. Where this is the case, symbols and hatchings should be used to ensure that the graphs retain their clarity and legibility in such circumstances.

Exhibit 29.6

y-axis formatting

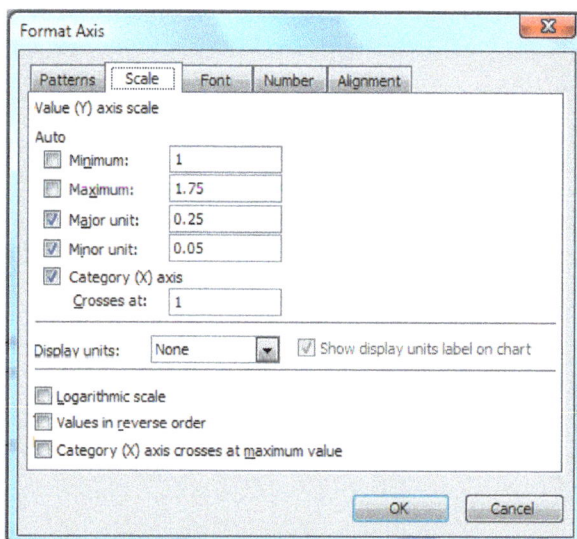

30 Model review and audit

30.1 Reviewing someone else's model

When reviewing a third-party model (either an old model, a model prepared by someone else in-house, or a model produced by a different organisation), it is necessary first to gain an understanding of the assumptions and methodology of the model. It may also be necessary to cross-check the spreadsheet against a checklist of data and assumptions.

When first presented with a model, after reading any information provided with it, spend some time looking at the model on screen in order to locate various key calculations and results sections. If the model has been prepared with a modular, logical layout, this should be an easy process. If the model has been prepared on a generally haphazard basis, it may be a time-consuming, frustrating and unrewarding (but none the less essential) process.

After an initial viewing, produce a comprehensive printout of the model and, thus prepared, begin to trace calculations through the model, making notes, in order to identify the calculations and data used to arrive at a given result. In order to do this efficiently, it is recommended that you begin with an important result (for example, equity IRR) and methodically trace **back** through the model, checking all calculations that ultimately feed into the result. Checking backwards from the result in this way minimises the work required in order to assess the validity of the key figure. If the result used is selected with care, most key calculations will have to be checked as part of the process of validating the result, and other results will become easier and easier to check.

This process avoids trying to understand and check every row of the model, which may be inefficient and difficult for a number of reasons. It is much easier to assess the validity of a calculation when its ultimate use is known. It is a waste of time to check redundant code, or code used to develop special analyses that are of no present interest.

If using recent versions of Excel, the audit tool is an invaluable aid in this process and should be used to the full. Beware, however, some functions, specifically certain uses of the Offset function, will not show any dependency on cells which they do in fact refer to.

It is essential to make methodical notes when undertaking this process so that you can follow your path back through the code and ensure that all calculations leading into a given formula have been checked in turn. Information acquired while checking can easily be forgotten if not noted down, and may result in calculations being checked several times if they feed into the result by several routes.

This process should ultimately provide a clear understanding of the calculation from the inputs through to the results for all the figures of interest.

31 Using models written elsewhere

31.1 Working with a third-party model

If some manipulation of an unfamiliar model is required (rather than simply a review as discussed in the previous section), then some techniques can be used to help when working with models which fall short of the ideal in terms of structure, methodology or quality. It is important to bear in mind that the process of becoming sufficiently familiar with an existing model is time-consuming. It can only lead to error or disappointment if a reasonable period of time is not explicitly allocated for this process before expecting to use the model to produce valid results.

31.2 Additions and enhancements

If the model falls significantly short of the desired structure and range of output or input values, it is possible to make 'quick and dirty' additions that will allow the model to be used for a number of runs without needing to make significant changes within the calculation sections of the existing model.

If the model either does not include a cash flow summary, or uses a format for the cash flow that is incorrect, inappropriate or unsuitable as a basis for the results required, then, rather than trying to restructure the given cash flow, simply add a new cash flow summary in the required format. The added summary can pick up values from the existing elements of the model and arrange them in the required format, allowing further results to be calculated based on the extracted values. This has the added advantage that unforeseen consequences will not arise from reorganisation of elements of the original model. Each item picked up in the new summary can be checked on the basis described earlier, if not already checked during the initial review process.

One problem with model structure that creates a great deal of work when trying to produce reasonable values, is a model structure that splits calculations between construction and operating periods, with each calculated on a different timeline – for example, monthly columns for the construction period and semi-annual columns during the operating period, with no incorporation of the construction period values into the semi-annual calculations. Obviously this prevents review of the whole project via the cash flow summary, and does not accommodate calculation of equity returns etc. In order to use such a model it is worth investing some time in transferring the results of the construction period calculations into the same timescale as the operating period values, allowing them to be easily incorporated into added cash flow and other reports. When doing this, care must be taken to ensure that the total values for a given period of time are not changed, most particularly an issue at the point where the construction period overlaps the first period of the operating section.

Note that all these adjustments assume that values from the original model are simply picked up in the new sections using an appropriate formula, and that no change is made to the original cells (other than where the review process indicates an actual error that you wish to correct).

31.3 Long-term use

The suggestions above are intended to help with a process of making a third-party model useable for the production of a number of specific runs or results. If a model is to be used in the longer term, to be developed as the deal progresses, then more concentration will be needed on becoming familiar with its detailed structure and operation. If the model is very unsuitable, then it might be better to start again from scratch, developing a model on a layout with which you are comfortable. Questions to ask when assessing this possibility might include the following.

- Is the model trivially simple?
- Is the model impenetrably complex?
- Does the model work in a robust and predictable way, or can it easily be made to do so?

If the answers to the above questions, or alternative evaluation thresholds, suggest that it would be better to replace the model rather than try to work with it, bear in mind when cross-checking the new model against the displaced version that **the model often becomes a library of obscure project information**. Be very certain that apparent anomalies in the old model really are errors, and not poorly documented representations of very specific project terms.

31.4 Procedure

The first step when preparing to work with a strange model is to follow the review procedure described earlier, checking all the results that you want to use in your own operation of the model, in so far as these exist in the model.

Once a basic understanding of the workings of the model, and of the effect of existing data items on the required output, has been acquired, steps can be taken as necessary to make the model more useable, including the removal of any built-in circular code (see Section 28.3.1), and new runs can be performed as required. Given the common requirement for some circular calculations, it will probably be necessary to add a recalc macro to the model if one has not been included already (see Section 7.4.2). Once a circular path is identified in the code, if possible correct the code to eliminate the circularity, or break the circle using the recalc macro.

To the extent that key information is unavailable or inaccessible, add new sheets to provide output in the format required. For example, if a suitable Net Cash Flow Summary is not included in the model, add one, in the same layout and format you would use in a model prepared from scratch, and use it to present the relevant figures from the original model sheets.

Ensure that the construction and operating periods tie together, making revisions as necessary to achieve this. Use masks and the SUMIF(...) or INDEX(...) functions if timing formats need to be re-organised.

When the model has all the required calculations and presentation sheets, spend some time carefully removing replaced or redundant code. To identify redundant code, use the formula audit tool. However, remember that this is not wholly foolproof. When removing calculations therefore, save a copy of the file before removing the material, and remove cells by deleting the rows containing the unwanted material, rather than simply deleting cell contents. This should then generate error messages when the model is recalculated after making the removal, alerting you to the non-redundant nature of the items removed.

If significant changes are to be made to a section of the calculation as part of the process of using the model (for example, the inclusion of an alternative finance structure) then, again, this is probably best accomplished by adding a new finance section, picking up values from the original model as required, and processing them according to the new assumptions. It is then necessary to carefully follow through the calculations feeding into the results and reports you wish to use, and ensure that all references to the original finance section are replaced by references to the new section.

32 Examples and exercises (See www.projfinmod.co.uk for files)

32.1 Introduction

This section provides sample data and assumptions, along with suggested layouts for models derived from them. It is intended to give an idea of some of the possible formats in which data may be received, as well as providing example layouts for models at various development stages.

The imaginary water project used as the main example has quite a complex structure, allowing a number of techniques to be illustrated based around one deal. It also allows exploration of the issues involved in analysing complex structures at the feasibility stage, where data is incomplete and time limited, requiring the model to be kept as simple as possible. **It should be noted that the water project is intended to illustrate principles, concepts and structures rather than to provide realistic data or assump-tions for an actual project of this sort**.

A number of files have been prepared to provide a framework for preparation for the exercises, illustrative solutions to the exercises, and further illustrations of specific modelling issues. These should be provided at the time of purchase, but in case of difficulty contact Euromoney publications, or contact the author via her website.

Filename	Description
SarvaCapex00543A.xls	Annual capital cost data
SarvaCapex00543Aadj.xls	Annual capital cost data adjusted for inclusion in the model
Sarvafeasblank.xls	Empty skeleton for Sarva project model
Sarvadataoutline01.xls	Solution for Excercise 2a
SarvaFeasEx2bSol.xls	Solution for Exercise 2b
Sarvacapex00638U.xls	Monthly capital cost data
Sarvacapex00638Uadj.xls	Monthly capital cost data adjusted for inclusion in the model
SarvaFeasEx3Sol.xls	Solution for Exercise 3a
MinimaxExample.xls	Illustrative calculation of minimum offtake level
SubsidyExample.xls	Illustrative calculation of subsidy

32.2 Feasibility model

This section examines the preparation of a feasibility model for the Sarva water project. It provides examples of initial information, and follows the process of developing this into a model, including the accumulation of the minimum set of data and assumptions required to produce a model.

Rather than providing a simple set of information upon which to base the example model, an attempt has been made to provide information in the confused and incomplete form that might realistically be available for first analysis of a new project. The process of extracting key data from the initial information, and of acquiring further information, thus forms part of the exercise. This process is seen as an essential aspect of the modelling procedure. The outcome of this part of the exercise – a full set of data for the feasibility model – is however provided as a sample solution, SarvaFeasEx2bSol. xls, and to allow the subsequent exercises to be attempted without having to complete the first stage.

32.2.1 Initial information

The following 'Meeting notes' are intended to represent the initial information available for a proposed water treatment plant in a small Mediterranean country with a sound economy and access to hard currency through its thriving tourist industry.

A new treatment plant is required for a rapidly expanding resort town, and the local state authority (AGS), has issued an invitation to bid (ITB) for the construction and operation of the plant. Together with the ITB, AGS have provided a copy of a feasibility study prepared four years ago by B&G, a well-known firm of consultants. The model is to be prepared for a water company, Speculative Projects International Limited (SPIL), interested in bidding for the project. They would expect to take a majority share in the project's equity, and to act as operator of the completed plant through their subsidiary, Secured Project Operations International Limited (SPOIL). Their local representative, Jeff Higgs, has compiled some information in addition to that provided by AGS, and is still working to collect data.

The deadline for submission of bids is quite short, and SPIL feel that they need to make a decision in the next 10 days as to whether they should commit the resources required to pursue this opportunity and prepare a bid. It is therefore necessary to produce a model as soon as possible that will give some preliminary information on the basic economics of the deal. A meeting takes place to discuss the available information, and the required output from the model. Present at the meeting were:

- Jeff Higgs, SPIL's in-country representative;
- Angie Sparc, from the Engineering Department;
- Mark Brigbane, from SPOIL;
- Jeremy Bond, head of the finance team and overall project team leader; and
- the modeller.

At the end of the meeting, the following notes represent the information assembled by the modeller as a basis for the production of the feasibility model.

Notes of a Preliminary Meeting on the Sarva Project

Project location
Sarva, a coastal town in Sunronia.

Project
Construction and operation of a water treatment works for the town of Sarva and certain surrounding villages. The plant will treat waste water and produce irrigation and/or potable water and dried slurry that can be sold for local agricultural use.

Basis for bid
The ITB specifies a maximum price per cubic metre of waste water treated (with specified minimum quality requirements for treated water and solids). The price assumes a specified maximum level of contamination of the waste water – the tariff contamination level (TCL) – but the plant must be capable of dealing with an unspecified higher level of contamination. The bid is to comprise a specified plant capacity with a full technical specification and precise description of the areas to be served by the plant, the required tariff for treatment of waste water within the TCL, and

---

continued

any adjustment required to the tariff for treatment of waste water with contamination above this level, together with the maximum level of contamination that can properly be dealt with by the plant.

The bid is to cover construction of the plant plus operation over 30 years from final completion, and is to include the pipeline network as well as the plant itself.

Revenue

Payment for water treatment will be made directly by AGS at the agreed tariff levels. Sale of products will be as arranged or assumed by the bidder, and is expected to impact the bid only by the indirect effect which any assumed revenues generated from sales will have on the possible level of treatment tariff that can be offered. Jeff Higgs is preparing some information as to possible levels of demand and price for products.

Treatment volumes

The projected volumes of waste water, and even the present volumes, are not guaranteed by AGS, but estimated values are given for the past two years. Accurate figures are not available because no co-ordinated system of waste water collection currently exists. Many homes have septic tanks that residents pay to have emptied by private companies, which are under no obligation to provide statistics to AGS. In the old town, some waste is still emptied into open drains venting directly into the sea, while in the outlying villages waste is often simply applied directly to fields and gardens. Some extrapolation can be made from the volumes of clean water supplied, but many homes are not connected to the mains supply and such homes may still contribute significant quantities of waste water from private supplies taken directly from local rivers or wells. It is intended eventually to compulsorily extend mains water supply to all users but, at present, proper treatment of waste is seen as a priority, partly because of the threat to the town's tourist industry from the increasing pollution of the streets, sea and beaches.

Figures are given in the B&G study for assumed waste volumes for the five years prior to preparation of the study, together with projected volumes based upon population growth figures prepared as part of a national study by the Sunronia government. Unfortunately, the figures that B&G projected for the past two years differ significantly from the estimated actual figures provided by AGS.

AGS are able to provide historic population data which is believed to be fairly accurate, together with their assumptions regarding population growth over the next 30 years. Jeff Higgs is trying to find out the assumptions upon which their projected growth assumptions are based, but it is not clear if this information will be made available. SPIL also has access to a World Bank survey, prepared two years ago, which gives population growth projections for the region. This will not reflect specific issues relating to Sarva, but does include estimates regarding the movement of population from rural to urban areas.

If it is decided to proceed with the project, then consultants will be used to prepare waste water volume projections: meanwhile, some sensible combination or selection of these data sets must be agreed in order to prepare the feasibility model.

In addition to projecting the total volumes to be treated, the model needs to be able to distinguish between various regions within the area to be covered by the plant, because the costs per treated cubic metre associated with connecting the outlying villages will be significantly different to those for the town itself, and it may be necessary to examine the project assuming that coverage of the villages is omitted or delayed. Because the treatment of waste in the villages has little immediate effect upon tourism, such modification of the scheme may be politically acceptable if it offers a sufficient tariff reduction or improvement to the service available in more critical areas.

Construction

Angie Sparc has prepared some very basic construction cost figures. She is waiting for figures from various sources before being able to provide a more sophisticated analysis. She would like to know what breakdown and format of the construction costs data would be best for the model. The current data is:

continued

	Full scheme (£m)	Town only scheme (£m)
Network	240	130
Civils	85	85
Plant and machinery	150	120
Total costs	**475**	**335**

The construction period will be approximately 5 years for the full scheme and 3.5 for the town only scheme.

Operation

The plant will be operational after 5 years for the full scheme, and after 3.5 years for the town only scheme.

Operating costs for a plant with the proposed capacity have been estimated by Mark Brigbane at £5 million per annum. These costs can be refined, but require more detailed information as to the plant size and type, and the anticipated volumes to be treated.

Finance

For this initial analysis, the model should assume that there will be two senior loans – an ECGD export credit loan and a commercial loan. Equity will comprise 20% of total funding and be composed of a mix of pure equity and sub debt in the ratio 10:90. Pure equity will be paid in first, then sub debt will be drawn, as needed, prior to drawing the senior commercial loan.

Assume that a six-month debt service reserve will be required.

Tax

Jeff Higgs has general information regarding the country's tax regulations, but it is believed that the provisions of a special Enterprise Support Scheme (ESS) may apply to the project.

Details of the ESS are rather obscure, but are thought to include a total tax holiday for the first five years of operations. There is also believed to be provision for a 5% cap on the employer's portion of state income tax for employees, and double capital allowances.

A withholding tax applies, equal to 10% of dividends paid to foreign lenders and investors.

No information is available yet about the actual timing of tax payments.

Accounts

Detailed information is not yet available. The working assumption is that profit constraints on dividends will apply. For the present, assume straight line depreciation over 10 years. It would be helpful to know if this assumption has a material effect on returns.

There is a reserve requirement, thought to be 10% of cumulative net profits, up to a maximum of 20% of invested capital.

Extract from the ITS

Definitions
Plant Owner Operator Company – POOC

2.4 Plant Capacity
2.4.1 The plant is required to treat Waste Water as described in 1.8.5. The bid must indicate the plant capacity for treatment of Waste Water in cuM/sec.

2.4.2 The bidder is also required to indicate the maximum possible contamination level for Waste Water that can be handled by the plant without failing to meet Minimum Quality standards (3.4.2).

continued

> **5.5 Tariff**
>
> 5.5.1 ACS will pay to the POOC a tariff per cuM Treated Waste Water, not to exceed $a25.32, provided that Minimum Quality standards (specified in 3.4.2) are met.
>
> 5.5.2 If Minimum Quality standards fail to be met at the weekly check (see 7.4), then payment will be suspended until such time as quality is restored to the Minimum Quality standard or better.
>
> 5.5.3 If the biological oxygen demand (BOD) of the Waste Water exceeds 180mg/l, then a higher tariff may be requested.
>
> If it is proposed that the POOC will require a higher payment in such circumstances, then the bid must include full details as to the calculation or amount of such tariff.

32.2.2 Exercise 1

> Based on the information in the 'Meeting notes', prepare a list of the data you need, and might realistically expect, in order to produce a working feasibility model. Prepare the list(s) in a form suitable for use to directly request data from the appropriate parties.
>
> You may find it useful to begin constructing the model in order to clarify your thoughts on the items needed and the best format in which to receive them.
>
> See Section 27.1 for information on getting started, and Section 12 for information on the format of received data.

32.2.3 Notes on Exercise 1

There are significant gaps in the information set out in the 'Meeting notes', which is intended to reflect the confusion common at this early stage in a deal. Some gaps will only be filled correctly after a considerable investment of time and resources. Workable approximations must be found for such values, and answers provided using more accessible data, in order for a feasibility model to be prepared that will give figures upon which any decision can reasonably be based. In order to begin the process of assembling a useable set of data and constructing a basic model, therefore, some essential information must be obtained, and estimates or guesses produced for some other items.

As a starting point, having reviewed the available information, it may be helpful to consider the data by category, ideally in association with the construction of a data section for the model. Putting the model together can highlight gaps in the information that might otherwise be missed. To prepare a data section, some decisions have to be made about the model in order to set up the worksheet.

- What period must the model cover?
- In what currency should the model be presented?
- What timeline should be used?

Capital costs and financing

For the capital costs, indicative total costs have been provided, with some indication as to the total construction period. An initial estimate of timing of expenditure can thus be made assuming steady expenditure over the construction period, but proper timings should be requested as timing can have a significant impact on interest costs, etc. Looking at the capital cost estimates provides a reminder that two possible approaches to the project may need to be considered: in view of the tight timetable, it is probably worth seeking confirmation that the alternative 'town only' case is required at this stage.

No indication is given as to whether the costs shown include any inflation, whether they should be further inflated, and if so at what rate, or whether they should be treated as fixed price contracts. It is important that this information be available, and it should be requested when advising the required format for future construction cost data. Given the proposed finance structure, it will also be necessary somehow to divide the capital costs between costs incurred in Sunronia and payments made to sources outside Sunronia, denominated in other currencies.

The basic finance structure has been specified, but many details will be required to model the two loans. A list of required data items must therefore be compiled for each loan, and the list in Section 15.3.1 can be used to assist with this. In addition to the loans and specific fees relating to the loans, there may be fees associated with the equity, as well as legal fees incurred in arranging the finance and developing the project documentation.

Operating data

The operating section is probably the most confused at present. It may be helpful to start thinking very carefully about the cost and revenue items that the model will be calculating, and the data needed to specify them.

There will be revenues for treatment of water and for the sale of by-products, irrigation water, potable water and dried sludge. There will presumably be fixed costs, incurred irrespective of the actual utilisation of the plant, variable costs associated with the treatment of waste water, variable costs associated with the drying of sludge, and variable costs associated with the production of potable water from ordinary treated water. Values will be needed for each of these, together with the basis for their calculation.

The operating cost estimate provided is given on a per annum basis assuming a certain set of operating parameters. This is of limited use because a key function of the model is to allow different scenarios and sensitivities to be assessed, and this requires costs to vary appropriately with other assumptions (for example, volumes of treated water). Details must therefore be sought as to the type and calculation of costs, as well as appropriate values, in suitable units, for fixed and variable costs.

The revenue calculation will differ according to whether the waste water exceeds the maximum biological oxygen demand (BOD) level specified for payment of the normal tariff. Because the tariff is specified for any level of contamination up to the TCL, it would seem sensible to make a conservative assumption that all waste water not exceeding the TCL will actually be at the TCL, and costs and capacity figures can be input and calculated on this basis. This assumption can be checked with the team. If this is not considered a valid assumption, then it should be possible to work with an assumption of average contamination levels, which should still allow a single, consistent set of data to be input for all flows not exceeding the TCL. Is the consideration of costs and revenues in relation to higher contamination levels required for this preliminary assessment? If required, what would be the best way to deal with this in the model? Can all cost and capacity variables be driven from a single input value, say average BOD or BOD as a percentage of the specified maximum BOD for basic tariff? If not, then can data be provided in 'sets' for a range of values to be analysed? Remember to try and minimise the model's complexity. If the team are, for example, looking at a combination of different BODs at different times of day or over a year, consider carefully whether it is necessary to include more than an average BOD value for flows charged at the basic tariff and for flows at higher contamination levels.

The amount of waste water treated by the plant would appear to depend upon two things – the waste water produced by the population and the capacity of the plant and network. Because both of these may need to be varied as part of the analysis process, it is probably worth specifying these two constraints separately.

The population data used for the waste water estimates seem very confused. Because population dynamics and per capita waste water assumptions are probably not within the modeller's area of expertise, it may be preferable to request data in the form of projected waste water flows. Given the uncertainties, however, there may well be a requirement to look at several population assumptions with several per capita waste water production assumptions, and this will be easier to do if these can be varied independently within the model, rather than having to input a full set of waste water figures for each combination. The assumptions used, however, should still be requested in a form suitable for use in the model. The model can easily include a selection of several sets of population data, and it would probably be helpful to make this clear when requesting the data.

Ascertaining the proposed capacity of the plant should be fairly straightforward, but the capacity of the whole system may build up over time as the network is completed. Plant and network capacity should therefore probably both be input. Alternatively, plant and network capacity could be combined into a 'system capacity' value for input into the model. This would not simplify the model significantly, however, and would require new figures to be input for every combination of plant and network capacity considered. It may therefore be preferable to specify these two items separately in the model.

The wording of the ITB suggests that plant capacity may vary according to the contamination level of the waste water. This should be checked with the engineering or operations members of the team.

Economic data

This area should be fairly simple at this stage. A general inflation assumption will be needed for each currency. There does not appear to be any currency protection provided through the proposed tariff arrangements, so currency devaluation may be important to the deal. It is worth checking whether this is the case or whether currency exposures can be hedged in some way, but the model will probably need to allow real currency appreciation or depreciation to be assessed.

Tax and accounting

These seem to be another area of confusion at present. An assumption as to applicable tax rates has been provided. Because they all appear to be chargeable on the net profits, the three types of tax indicated can probably be totalled and used in a single calculation.

The ESS may obviously have a significant impact on the project cash flows, and the model should probably allow it to be taken into account, even at this early stage. A data switch could be used to determine whether or not the ESS provisions are applied or not for each run, allowing its importance to the deal to be assessed. Of the information given, the tax holiday and double capital allowances would seem to be significant concessions. The cap on employer's state income tax payments for employees is probably not significant, particularly given the tentative nature of current data (including staff costs) and the absence of the other basic information needed to calculate the effect of this concession. This item will therefore be ignored by the model for the present.

Some further basic assumptions are needed to produce a tax calculation, including the assumed timing of payments in relation to the profits on which tax calculations are based. It may take some time to establish proper assumptions for all elements of the tax calculation, and it is probably best, therefore, to model tax at this stage using simple assumptions, ensuring that their arbitrary nature is made clear to those involved with, and using the model.

Advice is needed as to the methodology for calculation of capital allowances and the breakdown of construction costs into applicable depreciation categories.

For accounts, although final data is not yet available, working assumptions have been provided.

32.2.4 Request for further data: sample solution to Exercise 1

Review of the information provided, together with some preliminary work on the model, has led to preparation of a list of questions, issued on the understanding that further information requirements may well become clear as work progresses. The questions are divided into various categories to help the team members identify the items for which they are primarily responsible.

As team leader, Jeremy Bond needs to ensure that appropriate parties are approached concerning any questions not directly answerable by members of the team. He must also be kept informed as to the assumptions being made where no data, questionable data, or a choice of data is available, and must ultimately take responsibility for such assumptions. Together with the questions, a list is given of the information which the modeller proposes to include in the model, for review and confirmation.

Note on Model Data Following Meeting at Spil House

Following our meeting, I have prepared a summary of the data currently available in a suitable form for use in the model, together with a list of other data needed now or in the longer term in order to produce an analysis of the project. This is subject to further data requirements becoming clear as work progresses.

General model assumptions
1 Should the model at this stage be able to analyse both the 'full' and 'town only' cases?
2 What total period should the model cover (in years) to allow for any likely variations in the construction or concession period?

Macroeconomic assumptions
3 What is the currency of Sunronia (with customary abbreviation)?
4 What is the initial exchange rate between sterling and the Sunronian currency? Should any real appreciation be assumed between them, or can the model assume purchasing power parity for now?
5 What inflation rate(s) should be assumed for general UK and Sunronia inflation during the analysis period (construction plus concession life). Should a separate rate be included for any particular cost or revenue items?

Construction
The ideal format for construction cost data is the provision, for each category of costs, of a total expenditure figure as at some specified value date, together with a percentage profile for the timing of expenditure from financial close.

The breakdown of costs should be sufficient to support inflation, funding, depreciation, etc., calculations, and show any categories that are likely to be of interest and may be varied independently. Once these criteria are met, the breakdown should be kept as simple as possible.

It should be clear to what extent, if any, costs are quoted on a fixed price basis.

Clear guidance should be provided regarding the currency in which costs are denominated.

---

continued

As a temporary measure, the model will use the figures shown below, with timing of payments as indicated. Figures will be inflated from financial close at the general sterling inflation rate.

	Total cost (£m)	Paid In equal semi-annual amounts over...
Full scheme		
Network	240	Five years from financial close
Civils	85	Two-and-a-half years from financial close
Plant and machinery	150	Two-and-a-half years from financial close
Town only scheme		
Network	130	Three-and-a-half years from financial close
Civils	85	Two-and-a-half years from financial close
Plant and machinery	120	Two-and-a-half years from financial close

For immediate use, guidance as to actual anticipated timing of expenditure, a rough local/foreign split and appropriate inflation assumptions would be very helpful.

Would construction of the treatment works actually start at financial close, or would it be delayed so that the installed network and projected waste water volumes would allow the plant to be used as soon as it is completed?

Operation

Presumably, the volumes treated in any half year will be the lesser of waste water volumes produced, the capacity of the installed network, and the total capacity of the plant, assuming a given level of contamination?

Values for all these will therefore be required by the model, either as maximum values, with some sort of build-up profile, or as values for each half year over the analysis period.

The model needs a breakdown of operating costs between fixed costs (assumed costs incurred in each year, irrespective of utilisation of the plant) and variable costs (costs that vary according to the quantity of waste treated by the plant). Fixed costs should be quoted as an amount per annum, and variable costs as an amount per quantity of processed material – for example, per M^3 of waste water treated, potable water produced, etc. This information should allow costs to automatically reflect varying assumptions for operating levels.

An indication is needed for any division of operating costs between local and foreign operating costs.

What inflation assumptions should be used for the operating costs?

Is the model required, at this stage, to consider treatment of waste above the maximum BOD level specified for the base tariff?

What are the operating costs associated with production of potable water, and what are the constraints on production of potable versus ordinary clean water? WIl potable water sales be determined as the maximum possible production or by assumed demand?

How is the volume of sludge calculated? Will it all be sold? If not, the model needs assumed demand figures.

Sale prices are needed for potable water and sludge.

What assumption should be made for waste water volumes, given the range of conflicting data available. It would be very straightforward for the model to perform a range of analyses based upon say maximum, medium and minimum flow assumptions.

For initial analysis, the maximum permitted tariff of $a25.32/M^3$ will be used for treated waste water volumes.

Finance

The following data items have been assumed/are required for the finance section:

continued

	ECGD Loan	Commercial Loan	Subordinated Loan
Drawdown period (full scheme)	5 years	5 years	5 years
Drawdown period (town only scheme)	3.5 years	3.5 years	3.5 years
Construction period interest rate percent per annum	{ }%	{ }%	{ }%
Post-construction interest rate percent per annum	{ }%	{ }%	{ }%
Assumed facility size percentage above total drawings	5%	10%	N/A
Percentage foreign costs funded	85%	N/A	N/A
Local costs funded as percentage of foreign costs	15%	N/A	N/A
Percentage interest allowed rolled-up	85%	100%	100%
Percentage own fees funded	85%	N/A	N/A
Timing of 1st repayment (after fin. close)			
Full scheme	5.5 years	5.5 years	5.5 years
Town only scheme	4 years	4 years	4 years
Number of semi-annual repayments	{ }	{ }	{ }
Premium paid up-front as percentage of facility	{ }%	N/A	N/A
Up-front fees as percentage of facility	{ }%	{ }%	N/A
Commitment fees as percent per annum of undrawn facility	{ }%	{ }%	N/A
Currency in which loan is denominated	£ st	£ st	£ st
Repayment method	Equal Semi-annual Installments	Annuity Payments	Annuity Payments
Agency fees	£25,000 pa	£25,000 pa	N/A

Equity is assumed to be denominated in sterling, to be paid in as needed to fund any costs not met from drawings under the export credit facility, and to be calculated as an amount equal to 20% of the total calculated debt and equity drawings, of which 10% will be paid in as pure equity and 90% as subordinated debt.

Any costs during construction not met from drawings on the ECGD loan, pure equity, sub-debt and/or net revenues, are assumed to be funded from the commercial loan.

Presumably there will be legal costs associated with the financing, general documentation, etc. What provision should be made for such costs?

Tax and accounting

It is assumed that three taxes on profits apply – 34% corporation tax; 4.75% local levy; and 3.2% tourism tariff. Are any of these deductible when calculating the others, or can they effectively be totalled and applied as a single, composite rate?

Until further information becomes available, a set of simple tax assumptions will be used by the model (and any improvements on these basic assumptions would be very welcome):

1 interest and fees pre-operation will be capitalised and depreciated as for plant and machinery;
2 losses will be carried forward;
3 tax will be calculated annually, and paid in two semi-annual tranches in the following year;
4 tax will be charged at a composite rate of 41.95%; and
5 capital allowances will be calculated on a declining balance basis at 4% per annum on buildings and 10% per annum on plant and machinery (assume network costs split 80:20).

continued

In order to assess the effect of the ESS, the model will be written with a switch allowing the ESS to be included or ignored, as required. As for tax in general, some preliminary assumptions will be used by the model until more detailed information becomes available: (a) a 100% tax holiday for the first 5 years of operation; and (b) double capital allowances.

Withholding tax on profits presumably applies only to profits paid to shareholders outside Sunronia. Do we have any information as to the likely local/foreign breakdown of shareholders? The model will, in any case, calculate equity returns assuming no dividend withholding tax and assuming all dividends are subject to withholding tax, giving an indication of the IRRs for both types of investor, assuming that investments and returns are split between local and foreign investors on a consistent basis over the analysis period.

Dividends will be calculated as the lesser of available cash and cumulative net profits less reserves. The stipulated reserve will be calculated as the lesser of 10% of cumulative net profits and 20% of cumulative equity invested.

Accounting depreciation will be assumed to be on a straight line basis over 20 years for buildings and 10 years for plant and machinery. Interest and fees will be capitalised up to start of operations, and expensed thereafter. Capitalised interest and fees will be depreciated as for plant and machinery.

For all tax and accounting purposes, the values used will be the local currency equivalent amounts at the time of expenditure or income, with no adjustment, at present, for currency depreciation or appreciation.

During the preparation of the note, a draft data section was produced, including test data for values not yet provided.

Once the note has been distributed, responses from a variety of sources are received over the following two days. In so far as is possible with the information available, the model is being built up over this period.

New information is incorporated as replies are received.

32.2.5 Further data

Memo re Sarva Project data
From: Jeremy Bond
To: All members of the Sarva Project Team

(Note: Action Points other than model indicated by '*')

Addressing the points in the notes circulated following the SPIL House meeting:

General model assumptions
I believe that the town only case may be relevant to the decision-making process and, if possible within our very tight time constraints, it would be very helpful to be able to run some cases on this basis.

I think a 45-year analysis period will be adequate. For now, assume a 30-year concession period from start of operation.

Macroeconomic assumptions
The currency of Sunronia is the 'solar', abbreviated to $a. The current exchange rate is $a50.3 = £1 sterling and we would need to be able to explore the possible impact of real exchange rate movements.

continued

Assume UK inflation of 2% p.a. historically, 3% for the first six years of the model, and 3.5% thereafter. For Sunronian inflation assume a constant 4% p.a. for now. We will need to check the importance of inflation assumptions to the deal with some sensitivities. Unless otherwise stated, all figures can be assumed to be given as at today's date, with financial close occurring in 12 months time.

Could those providing cost and revenue data please indicate whether any item should be inflated at a rate significantly different to general inflation, and whether one-year's inflation to financial close is inappropriate for any reason.

Construction

I understand that the construction contract is expected to be 100% fixed price. For the present assume that 60% of all construction costs will be foreign supplied.

Angie Sparc will provide timing of expenditure, a more detailed local/foreign split if available, and the basis for a breakdown of costs between depreciation categories (see below). Figures for both full scheme and 'town only' case required.

In addition, the model should include a development fee, payable to SPIL at financial close, equal to 150% of our costs in developing the project up to financial close. Use an estimate of £1.25 million for the development costs, mainly spent over the six months prior to financial close.

Operation

The assumption re calculation of treated volumes would appear to be correct but could anyone who thinks differently please let me know. (Any comments Angie or Mark?)

For the moment I think the model should only consider waste water with contamination within the range covered by the basic AGS tariff. Be conservative and assume that all waste water is at the maximum contamination level covered. I wonder if we might be interested in offering a higher limit, or no limit, for contamination levels covered by the base tariff. What are the issues here? This is not required, however, for the initial approvals process.

Mark Brigbane is to provide detailed operating data, as requested in the original memo. If necessary, arrange a meeting specifically to discuss operating data in the model.

Jeff Higgs is to provide initial estimates, in the next two days, of the demand and sale price for three by-products – irrigation water, potable water and dried sludge. Estimate will indicate whether figures are constrained by anticipated supply or demand.

Given the total confusion about projected waste water figures, I think the model should be prepared on the assumption that low, medium and high population figures will be provided. Who should prepare these? Figures need to be available within five days at most in order to allow the model to be checked and sensitivity cases run in good time. The population figures should be used with various daily per capita volume assumptions to calculate the projected waste water flows. I would suggest 1 cuM and 0.75 cuM for initial analysis, unless specific information is available for Sarva.

Please include provision for a management fee, payable from one year prior to the start of operations, initially taking a value of £500,000 pa, inflating at the general sterling inflation rate.

For now assume 1 month receivables and 2 months payables delay.

continued

Finance

	ECGD Loan	Commercial Loan	Subordinated Loan
Drawdown period (full scheme)	5 years OK	5 years OK	5 years OK
Drawdown period (town only scheme)	3.5 years OK	3.5years OK	3.5years OK
Construction period interest rate percent per annum	6.85%	*reference rate plus 3%*	9.00%
Post-construction interest rate percent per annum	6.85%	*reference rate plus 2.75%*	*same as pre-completion rate*
Reference rate percent per annum	N/A	4.0%	N/A
Assumed facility size percent above total drawings	5% OK	10% OK	N/A
Percentage foreign costs funded	85% OK	N/A	N/A
Local costs funded as percentage of foreign costs	15% OK	N/A	N/A
Percentage interest allowed rolled-up	85% OK	100% OK	100% OK
Percentage own fees funded	85% OK	N/A	100% OK
Timing of 1st repayment (after fin. close)			
Full scheme	5.5 years OK	5.5 years OK	5.5 years OK
Town only scheme	4 years OK	4 years OK	4 years OK
Number of semi-annual repayments	40	40	50
Premium paid up-front as percentage of facility	12%	N/A	N/A
Up-front fees as percentage of facility	1.5%	1.5%	N/A
Commitment fees as percent per annum of undrawn facility	0.4%	0.4%	N/A
Currency in which loan is denominated	£ st OK	£ st OK	£ st OK
Repayment method	Equal Semi-annual Installments OK	Annuity Payments OK	Annuity Payments OK
Agency fees	N/A	£25,000 per annum OK	N/A

Equity and funding basis assumptions OK as indicated. Include £250,000 for legal fees.

Assume that lenders will require a maintenance reserve account, funded from available cash, equal to 100% of major maintenance costs in next 12 months, plus 70% of major maintenance in 12 months after that, then 40% of next 12 months, and 10% of the next 12 months of maintenance costs.

Tax and accounting assumptions

*Jeff Higgs is seeking confirmation and clarification on all tax and accounting assumptions, and the initial assumptions should be replaced as actual data becomes available.

In the meantime, the assumptions indicated in the original memo seem fine.

The calculation of IRRs with and without withholding tax is fine for now. Could you also calculate an overall SPIL return that includes development costs/fees and management fees. If it is easy to do, could you calculate this assuming that SPIL takes 10%, 25%, 30% and 80% of the equity. If this is difficult, use the 25% figure only.

SPOIL International
6th to 8th floor, Zephania House
54, Betjemin Street
Reading, Surrey XY50 1ZA

From: Mark Brigbane
Director, Business Development
Re: Sarva Project operating data

Volumes

The capacity of the plant and network will be assessed to be sufficient to meet all anticipated requirements.

The build-up of flows through the plant will depend upon the assumed population figures.

Operating costs

The operating costs will be 90% fixed and 10% variable with the size of the plant. Using the original estimates, therefore, £4,500,000 per annum will be fixed and £500,000 per annum variable. Assuming plant capacity of 40,000 cuM/sec, this gives variable costs of £12.5/cuM.

Assume 15% local (UK) and 85% foreign (Sunronia and either France or Germany).

Assume 3% inflation for the first 3 years, 5% for the next 10 years, and 4% thereafter.

Contamination levels

The ITB specifies a maximum contamination level of 180mg/l. The costs provided reflect this assumption.

Potable water

Add a further £200,000 per annum for potable water treatment. This will allow production of 30,000 cuM potable water pa. Higher production would require plant redesign with different capital costs, and a new cost estimate will be provided if required.

Sludge volumes are calculated from the solids component of waste water, the volumes treated, and the final moisture content of the dried sludge.

I think this addresses all points in your memo. If you need to check any points of detail, I suggest you contact Philip Green (pgreen@SPOIL_it.com)

Mark Brigbane

SPIL ENGINEERING BUDGET SHEET
Originator: Angie SPARC
File: SEN\00543A
Plant/Project Title: Sarva Waste Water Processing Plant

See accompanying Excel file: **SarvaCapex00543A.xls**

Please find attached preliminary capital cost figures for the Sarva water project, both full and town-only schemes. The figures are broken down into local and foreign denominated costs for each cost category, and given as annual expenditure profiles. I have also included provisional figures for major maintenance costs over a 30 year operating life.

Hotel Mirabelle-Sarva
3100 Bd. Souliereena – Sarva – Zona Es Maritina
Phona/Fcsimo – 88 097 453

From: J. Higgs

Re: Treatment works by-products.

There is currently use of untreated waste water for irrigation purposes, either directly by families using their own waste water on their land, or via sales by the waste companies who empty the septic tanks.

The septic tank water has the solids removed in settling ponds, but is otherwise untreated, and is sold at very low prices. It will be hard to convince farmers that there is sufficient benefit in using clean water on their land to justify a price differential compared with their existing supply, limiting our pricing. On the other hand, connection of the network will steadily reduce the supply of septic tank water and demand levels may sustain a higher price if little alternative is available.

The existing price is between $a1.5 to $a3.0 / cuM and estimated demand is 500,000cuM per annum. Demand is highly seasonal, with virtually no irrigation between December and mid-March and peak requirements in August.

The existing market for dried sludge equivalent (untreated solids from septic tank companies) is moderate. However, two large-scale farming projects are currently starting up to cater to the growing hotel and cruise market, and initial approaches suggest that they would be interested in entering into fairly large contracts to secure a reasonably priced, guaranteed supply of organic material.

Current use is estimated at approximately 18,000 tonnes per annum. The two new farming ventures have indicated that they would be interested in taking between 6,500 and 8,000 tonnes pa.

The sale price for septic tank solids appears to be negotiated for each tanker-load, and can be anything between $a4 and $a35 per tonne. The quality of this material is also highly variable, although it is not clear to what extent farmers are able to assess this when purchasing, and hence whether consistent quality would be a consideration when setting the price.

Potable water is always in demand. Prices are high, and there should be little difficulty in selling the maximum production from the plant at a price of around $a3 to $a4 per cuM.

Re the tax and accounting assumptions, I think it will be impossible to gain much useful information in the required timeframe. I would suggest that we use the simple assumptions indicated in the note on the model data, and engage a local accountant if it is decided to proceed with the project.

All is progressing well here. Could I see the numbers as soon as they are available please?

Best regards,

Jeff Higgs

Memo re Sarva Project data
From: Jeremy Bond
To: Jeff Higgs
cc: All members of the Sarva Project Team

Jeff,

Reviewing your note, I would suggest that we use the following assumptions in the model:

Irrigation water $a2.8/cuM with a demand of 500,000 pa. We can currently ignore seasonal variation, but this should be included in the model as soon as the decision is made to proceed.

For dried sludge, the model should assume that all production is sold. Use a base case sale price of $a80 per tonne but be prepared to use higher figures if required.

Assume all potable water produced is sold, with a sale price of $a3.50 per cuM. I would suggest that the first figures assume that the maximum possible amount of potable water is produced.

Also, it occurs to me that we have no assumptions in the data regarding revenues from charges for connection to the network. Does the ITB specifically exclude this, or is there some scope for collecting such charges, either direct from consumers or from AGS?

Jeremy

Memo re Sarva Project data
From: Jeremy Bond
To: All members of the Sarva Project Team

Following discussions with Jeff Higgs, it appears that there is no mention of connection charges in the ITB, and there has been no reference to such charges in any discussions that Jeff has had with AGS. They are therefore not precluded, but we need to have a feel for the cash flows using the ITB tariff before deciding whether or not we should explore the inclusion of connection charges using the model.

Jeremy

SPOIL International
6th to 8th floor, Zephania House
54, Betjemin Street
Reading, Surrey XY50 1ZA

From: Philip Green
Senior Operations Manager, Waste

It was a pleasure to meet you, and very interesting to discuss the details of the Sarva project and the modelling issues involved.

Following our meeting, I have attempted to complete your pro forma data section, along with the changes we discussed, and the figures are attached. I have spoken to Mark and he has now officially assigned me to a support role on the Sarva deal, so I suggest that you continue to talk to me directly as further information is required.

continued

I believe I now have a good understanding of your requirements for the model, and will be interested to see the process of developing the numbers. I think it would be a good idea to pursue your suggestion that I review the input and output figures relating to operations, in order to confirm your understanding of the data I have provided and the operating processes and procedures that they represent.

As a matter of interest, I have received a copy of a memo from Jeremy Bond in which I note he suggests that you do not currently analyse treatment for wastes with contamination exceeding a BOD of 180mg/l. I do not yet have a real feel for the finance issues in this deal, but I wonder if you are aware that this is an extremely low contamination level? I would not expect waste water flows for a project such as the Sarva Project to fall below contamination levels of BOD 300mg/l.

Regarding assumed volumes of waste water, unless better information is available I would suggest passing all the available data to the SPOIL Business Planning Unit. The people there do this type of thing for a living, and you should request the low, high and medium population forecasts and per capita estimates required. If you would like to contact them directly, I would recommend speaking to Mary Barclay, direct line 7872. Alternatively, if you confirm that you would like this work done, I can contact them for you, and get them working on it ASAP.

I look forward to working with you further on this.

Best regards,

Philip Green

Enclosures: Pro formas.

OPERATING DATA: PRO FORMA A

<u>Full Scheme (assuming contamination at maximum level for basic tariff)</u>

Plant Capacity: 3.00 cuM/sec waste water treated.

Each cuM of waste water would generate approximately 0.69 cuM of irrigation water.

Potable Water Production Capacity = waste water capacity × 65%.

Sludge Production = 0.00019 tonnes dried sludge per cuM waste water treated.

Variable Operating Costs:
Local = $a1.50/cuM waste water treated;
Foreign = £0.01/cuM waste water treated.

Fixed Operating Costs:
Local = $a14.8 million/year;
Foreign = £500,000/year.

Variable Operating Costs:
Local = $a0.06/cuM potable water produced;
Foreign = £0.02/cuM potable water produced.

All operating costs can currently be assumed to inflate at the appropriate general rate.

Network Capacity (cuM / sec)

Year 2	Year 3	Year 4	Year 5	Year 6
0.60	1.80	2.40	3.20	3.20

OPERATING DATA: PRO FORMA B

Town Only Scheme (assuming contamination at maximum level for basic tariff)

Plant Capacity: 2.40 cuM/sec waste water treated.

Each cuM of waste water would generate approximately 0.69 cuM of irrigation water.

Potable Water Production Capacity = waste water capacity × 65%.

Sludge Production = 0.00019 tonnes dried sludge per cuM waste water treated.

Variable Operating Costs:
    Local = $a1.50/cuM waste water treated;
    Foreign = £0.01/cuM waste water treated.

Fixed Operating Costs:
    Local = $a12.2 million/yean
    Foreign = £450,000/year.

Variable Operating Costs:
    Local = $a0.06/cuM potable water produced;
    Foreign = £0.02/cuM potable water produced.

All operating costs can currently be assumed to inflate at the appropriate general rate.

Network Capacity (cuM / sec)

Year 2	Year 3	Year 4	Year 5	Year 6
0.60	1.80	2.40	2.50	2.50

SPOIL International
6th to 8th floor, Zephania House
54, Betjemin Street
Reading, Surrey XY50 1ZA

From: Mary Barclay
Associate Manager, Business Planning

Please find below estimates requested via Philip Green for a proposed waste water treatment plant in Sarva, Sunronia.
    Figures assume a current population of 120,000 plus an average tourist population of 80,000 over the year for the full scheme; 80,000 residents and 72,000 tourists in the town only case.

Low Population Case
Growth in the resident population of 2% per annum for 5 years, and 1.5% per annum thereafter.
    Growth in the tourist population of 1% per annum until a maximum level of 84,000 is reached.

continued

Medium Population Case

Growth in the resident population of 2.5% per annum for 5 years, 2.0% per annum thereafter.
   Growth in the tourist population of 1.5% per annum until a maximum level of 93,000 is reached.

High Population Case

Growth in the resident population of 2.75% per annum for 5 years, 2.50% per annum for a further 5 years and 1.5% thereafter.
   Growth in the tourist population of 1.5% per annum.
   Tourist population maxima are for whole country. For city ony scheme adjust maxima in proportion to the tourist initial populations.

Per capita waste water production (cuM/day)

	Low	Medium	High
Residents	0.80	0.85	0.90
Tourists	1.10	1.20	1.35

In addition, there is an estimated commercial/industrial output of 15 million cuM per annum, expected to grow at 0.5% per annum for 5 years only.
   I would expect the average BOD for the above flows to be 310 mg/1 for residents and tourists, and between 200 and 400 mg/1 for commercial waste water.
With best wishes,

Mary Barclay

32.2.6 Exercise 2

(a) Based on the information so far and using the blank model skeleton 'Sarvafeasblank.xls', prepare a data section in a suitable format (see Section 12).

For values provided in a spreadsheet, process into the required format before pasting into the model.

(b) Using the data section prepared for (a), or the illustrative data file, Sarvadataoutline01.xls, prepare a feasibility model for the Sarva project, bearing in mind the current accuracy of the data, the importance of various assumptions and the time available. Refer to Sections 1.3 to 11 for general information on model layout and structure and Section 27.1 for help on producing a model from scratch. For detailed information on each model sheet, see Sections 12 to 26.

32.2.7 Notes on Exercise 2

Notes on responses to the modeller's data memo

First memo from Jeremy Bond. This memo is exactly what is needed to progress the assembly of a useable set of data for the model. In so far as it lies within his area of knowledge, Jeremy has given decisions on the data to be used. Where further input is required, he has mostly assigned responsibility to individuals, with clear instructions as to what is required, and without losing sight of the time constraints.

This memo provides data in relation to:

- the need for full/town only cases;
- the period analysed by the model;
- inflation, exchange rates and treatment of currency devaluation;
- the nature of the construction contract;
- development costs/fees;
- the basis for establishing and calculating treated water volumes;
- contamination level assumptions;
- per capita waste water usage;
- management costs/fees;
- finance assumptions;
- pro temps tax and accounting assumptions; and
- required equity IRR output.

Note From Mark Brigbane. This note is interesting in that it appears to have completely missed the point on virtually all issues. It is important that the modeller can recognise responses that are actually red herrings and so avoid wasting a lot of time trying to incorporate illogical, inappropriate or misleading information into the model.

The response about waste water volumes simply suggests that the chosen plant design will be adequate to meet anticipated requirements. This implies that treated flows would equal produced flows in all cases. If projected waste water flows exceed the capacity of the plant or network assumed for construction cost purposes, then any cases run on this basis would either understate capital costs or overstate net revenues. What is required is guidance as to the appropriate figures, reflecting any changes over time, for each of the three possible constraints – network capacity, plant capacity and waste water flows.

The guidance given regarding operating costs is incomplete and appears fundamentally to misunderstand what is needed in terms of fixed and variable costs. The model requires cost figures split between costs that will not vary depending upon the amount of waste water treated in each half year, and costs that will vary according to assumed volumes of waste water passing through the plant (or by-product production), not according to the assumed capacity of the plant. The local/foreign split needs to be given for each type of cost, because it is unlikely to be the same for fixed and variable costs. Mark also appears to have misinterpreted the description of 'local' and 'foreign'. Local is intended to represent costs incurred in the country in which the project is to be located, while foreign indicates all costs paid in other countries, and hence, presumably, in other currencies.

The inflation information shows variation over time, using rates that differ from the currently assumed general inflation rates. No distinction is made between inflation for local and foreign costs. The assumption behind this data is required if it is to be used in preference to the general inflation rate.

The response regarding any association between costs and contamination levels merely confirms the basis for the data provided, without attempting to give the information needed to support the running of sensitivity cases.

Similarly, the potable water figure gives no information that could be used for sensitivity cases assuming other levels of potable water production. Because production may be less than capacity, if demand-driven, sensitivities may well be run without any implications for capital costs. In addition, this figure raises questions as to the data already given. Does the £5 million figure already include any costs for potable water production?

The reply regarding sludge describes the calculation without actually giving any information to allow its inclusion in the model.

It is apparent from the later note from Philip Green that the modeller took advantage of the one useful piece of information in this note.

Engineering budget sheet from Angie Sparc. This is a straightforward and informative note, accompanied by a spreadsheet giving amounts and timing of construction and major maintenance cost expenditure ready to be adapted into a suitable format for use in the model.

Memo from Jeff Higgs. This fax contains much useful information, although in many cases insufficient guidance is given as to the values to be used in the model. A greater or lesser amount of guidance is given for demand levels and sale price of irrigation water, dried sludge and potable water, together with some guidance as to the tax and accounting assumptions to be used in the model.

Two further memos from Jeremy Bond. The first of these memos converts the general information given by Jeff Higgs into specific assumptions for use in the model. It also considers the implications of seasonal variation in sales of irrigation water, and decides to postpone reflection of this issue until later on in the analysis. This would seem a sensible choice at this stage because the decision to proceed with the project or not is unlikely to be affected by the precise timing of revenues within the year. Given that the actual start dates, etc., are far from precise at this stage, any reflection of seasonal timings in relation to the project timetable will in any case be largely based on guesswork. As the deal progresses, however, such details will become more important and will be more accurately determined, making it appropriate to include them in the model.

The issue of connection charges is raised. Although it seems they may not be needed immediately, the modeller should be on the alert to include this revenue stream if it is needed to make the project feasible.

Letter from Philip Green. This is a useful and informative note, giving the requested information together with assistance in other areas. Philip also offers some information regarding contamination levels that may be very important.

Both full scheme and town only values are given for the following:

- plant capacity for waste water treatment, irrigation, sludge and potable water production;
- fixed and variable operating costs, local/foreign;
- operating costs associated with the production of potable water; and
- network capacity.

Letter from Mary Barclay. This seems to give all the information required for modelling purposes, although the assumptions upon which the figures are based would be helpful for those required to make decisions using the data.

Data is given for:

- low, medium and high population figures;
- low, medium and high per capita waste water figures; and
- commercial/industrial waste water figures.

In addition, estimated BOD levels are given for various types of waste water flow. This is presumably in reply to an additional question raised by Philip Green as a result of his own concerns regarding the assumed contamination level used for the analysis.

Notes on data items

Macroeconomic assumptions. At present only two inflation rates need to be considered – an overall rate for sterling and solars.

Construction costs. These figures are given as annual values which need to be converted to semi-annual figures for inclusion in the model. At this stage it is probably appropriate simply to divide costs evenly across the year.

The data is supplied as sterling or $a expenditure amounts in each year. To simplify later changes to amount, timing or exchange rate assumptions, this is best input as total amounts and percentage expenditure profiles.

Ideally converting from annual expenditure figures to semi-annual percentage values can be done in Excel, in an expanded version of the file in which the data is supplied, prior to pasting the resultant values into the model.

Jeremy Bond has requested inclusion of a development fee, based on specified development costs of £1.25 million, spent prior to financial close. The development <u>fee</u> will be a cost to the project and income to SPIL, whilst the development <u>costs</u> are neutral for the project, but a cost to SPIL, needing to be taken into account when calculating a specific investor return for SPIL. The costs can be included in the 'Pre-year 1' column with a specified date allocated to them for calculation of investor returns using the XIRR function. Note that as project negotiations progress towards Financial Close, an increasing proportion of the development costs will comprise sunk costs and will no longer be relevant for SPIL's investment decisions regarding the project.

Operation. A full set of operating data seems to have been provided, although it is important to remember that this is all based on an assumed contamination level, and new information might be required if any other contamination level came to be used. Given the comments from Philip Green and the information from Mary Barclay, it seems likely that some variation will be required in the contamination assumptions. It is far from clear, however, how such variation will be specified, and which values it will effect. It is probably best, therefore, to make no specific provision for this in the draft model, but to ensure that the structure and layout of the model are such that changes can be made easily and quickly.

The network capacity figures have been supplied as annual values. As these are capacity figures in cuM/sec, it would be incorrect to halve these to reach semi-annual values. At present it is probably best to adopt the simple solution of using the average figure given, over the whole year – i.e., to use the given figures in both halves of the relevant year.

A management fee is now required, payable to SPOIL. This needs to be calculated as a distinct item because, although a cost to the project, it can be included as a revenue item when looking at equity returns for SPIL.

Finance. The present financing structure is quite simple, as it is intended merely as a general example of the type of finance structure that might be possible for the deal. On this basis, whenever a choice arises between two or more methodologies for modelling the finance structure specified, it would be best to assume that the simplest solution is applicable.

Tax and accounts. Although still very preliminary, some complexity will be needed in the tax calculations to include the ESS provisions on an optional basis. This should be constructed carefully to allow data to be changed later. (See Section 5 on the use and construction of switches.)

32.2.8 Sample solution for Exercise 2a

Sarvadataoutline01.xls shows the layout and content of an example data section and provides as an illustrative solution to Exercise 2(a). It can also be used as the basis for Exercise 2b.

32.2.9 Notes and example solution for Exercise 2b

A sample solution for Exercise 2b is provided in the file SarvafeasEx2bsol.xls.

The 'Worklines, masks, factors and counters' section will be developed as the model is built, alongside the sheets discussed below. Reference will be made to elements added to this section as they arise.

The model is semi-annual, and has a timeline covering 45 years from financial close.

A title has been added indicating which case is being run according to the value for the 'Full Scheme or Town Only' switch in the data. (For information about switches and the use of strings, see Sections 5 and 9.3.1.)

Capital costs

See Section 14 for a full explanation of the layout and content of this part of the model.

The capital costs section should pick up the 'selected' values from the data section. The construction costs are optionally assumed to be fixed price or inflated. For the foreign cost values, which are denominated in sterling but presented in solar, currency devaluation must be reflected in these figures, as described in Section 8.

Development fees are assumed to be a sterling-denominated figure subject to inflation. This figure is input into data as a sterling development cost amount, immediately converted to solars at the initial exchange rate. The converted cost value is then multiplied by an input factor and by the total currency devaluation factor at Financial Close.

In support of this section, sterling and solar inflation and devaluation factors were set up in the Worklines sheet, along with the required timing masks.

As a simple check at this stage, set UK and Sunronian inflation assumptions to the same values and check that foreign Network Costs, Civils and Plant and Machinery have totals equal to the input amounts. (Remember to restore the inflation rates after checking in this way.)

Funding

See Section 15 for a full explanation of the content and layout of the 'Finance' sheet.

The funding structure specified at this stage of the deal is quite simple, the main issues relating to the handling of currencies. Equity and loans are drawn as required to meet costs, so at this stage no special deposit for excess funds is required in the calculation.

Interest and repayments are assumed to be paid at the end of the period in which they are calculated. Drawings are assumed to be made evenly over the period.

For the up-front fees and the equity and sub-debt calculation, inherently circular calculations should be broken using a recalc macro (see Section 7). Values are calculated in the recalc macro for total loan drawings (i.e., principal and rolled-up interest) for each loan (except the sub-debt rolled-up interest), and for total equity. These figures are calculated in solar equivalents at the initial exchange rate by dividing the principal drawings in each period by the applicable mid-period total devaluation factor and the rolled-up interest by the end-period total devaluation factor. The facility sizes and total equity amount are then converted to values as at financial close by multiplying by the total devaluation factor at Financial Close. The equity figure and sub-debt facility size are then calculated from this total funding value.

The loan principal drawings are calculated based upon the construction costs and fees. All these are already presented in solar equivalents at the time of expenditure, so no currency adjustment is required in the drawdown calculation. Drawdown masks are set up in the worklines, etc., section to control the period over which drawings are made (see Sections 3.1.3 and 15.3.2.5).

Repayments are sterling repayments of a sterling loan amount, presented in the solar equivalent at the time of payment. Each repayment is therefore calculated based upon a solar loan balance adjusted for currency devaluation to the end of the period. This is done by simple inclusion of the calculated currency adjustment figure in each period in the repayment calculation. The equal semi-annual instalments are calculated by dividing by the value in the repayment mask, provided that value exceeds zero.

The annuity repayments are calculated using the PMT() or PPMT() function to calculate the repayment in each period based upon principal, interest and number of payments. If using the PMT() function, the interest payable must be deducted from the calculated figure to provide the repayment amount. For the subordinated loan a target balance is calculated, representing the balance if annuity repayments are made. The actual repayments are calculated in each period as the lesser of the available cash (after paying interest) and the difference between the existing balance and the target balance at the end of the half year.

A check-line can be used to total interest and repayments and divide them by the total devaluation factor at end of period. This shows whether the total amount of principal plus interest remains constant throughout the repayment period. In combination with a check that the last repayment exactly repays the outstanding loan balance, this confirms that the annuity calculation is operating correctly.

The interest calculation is carried out on a simple average balance basis, taking the outstanding balance at the end of the previous period, plus half the drawings, each adjusted for currency devaluation to the end of the period. For the balance outstanding this is achieved by dividing by the previous period's end-period total devaluation factor and multiplying by the current period's end-period total devaluation factor. For drawings, the drawings are divided by the mid-period total devaluation factor and multiplied by the end-period total devaluation factor.

The interest rates are picked up in the Funding sheet, allowing the pre and post-completion rates to be selected in the correct periods (see Section 15.3.2.4), and ensuring that any subsequent requirement to input a rate varying over time can be accommodated by simply changing these rows, rather than by having to change the interest and annuity payment formulae directly.

Rolled-up interest is calculated for both senior loans as the calculated interest multiplied by the appropriate loan drawdown mask and the percentage interest rolled-up, as specified in the data. For sub-debt interest is rolled up whenever it cannot be paid, throughout the loan life.

The currency adjustment is calculated as the previous period's balance outstanding, divided by the previous period's total end-period devaluation factor, plus loan drawings divided by the mid-period total devaluation factor, all multiplied by the end-period total devaluation factor minus one.

The loan balance is an end-of-period value, calculated as the previous period's balance, plus principal drawings, rolled-up interest and currency adjustment, less repayments.

The commitment fee calculation is simplified to minimise problems with circularity. In each period in which drawdown is permitted for the loan, the fees are calculated based upon the previous period's balance outstanding, adjusted for currency devaluation by half year. It is important to ensure that the facility amount is also properly adjusted for currency devaluation.

A debt:equity ratio is calculated on the Summary sheet, to check that the figures reflect the ratio specified in the data. This ratio is calculated using equivalent solar figures at a constant exchange rate, reflecting the ratio in the underlying currency.

To facilitate initial checking of these calculations, the effects of currency changes can be temporarily removed by setting the post-year one sterling and solar inflation rates to the same value and recalculating the model using the recalc macro. The relationship between drawings and repayments or facility amounts can then be checked very easily, as can equity drawings. Inflation rates can then be restored to the original values once the check is completed.

Operations

See Section 16, for a full explanation of the content and layout of this part of the model. This section requires the reduction of various bits of information into a clear, logical presentation leading to calculation of revenues and operating costs.

For the revenues, the initial revenue stream is the payment received for treatment of waste water. The treated waste water volumes therefore need to be calculated as the minimum of waste water produced, network capacity and plant capacity. The operating section therefore starts with these three items. Plant and network capacity are calculated from data input, using an operating period mask added to the worklines, etc., section to control the timing of the availability of plant capacity. At present, the timing of operations attempts no accuracy beyond the semi-annual periods of the model, so capacity figures in cuM/sec are simply converted to cuM by multiplying by 60 seconds × 60 minutes × 24 hours × 365/12 days per month, and by the number of operating months in each half year, calculated in the Worklines sheet. The operating mask reflects the input concession life.

The projected levels of waste water production use the information given in the data for initial population levels, population growth and per capita usage. Because they are an important element of the calculation, and one which will be varied from run to run, the selected per capita values are automatically shown in the row descriptions for calculated waste water flows (see Sections 5.1 and 9.3.1 for information on the use of strings and switches).

The treatment charge is denominated in solars, so no currency adjustment is needed; the charge can simply be escalated from the appropriate value date with the general solar inflation factor, mid-period.

Solar values per period are presented in millions, while most production and sales volumes are presented in thousands of cuM. It is important to ensure that calculations correctly reflect these assumptions.

The by-products need to be calculated with reference to the amount produced and the amount that can be sold. For potable water, at present it is assumed that only as much as can be sold will be produced, and that irrigation water will be produced for all the treated waste water not used to produce potable water. Given this assumption, the calculations are quite straightforward, using the calculated treated waste water volumes and the input data items relating to by-products.

As for the waste water treatment tariff, the by-product sales prices are assumed to be denominated in solars and therefore simply require inflating at the general solar rate, with no currency issues.

An additional mask can be created for the management fee, which must commence one year before the start of operations. The operating costs calculations are otherwise straightforward, although it must be remembered that foreign-denominated costs must reflect currency devaluation.

In order to facilitate comparison of potable water production versus sale of irrigation water, the operating costs associated with production of potable water are calculated as a separate item and the net revenues from potable water sales are calculated as an information line. This is then used to calculate a net revenue figure per cuM treated waste water. This can be compared with the inflated figures for irrigation water sales as a per cuM treated waste water figure.

Tax

See Section 17 for a full explanation of the content and layout of this part of the model.

There is a special requirement with this tax section to include an optional tax structure – the ESS. This can be put together in a number of ways. In this case the simple tax calculation was put in place, and the necessary adjustments for the ESS were then added to the basic structure.

The capital allowance calculations have been split between the tax sheet and the worklines sheet. The costs to be depreciated are shown broken down into several categories, including a category for capitalised interest and fees, corresponding with those listed in the input table of capital allowance assumptions. See Section 17.1 for a detailed explanation of capital allowance calculations.

The additional capital allowances available under the ESS are calculated in the worklines sheet.

Because there is a tax holiday under the ESS, the tax rate is picked up and shown across a row in the tax section. This allows the tax holiday to be modelled easily by changing the rate to zero for the period of the tax holiday using a mask in the worklines section, and illustrates the assumption being used when printing or reviewing the tax section. For simplicity, given time constraints and the largely speculative nature of the tax assumptions being used, the number of years for the tax holiday is calculated with reference to the annual mask included in the tax calculations, ensuring that a single rate is assumed for any given year of the tax calculation. The mask is calculated to take a value of zero in periods to which the tax holiday applies, and of one thereafter. The mask must therefore take a value of one throughout if the ESS provisions do not apply. It has been assumed that the tax holiday applies from the year in which operation commences.

The earned interest calculation had not been included in the model at the stage when the tax section was being input; a blank row on the Deposits sheet was therefore labelled 'Total earned interest', and used in the tax calculation. When the model Deposit sheet was completed, it was ensured that this row was preserved and contained the appropriate values.

Tax is assumed to be paid in two semi-annual tranches in the year following its calculation. As tax payable has been calculated as an annual figure, this is calculated as (tax payable in the previous period plus tax payable two period's previously) divided by two.

Profit and loss

See Section 18 for a full explanation of the content and layout of this part of the model.

This section is quite standard, although it does include a reserve calculation. Depreciation is calculated in the Worklines sheet.

Earned interest initially picked up the blank row labelled 'Earned Interest' and used in the tax calculation.

A row calculating cash flow available for dividends is taken from the 'Cascade' sheet.

Returns

See Section 21 for a full explanation of the content and layout of this part of the model.

It is required that returns be calculated with and without reference to withholding tax on dividends, and that overall returns and specific returns to SPIL be calculated.

Given the quality of data available so far, simple IRR calculations have been used for most return calculations.

The complications for the section arise less from the different returns to be calculated than from the consideration of currency issues. Returns are initially calculated on the nominal solar figures calculated by the model, giving nominal solar IRRs. The investors are, however, assumed to be partly or wholly UK based, and both nominal and real returns need to be considered on this basis. It was decided to maintain the principle of keeping all values in a single currency within the calculation sections. Nominal returns are therefore calculated by removing currency devaluation from the figures. The resultant figures are clearly labelled to indicate that they are not on the same basis as other, nominal solar figures. Devaluation is removed simply by dividing by the mid-period total devaluation factor, giving figures that should reflect sterling inflation, with a consistent exchange rate, allowing an IRR to be calculated which will be the nominal UK figure. These figures can then be divided by the mid-period sterling inflation factor to give figures upon which real UK IRRs can be calculated.

As requested, cash flows to SPIL have been calculated. Little extra work is required to produce this for a range of assumed SPIL shares, so the full range of rates requested by Jeremy Bond have been analysed. For SPIL purposes, the development costs should be taken into account as a cost, with development fees added back as a revenue item, together with management fees. For these calculations XIRR has been used to capture the timing of the development costs.

Cover factors

See Sections 10 and 22 for a full explanation of the content and layout of this part of the model.

Cover factors are generally calculated on a nominal basis, as has been done here. In practice, however, because both loans are denominated in sterling, it is not the nominal solar cash flow that is relevant to debt service, but the equivalent sterling cash flow, requiring adjustment to the loan balances and cash flows used for the FNPV cover factor calculations.

In periods where no debt service or loan balance exists, the cover factor calculations take a value of "", allowing the minimum cover factor to be picked up correctly using the MIN(...) function, which ignores empty cells.

Cash balances

See Section 20 for a full explanation of the content and layout of this part of the model.

The debt service reserve account (DSRA) is entered here as a simple deposit funded from post-tax and finance cash flows to give a balance equal to the following six month's debt service. The interest is calculated assuming that transfers to and from the deposit occur at the end of each half-year period – i.e., based upon the previous period's closing balance. At present, there is no assumption of any surplus funding during the construction period, so no earned interest need be included in the calculation of available cash offset before calculating equity and loan drawings. If such a calculation were to be included, it would be advisable to use earned interest in the period after that in which it is calculated, ensuring that a circularity is not established between loan interest → DSRA required balance → DSRA earned interest → loan drawings → loan interest.

A maintenance reserve account (MRA) is funded from available cash after transfers to and from the DSRA, according to the target specified in the inputs.

The cash balance contains surplus net cash that cannot be distributed. As well as contributing to distributed dividends, transfers are also made from the deposit to cover cash flow shortfalls.

The empty row used as the 'Interest Earned' row for Tax and P&L calculations, is used as the 'Total Earned Interest' row as the calculations are entered, ensuring that earned interest is picked up correctly by existing calculations.

Balance sheet

Given the time constraints, no balance sheet was included at this stage. For information regarding the balance sheet, see Sections 28.2.17 and 32.3.

Net cash flow

See Section 23 for a full explanation of the content and layout of this part of the model.

The net cash flow summary section is largely a drawing together of values calculated elsewhere and presented here for convenience. It has been built up as other sections were input, allowing, for example, the matching of funding with costs to be quickly and easily checked as code is input.

Key inputs and results summary including investment period Sources and Uses

See Sections 24 and 25 for a full explanation of the content and layout of this part of the model.

The sources and uses during the invesetment period provides a good cross-check with the net cash flow summary and the funding calculations.

This summary sheet will develop as the deal progresses. For now, the input section includes formulae using strings to describe the key assumptions, based upon the switches set in the data.

Worklines, masks, factors and counters

See Section 13 for a full explanation of the content and layout of this part of the model. Additional information about specific masks, counters and factors can be found in Sections 3, 4, 8, 13, 14, 15, 15.3, and 16.

Macros

A recalc macro has been set up (see Section 7.4.2), which calculates the total drawings for each loan used as a basis for the loan fees etc., together with the total equity amount, calculated according to the debt:equity ratio specified in the data. All these figures represent sterling values, calculated in solar equivalent as at financial close.

32.3 Onward development

This section builds on the feasibility model constructed in Exercise 2, and explores the process of development as more details become available and as data begins to firm up. One would expect most data items to be revised, and many calculations to be refined, as the deal progresses through to financial close. This section aims to examine a small selection of these changes and to illustrate particular techniques, rather than give a complete reflection of the likely developments for a deal such as the Sarva Project.

Further data and information on the Sarva Project

Memo re Sarva Project data
From: Jeremy Bond
To: All members of the Sarva Project Team

Thank you for all your hard work so far. Despite the failure to meet threshold IRR targets in the preliminary modelling exercise, I am happy to tell you that (partly in the light of the information below) we have decided to proceed with bid preparation for this project.

Now the real slog begins!

I have received some important information from Jeff Higgs that suggests we should be bidding on a slightly different basis to that implied by the first reading of the ITB.

Following up on information from SPOIL regarding contamination levels, Jeff has obtained information indicating that AGS are expecting bids to be assessed on charges for contamination levels exceeding the tariff contamination level (TCL). It seems likely that the TCL has been deliberately set at a level well below any likely realistic BOD in order to present a politically attractive 'standard' tariff, while allowing bidders to set a realistic charge by means of payment for 'excess' contamination, which will, in fact, apply to all treated flows.

Obviously we will need to look carefully at the risks involved in such a structure and ensure that we can be properly protected without compromising the political objectives of AGS, but I think we should proceed with some further work on the figures immediately.

What we now want is for the model to give us the tariff needed to meet our return requirements in the base case, and meet basic financing criteria in the 'worst' case. Assume that we will need an overall real IRR of 20% per annum in the base case, with a minimum loan life cover factor of 1.05 in the worst case. This should still be applied for both the full and town only schemes.

See below for a preliminary definition of 'base' and 'worst' cases.

More detailed capital costs are now available giving a monthly expenditure profile, and I feel this should now be included in the model and reflected in the funding calculations.

Philip Green will provide information on any cost implications associated with higher contamination levels. We will need to consider the costs associated with increased BOD, the maximum BOD level to be covered by our tariff, and whether we should have incremental charges for different levels, or a single charge for levels above the TCL and below the specified maximum treatable by the plant. For now, however, I think we should use a conservative (i.e., high) average contamination assumption, and base all costs and tariffs on that assumption for all treated flows. Aside from practical issues of plant operation, the half-yearly average figures are probably exactly what concern us for now anyway.

The model will still also need to run a 'compliant' case, assuming flows contaminated up to the TCL guaranteed value.

It would be very helpful if the cash flow summary could be additionally presented on an annual basis and if a balance sheet could be added. Realised exchange losses on debt repayment can be expensed in the P&L, and the balance sheet loan balance and repayment values should be based upon nominal solar drawings.

Data item	Base case	Worst case
General Sunronian Inflation (all)	4%	5%
Construction Costs	100%	110%
Population Figures	Med	Low
Per Capita Use	Med	Low
Time to Plant Completion		
Full Scheme	5 years	6 years
Town Only	3.5 years	4.5 years
Operating Costs	100%	110%
Potable Water Sale Price $a/cuM	2.3	1.8

SPIL ENGINEERING BUDGET SHEET
Originator: Angie SPARC
File: SEN\00638U
Plant/Project Title: Sarva Waste Water Processing Plant

See accompanying Excel file: **SarvaCapex00638U.xls**

Please find attached revised capital cost figures for the Sarva water project, both full and town-only schemes. The figures are broken down into a monthly expenditure schedule.

SPOIL International
6th to 8th floor, Zephania House
54, Betjemin Street
Reading, Surrey XY50 1ZA

From: Philip Green
Senior Operations Manager

I am pleased to hear that the figures are to be based upon a more realistic contamination assumption. I would recommend that you use the average figures provided by Mary Barclay, of 310mg/l for residents and tourists and 400 mg/1 for commercial waste. Assume that this would give a 20% increase in variable operating costs and a 2% reduction in plant maximum capacity.

I think this should cover it for now. Please note that, although fairly rough estimates, these figures should be recalculated for any intermediate values, not assumed to vary linearly with BOD.

Best wishes

Philip Green

32.3.1 Exercise 3

(a) Based on the new information and the feasibility model prepared for Exercise 2, adjust the data, capital cost and funding sections to reflect the monthly capital cost expenditure profile now supplied. See Section 3.2 for information on expanding timing detail in the model.

(b) Using the model as adjusted in (a), add provision for runs at the specified higher contamination levels. See Sections 5.1 and 5.2 for information on using switches in the model.

(c) Using the model as adjusted in (b), add a case control table to allow the base and worst cases to be run automatically for the scenarios under review. See Section 9.4 for information on case control tables.

(d) Using the model as adjusted in (c), include a mechanism that wholly or partially automates the calculation of a target tariff to meet the specified cover factor and return constraints. See Section 11 for information on optimising revenues to meet target constraints.

(e) Include realised exchange losses on debt repayment in the profit and loss calculation, and add a balance sheet to the model prepared for (d).

(f) Add to the model as adjusted in (e) an annual summary of the net cash flow report. See Section 3.4.

32.3.2 Notes on Exercise 3

The exercise is intended to illustrate some techniques often needed to develop a model beyond the feasibility stage, through the development process to its final form, reflecting all manner of specific and detailed assumptions. It is assumed that the exercise will be performed using the feasibility model prepared for Exercise 2b.

Notes on Exercise 3(a)

Jeremy Bond in his memo requests that the model now handles the capital costs on a monthly basis, and that this be reflected in the funding calculation. This will necessitate calculation of appropriate monthly inflation and devaluation factors. This facility is being added to a reasonably extensive existing model, with many calculations already referring to the capital cost figures. Most of the calculations outside the funding section will continue to operate correctly based upon semi-annual capital cost figures. It is therefore safest and most efficient to preserve the existing capital cost rows, changing the formulae to become semi-annual sub-totals of the calculated monthly figures, thus ensuring that calculations other than those being specifically converted to a monthly basis can continue to pick up the correct figures without any amendment. This applies similarly to the funding calculations.

Notes on Exercise 3(b)

The model is now required to run assuming one of two possible assumptions regarding contamination levels. Philip Green's letter indicates that the two cases will have different values for plant maximum capacity and variable operating costs. The basis for the analysis indicates that the two cases will also use different waste water treatment tariffs. It would therefore be helpful to control the two cases by the operation of a single switch that will change all three items to the values required for the selected run. A little thought should be given as to the means by which this is included in the data section in order to incorporate the options without including too many obscure data items.

Notes on Exercise 3(c)

A 'base' case and 'worst' case have now been defined, and it is a good time to set up a sensitivity table to allow standard cases to be run and re-run easily as the data evolves. Bear in mind that in addition to the base and worst cases, the model is also considering several separate scenarios – for example, full scheme, town only scheme, TCL assumed and higher contamination level assumed. Base and worst cases will presumably be needed for all these scenarios.

Prior to setting up the sensitivity table, it will be necessary to identify and incorporate any additional data and calculations required to allow the 'worst' case to be run. Reviewing Jeremy Bond's memo, new provisions would seem to be needed for:

- a construction cost sensitivity factor, allowing a flat percentage adjustment to the construction costs; and
- an operating cost sensitivity factor, allowing a flat percentage adjustment to the operating costs.

Because the original model has been constructed with care to allow easy running of sensitivities, all the other items that need to be changed to run the worst case can be controlled by using different values for existing data items.

Once the new provisions have been included, include values in the case control table for all data which varies between the different cases to be run.

Notes on Exercise 3(d)

The purpose of the model has now changed slightly when considering the higher contamination case. The issue is no longer simply to analyse the project based upon given tariff constraints. Rather, it is now required that an indicative tariff be calculated that is as competitive as possible, but still meets minimum requirements as to returns and financeability. The process is complicated by the fact that the two specified requirements are based upon different sensitivity cases. There are a number of ways of approaching this issue. Bear in mind that the process will probably involve calculation of a tariff as specified, then use of that tariff for a number of sensitivity cases. The model must not, therefore, automatically recalculate a new tariff for every run. There must be an option to either calculate a tariff, or to use a tariff previously calculated and stored or manually input.

The simplest way to find the required tariff is probably to create a procedure for calculating it by running both base and worst cases, targetting the appropriate value in each case, and using the higher of the two calculated tariffs. This figure can then be used for all further runs of the given scenario. This optional calculation should operate through the recalc macro, controlled by a switch in the data, allowing all values to iterate to a solution together, and maintaining the principle of defining the case being run via data input.

Remember to ensure that any new data items are included in the sensitivity table if they are to vary between cases.

Notes on Exercise 3(e)

For this part of the exercise it is necessary to calculate loan balances and repayments based upon the nominal loan drawings in solar equivalents at the time of drawing, rather than upon the adjusted solar figures reflecting currency devaluation. The difference between repayments calculated on this basis, and the actual values, is then to be deducted from the profit and loss calculation. These nominal figures are also used in the balance sheet for debt and repayments over the next 12 months.

The balance sheet is otherwise straightforward.

Notes on Exercise 3(f)

This is a fairly simple exercise in applying timeline conversion techniques. A copy of the NCF sheet should be created and given an annual timeline. Surplus columns should be deleted and formulae replaced with SUMIF(...) or INDEX(...) functions giving annual values based on the semi-annual values in the NCF sheet. If the layout of the annual summary is identical to that of the semi-annual cash flow, then an appropriate formula can be entered for the first row and simply copied to all rows in which figures are to be converted. If the layout is to be changed, it may still be worth beginning with an identical layout, then removing or adding rows once the formula has been copied to all required corresponding rows.

32.3.3 Sample solutions for Exercise 3

A sample solution is provided in file 'SarvaFeasEx3Sol.xls'.

Sample solution for Exercise 3(a)

The amendment to the data section is quite straightforward. Because only the capital cost section should use the input capital cost data values, and will now be using the monthly figures, the original semi-annual input figures become redundant and should now be wholly replaced by the monthly inputs. On the capex sheet, rows for the monthly figures should be inserted above the original rows, which should be amended to total the new monthly values.

The worklines sheet now needs amending to include monthly values for capex timing masks, for both inflation rates and for currency devaluation.

The funding section must now reflect the monthly accuracy of the capital costs. When including this, an attempt has been made to minimise the number of items displayed on a monthly basis, to avoid unnecessary and confusing expansion of the number of rows in the funding calculations. Consideration has therefore been given to which figures are actually required on a monthly basis, and to what extent figures merely need to reflect the monthly timing assumptions without giving a more than semi-annual presentation. Certain figures, such as interest, certainly need only a semi-annual presentation as they are assumed actually to be paid at six-monthly intervals. The example has been prepared on the assumption that monthly schedules will be required for loan and equity drawings, and hence for the net funding requirements which support them. At this stage of the project the need for such figures is perhaps limited, but as approaches begin to be made to lenders and investors, these figures will almost certainly be requested.

New rows have been added to the export credit loan calculation, giving drawings on a monthly basis, totalling into the existing 'Principal Drawings' row. These drawings used the monthly figures calculated for network, civils and P&M costs in the capital costs section, plus the appropriate percentage of up-front fees and development fees in the month of Financial Close. Interest is calculated based upon an average balance calculated using average balance factors from the Worklines section. The average balance assumes drawings at the mid-point of the month in which they arise.

To support the equity and commercial loan calculations, monthly figures are calculated for the funding requirement after drawdown of the ECGD loan. Interest payable and interest rolled-up are respectively added and subtracted from the month 6 figures.

Monthly figures are calculated for equity drawings, using the post-ECGD funding requirement figures. The total equity figure against which the monthly drawings are compared is adjusted in each month for currency devaluation. The total of the monthly equity drawings in each half year is picked up in the original 'Equity as Drawn' row.

The subordinated loan is drawn next, with the principal drawings constrained by the debt:equity requirement and the specified percent equity from pure equity or subordinated debt.

Monthly commercial loan drawings are calculated based upon the monthly funding requirement after pure equity and sub debt drawings, with an average balance calculated using the monthly drawings, as for the ECGD loan. Monthly drawings are totalled into the original, semi-annual 'Principal Drawings' row.

Cross-checks for the new calculations were carried out, checking that the net cash flow still showed funding exactly matching costs, and that repayments exactly repay the loans over the correct period. A quick check of the calculation was done using a run with equal inflation rates input for sterling and solars, eliminating currency devaluation effects from the figure and so simplifying the process of checking the non-currency related calculations.

Sample solution for Exercise 3(b)

The methodology for including a switch between the TCL and a more realistic higher contamination level was considered carefully for this exercise. The changes to plant capacity and operating costs have been specified as a percentage increment and could be applied via a sensitivity factor. This approach could, however, lead to confusion if sensitivities were then required for these figures. In view of this, it was decided to include a specific adjustment to these values for the high contamination case. A switch therefore selects between two sets of values for the relevant items, with a formula picking up the selected figures replacing the existing input value in the data section, allowing the chosen figure to be instantly incorporated into the model without changing any calculation code.

Sample solution for Exercise 3(c)

The first stage in this exercise is the inclusion of the sensitivity factors for capital costs and construction costs. This is most directly done by adding the factors to the data, each taking a value of 1 for the 'base' case, and multiplying the construction costs in the capital costs section and the operating costs in the operations section, by the appropriate factor. It is important to ensure that the factor is applied to all the relevant figures, but is not applied more than once to any given item. In the example, the factor is included in the capital cost section at the point where the total figures are multiplied by the expenditure profile. For the operations section, the factor is again applied in the formulae at the point where the annual or per cuM costs are picked up from the data. The application of the factors can be checked very easily, because the construction and operating cost totals on the capex, ops or NCF sheets, should vary in exact proportion to any change to the factor.

Once the new sensitivity factors are in place, the sensitivity table can be constructed. This should include all the items necessary to completely specify the runs to be included in the table. The runs selected in the example are:

- full scheme base case assuming realistic contamination levels;
- full scheme worst case assuming realistic contamination levels;
- full scheme base case assuming TCL;
- full scheme worst case assuming TCL;
- town only base case assuming realistic contamination levels;
- town only worst case assuming realistic contamination levels;
- town only base case assuming TCL; and
- town only worst case assuming TCL.

The items required to specify this range of cases are included in the case selection table layout added at the top of the data sheet. The values in the 'selected values' column have been incorporated into the data section one-by-one, replacing the value entered for each item in the original data section with a formula that picks up the value for that item in the 'selected values' column. When this process is complete, check that selecting the full scheme base case still gives the same values as before the table was included, and that the results change appropriately when a '2' is entered to select the full scheme worst case.

Sample solution for Exercise 3(d)

As discussed earlier, there are many possible 'correct' solutions for this part of the exercise. The chosen sample solution allows a tariff to be calculated to achieve either a specified equity return or a specified cover factor. A switch in the data determines whether the tariff is calculated or input, and a further switch selects which target is used to determine the calculated tariff. The sensitivity table will specify appropriate targets for 'base' and 'worst' cases, and the value of the calculated/input switch can be set as required for each run, via the case selection table.

The assumed methodology is that tariffs will be calculated for the base and worst case for a given scenario. The higher of the two calculated tariff figures will then be entered in the case selection table as the input tariff figure for all runs based on that scenario, and the tariff switches set to select an input tariff. All cases for the scenario can then be run and assessed using the new tariff figure. This approach was selected because it was considered to be reasonably quick and efficient, easy to model in a fairly short timescale, and likely to operate properly even as major changes are made to the model.

The process of iterating to a tariff for the selected criterion is performed via the recalc macro. The model calculates estimated tariffs to give the specified return and cover factor values. If a calculated tariff is selected via the data switch, then the recalc macro picks up the appropriate calculated tariff and the model uses the tariff copied into the 'numeric values' row of the recalc macro. If an input tariff is selected, then the calculated tariff in the recalc macro takes a value of zero or picks up the input figure, avoiding fruitless iteration, and the model uses the input value for the currently selected case.

The process of iteration could be performed entirely by adjustment between the last 'too high' and 'too low' values. It is, however, helpful to use some calculation to shorten the iterative process. If there were no tax and profit constraints, it would be possible to calculate an appropriate tariff with no iteration. The operation of losses carried forward, etc., means, however, that this is prohibitively complex. Calculation of the change necessary to achieve the required returns or cover factor, ignoring the effects of tax and profit constraints and of earned interest on deposits, can be combined with iteration through the recalc macro to produce the required tariff to an appropriate level of accuracy within a reasonable number of iterations.

For the calculation of a tariff to give the required return, the change in tariff is calculated as minus the NPV of the real-terms overall cash flow to equity investors discounted at the target IRR rate, divided by the equivalent NPV of real-terms waste-water treatment revenues. Once the change has been calculated, the macro tariff formula increments the numeric pasted tariff figure in the row below by the calculated percentage change, adjusted by any damping factors.

Calculation of the tariff adjustment to achieve a target cover factor is estimated in a similar way, but based on the difference between maximum debt multiplied by the target LLCR and the NPV at completion of CFADS discounted at the loan interest rate. This amount is then expressed as a percentage of the NPV of gross waste water treatment revenues, also discounted to completion using the loan interest rate. This percentage is then used to adjust the tariff value.

Once the necessary calculations are put in place, the relevant switches and values are added to the case selection table, and the process of calculating tariffs for all scenarios can begin.

Sample solution for Exercise 3(e)

Worklines were set up for both loans, calculating the loan balances and repayments based on the total of the solar equivalent of drawings as made. The difference between the actual repayments and these calculated values, the realised foreign exchange losses on the loan principal, were then deducted from the profit and loss calculation. A simple balance sheet report was then inserted.

Sample solution for Exercise 3(f)

A copy of the semi-annual NCF was added to the model and an annual timeline entered in place of the semi-annual headings. The values on the semi-annual NCF were then picked up as annual totals using SUMIF(...), annual balance, using INDEX(...), or annual per-unit figures using division.

Row totals were adjusted to the new timeline, calculating the total for each row, rather than simply picking up the corresponding totals from the semi-annual net cash flow, providing a quick check that the annual summary is picking up the correct values in each row.

32.4 Alternative deal examples

The above exercises and examples have illustrated the basic operation of a fairly standard model, using an input tariff or a single calculated tariff. The possible structures for a project finance deal are of course infinitely varied, but it may be useful to look at a few specific alternatives.

32.4.1 Optimised purchase/offtake arrangements

In structuring a project finance deal, the desire of lenders to minimise risk and secure project cash flows can conflict with the aims of equity investors to maximise the possible returns achievable. Thus lenders might wish to see revenues secured via advance offtake arrangements, or fuel costs limited via advance purchase arrangements, while equity investors might aim to take full advantage of market possibilities to sell at higher prices or buy at lower prices than those achievable via advance arrangements. In order to structure a deal to best meet the conflicting needs of both, the levels of sales or purchases required to satisfy the lenders' minimum requirements can be calculated by the model, with the remaining sales and purchases being at assumed market rates.

If the advance contracts are to be for a given amount of production throughout the loan or project life, then the recalc macro can be used to establish the required figure. Care must be taken when modelling this sort of calculation to ensure that (as well as meeting given criteria such as cover factors) over the analysis period the calculated figures actually provide sufficient funds when they are required. It may be necessary to include a deposit calculation to even out cash flows for such a calculation. It may even prove necessary to use a figure that exceeds the required cover in order to provide sufficient cash flow when it is required.

The illustration in MinimaxExample.xls assumes that the pre-contracted revenues are simply required to ensure that project costs and debt service can be met in all periods.

Because the revenues available for debt service will be net of taxes and all other costs, it would probably be simplest to establish pre-contracted revenue levels using a run excluding all other sales, avoiding the need to separate the costs and tax relating to pre-sale revenues within the model. As with tariff calculations, once calculated the pre-sale/ purchase figure can then be fixed and used in conjunction with sales of remaining production/capacity at market rates.

32.4.2 Calculated subsidy/grant

It may be the case that a free, subsidised or subordinated contribution to funding of capital costs will be available, and the amount of such subsidy will form part of a proposal or a competitive bid. In such cases, the required level of subsidy can be calculated, given a target equity return or cover factor and fixed cost and revenue figures. The subsidy will generally need to be calculated using the recalc macro. As for tariffs, the recalc macro can be used in conjunction with an estimated calculation in the model to establish the appropriate level of subsidy. If more than one criterion must be met (for example, equity return and cover factor), then both can be accommodated by the macro, provided they are applicable to the same case – i.e., both for the 'base' case or both for a specified 'worst' case. If a required subsidy adjustment is calculated for both criteria, the macro can simply select the higher calculated value. See 'Subsidyexample.xls' for an illustration of this type of calculation.

CPSIA information can be obtained
at www.ICGtesting.com
Printed in the USA
BVHW050937250319
543613BV00033B/2825

9 780995 673007